BEST 100 MILE BIKE ROUTES

HarperSport
An imprint of HarperCollins*Publishers*
77–85 Fulham Palace Road,
Hammersmith, London W6 8JB

www.harpercollins.co.uk

First published by HarperCollins*Publishers* 2014

1 3 5 7 9 10 8 6 4 2

A catalogue record of this book is available from
the British Library

Images on pp. 1, 2–3, 6–7, 16–17, 40–1, 58–9, 86–7,
112–13, 144–5, 170–1, 192–3, 214–15, 230–1
© Shutterstock.com

ISBN 978-0-00-746521-7

Printed and bound by
South China Printing Company

To my best riding buddy, Dr Peter Berman, who
died far too young and long before we could
do these rides together. I did some bits of them
with you though, mate, for which I'm eternally
thankful.

I'd like to thank my wife Kathleen for all the
work she did on this book. Thanks also to
Mark Bolland at HarperCollins who worked so
hard to correct my tendency to place-name
dyslexia, and my confusion over which is right
and which is left when giving directions. And,
finally, thanks too to a man who is as talented
as he is modest, Andy Jones, for additional
photographic material.

BEST 100 MILE BIKE ROUTES

CHRIS SIDWELLS

HarperSport

THE ROUTES

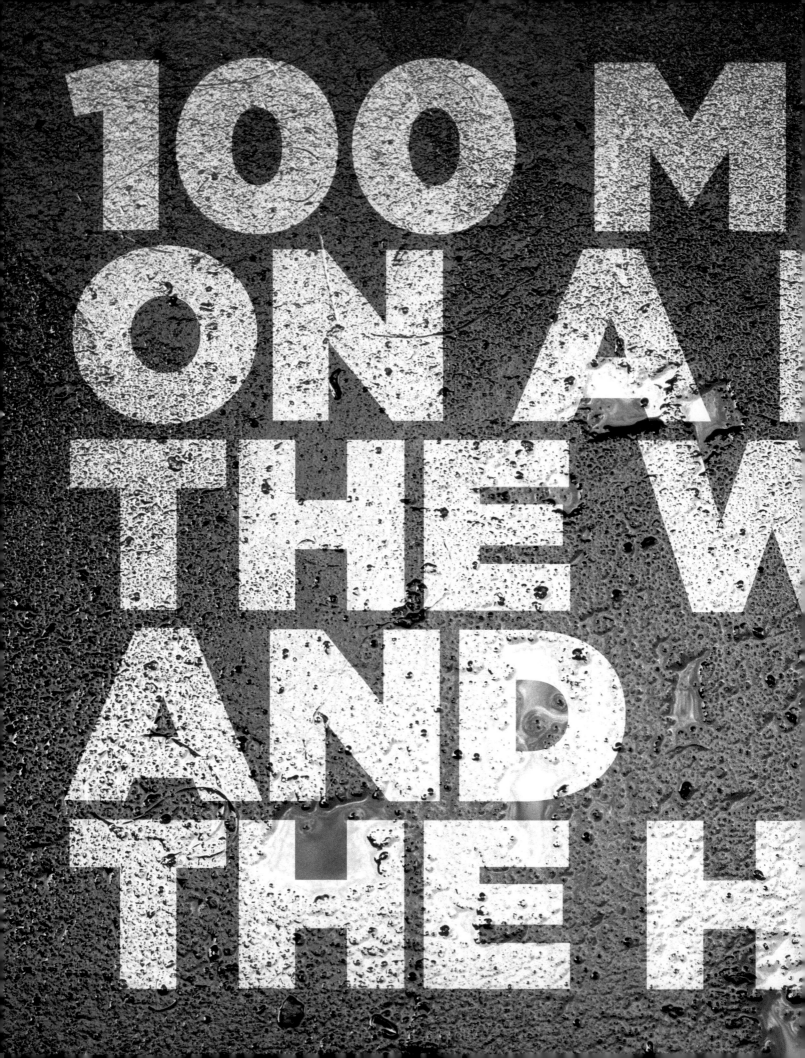

One hundred miles has a very special status in cycling. We use 100 miles as a fundamental unit of long distance. It's a good drive or a long train ride, which makes travelling 100 miles using your own power extra special but very achievable on a bike. Bikes were made to travel long distances, they support our bodies and transfer our power efficiently, but of all the distances you can ride why is 100 miles such a prize for cyclists?

It's partly the shape of the number, partly the way it looks and trips off the tongue. Plus, in our heads it's much more than one mile further than 99. Cyclists pride themselves on riding 100 miles and always have. I have a friend in his 70s who rides 100 miles every Sunday. If he returns home and his computer says 99, he'll ride around the streets until 100 pops up. He's always done it, and he always will for as long as he can ride a bike.

One hundred miles is a prize, it's a badge to be worn, something cyclists do because they can. But more than doing it for its own sake I've used 100 miles as a device in this book. It's a look at the best places in Britain to ride, delivered in 100-mile units. I hope it encourages you to experience the roads, views, hills, forests, towns, villages, lakes, rivers and sea of this beautiful island, and to discover them all from the unique perspective of riding a bike. I think it's a great way of meeting the enduring challenge of riding 100 miles in a day.

WHAT BIKE?

Bikes are wonderful machines. Any well-maintained bike can travel 100 miles if you provide the power, but some bikes make the experience easier and better. Road bikes are the most suited to travelling long distances on metalled surfaces, but mountain bikes, hybrids or cyclo-cross bikes will get you there so long as you swap their knobbly tyres for slick ones.

The main thing is to enjoy the experience of riding 100 miles, and for that you need comfort. Unless you are used to riding one, or you are an experienced racer, out and out race bikes probably aren't the best. They are built for speed and tend to be very stiff so all your energy gets transferred into the back wheel, but that means they can be quite harsh to ride. If you are buying a new bike with regular 100-mile rides in mind then the best place to look is in the cyclosportive category of your favourite bike manufacturer's range.

Cyclosportive bikes have lower gear ratios than race bikes, and they are more comfortable, something achieved by the shock absorbency of the materials they are made from and by their design.

Above: **A top-end road race bike like this, using technology such as an aerodynamically shaped frame and wheels, performs well over all distances. But it's built for speed as well as endurance, and for riding in a fast-moving bunch. A bike like this can feel harsh over 100 miles, unless your body is well conditioned to riding it.**

EXTRA KIT

There are some extras you need in order to ride 100 miles. An under-the-saddle bag is the best way to carry spare inner tubes, a multi-tool device, tyre levers and some money. You also need cycling-specific drinks bottles to carry in special cages that fit on your bike frame. And you need a good, reliable pump in case of punctures. Front and rear lights are a must if there is any chance of the ride starting or ending during the hours of darkness, and having small, flashing front and rear LED lights on your bike helps increase your visibility to other road users. Mudguards make riding in wet conditions much more comfortable. They don't have to be permanent fixtures on your bike – there are some very good ones that can be attached and detached in seconds. A cycle computer keeps you in touch with how many miles you've done, and a GPS device allows you to enter the ride route before you start, which is a big help. You should also build up a good wardrobe of cycling-specific clothing, with items that suit all weather and riding conditions, before attempting to ride 100 miles.

Below: **A cyclosportive bike is a much better option for long-distance riding, especially if you're doing it alone or in a small group. This bike has a bag for spares attached under the saddle, and thin, easily fitted mudguards to keep the rider dry and comfortable.**

BIKE PREPARATION

It's bad news when your bike lets you down, but it can be avoided by maintaining it. Do it yourself or let a bike shop do it, but regular servicing, prompt replacement of worn parts, and cleaning and lubricating your bike all ensure its dependability, but they also make riding it a pleasure.

Check your tyres for wear and cuts in the tread before every ride, and check that everything fastened to your bike, like bags, lights and a pump, is secure. Check the frame for cracks and dents, and if your transmission and/or brakes aren't in tip-top condition, get them fixed. Regular cleaning and lubrication are important, too. Clean and lubricate your bike after any wet ride, and if you don't have time to clean it all, at least clean and lubricate the chain and gears. Otherwise clean, inspect and lubricate once a week if possible, but not less than once a fortnight.

TECHNIQUE

Low gears are crucial, and not just for coping with hills. They are one of the secrets that make riding 100 miles achievable and enjoyable. Gearing down spreads the load on your legs over more pedal revolutions. Think of it this way: it causes less strain to lift 100 kilograms in ten 10-kilogram lots than it does to do it all in one go, but in both cases you still lift 100 kilograms. By pedalling a low gear quickly you can apply the same power as pedalling a high gear slowly, but the strain on your legs is less.

Cyclists call this fast pedalling style spinning, and spinning is a good word to keep in mind to reinforce the need for it while riding. It feels strange at first but with practice spinning becomes second nature. Watch the top guys in races like the Tour de France to give you a feel for what it looks like. Don't force your pedals around – spin them.

Spreading food and drink intake over the whole distance is crucial, too. Eat and drink little and often, and start doing it early. If you wait until you are hungry or thirsty you compromise the ride, and certainly compromise enjoying it. If you have a cycle computer or stopwatch with an alarm, set it to bleep every half hour to remind you to eat and drink. And there's nothing wrong with stopping once, twice or as many times as you like on a ride for a sit-down eat and a cuppa in a cafe. Doing it just makes cycling better.

I've tried to indicate any danger points if they occur on these rides, but it's up to you to gain experience of riding on the road, and to feel comfortable and be competent at handling your bike, and you must know the law as it applies to cyclists. There are lots of manuals and courses to help you ride better, but there are two big things to remember. Always ride downhill at speeds at which you feel in control, and bikes are only under control when you brake or accelerate when riding in a straight line. Do either when you are not going straight and you risk a skid or even falling off.

TRAINING TO RIDE 100 MILES

This doesn't need to be as time consuming as you think. You need to be physically fit in a general sort of way to ride 100 miles, and you need specific cycling strength and endurance in certain parts of your body so you don't encounter ride-stopping problems like saddle soreness or back and neck pains.

To do this it's best to think about conditioning before training. What you are trying to do is condition your body to meet the demands of riding 100 miles. That means making certain changes to it, and it's your training that does that.

So what are the demands of riding 100 miles? The overriding demand is that your body has to keep working at a moderate intensity for a long time doing the same thing over and over again. Now, you might think that a good way to condition yourself would be to ride a little bit further each time you train until you can ride for 100 mile. This will work but it takes a lot of time spread over a long time period. There are shortcuts.

Opposite: The ideal line through any bend is to start out in the road a bit, cut into the bend and end it slightly out. Of course, this depends on whether there are any other road users around you and that the line doesn't take you through a bad or loosely surfaced part of the road.

Right: When climbing hills it's more efficient to stay seated and pedal a low gear. Hold the tops of the handlebars, or the brake lever hoods, and point your elbows out slightly to open up your chest so you can breathe deeply.

Shorter bouts of riding at a higher intensity than you can keep up for 100 miles will help condition you in a much shorter time to ride 100 miles. A few longer rides at 100-miles intensity, increasing the duration of each ride, will condition your body to meet the mechanical demands of riding 100 miles, so you'll avoid saddle soreness. Plus a general strength training programme, paying particular attention to strengthening your core muscles, will eliminate any weak links. Weak links can make riding 100 miles harder than it need be, or it could even prevent you doing it.

You could buy one of a number of books with training programmes that help you prepare for riding 100 miles, or you could hire the services of a coach or trainer, but as a general guide you should try to ride your bike three or four times per week and do strength training twice per

week, but on different days. You can substitute cycling sessions with running ones, provided you are used to running, but you will get the best results if the majority of your training sessions are on a bike. And before starting a training programme for a 100-mile ride you should have done enough riding that you can complete two hours at a reasonable pace quite comfortably.

Within a one-week framework two bike sessions should be ridden at a faster pace than you will ride 100 miles. These sessions should consist of riding at a constant hard pace, but without ending totally exhausted at the end, or split into intervals where you ride even harder but only for five to ten minutes, say, interspersed with periods of easy pedalling.

The latter is called interval training – it's very effective, and you can approach it in a number of ways. One way when training to ride 100 miles would be to set up a ten-week build period to a targeted 100-mile ride. During the first weeks you do short intervals with longer rests. Something like one minute as hard as possible followed by two to three minutes riding easy, repeating that ten times during a ride. Do intervals sessions like that for three weeks then do a week with no intervals, just steady riding. After that, try three weeks of riding three to five minutes as hard as you can, with the same length of easy riding between each one, repeated three to five times. Do a week of steady riding after that and follow it with three weeks where you ride 10 to 20 minutes as hard as you can, with five minute easy riding between, repeated twice.

So that's two days per week and each training session should have one day of doing something easier between

it. For people working a five-day week this training could be done on Tuesdays and Thursdays, which leaves the weekend. For most people this is the best time to do a longer ride.

Start with two hours, then add 15 minutes onto the ride for each of the following two weeks, and in the fourth go back to riding for two hours. The next three weeks should go 2 hours 15 minutes, 2 hours 30 minutes then 2 hours 45. Then cut your long ride to 2 hours again before another three-week build-up of 2 hours 45, 3 hours and 3 hours 15, and repeat the process until you can ride for four hours at a comfortable pace without feeling shattered at the end of it. One hundred miles will be a doddle now.

The strength and conditioning days could be done in a gym or at home if you have the equipment. Strength and conditioning sessions should include leg exercises such as squats, lunges and dead lifts or leg presses. You should also do a range of core exercises, and a Swiss ball is very effective for that. Upper-body exercises like the bench press and rowing help condition shoulder and arm muscle that can become fatigued riding 100 miles. Get a good instruction book, or ask the gym instructor to show you how to do these exercises properly. Doing them in strict good form is essential.

Above: **When hills are too steep to climb in the saddle it's necessary to get out of it in order to bring more muscles in your upper body into play. Try to do this smoothly, and pedal smoothly, too. Keep the body vertical and let the bike move from side to side as you push and pull upwards.**

NUTRITION FOR 100 MILES

What you eat and drink in training can be divided in two: what you eat and drink to support your training, and what you eat and drink to fuel it. Supporting training involves eating sufficient high-quality and varied food so your body can respond to the stimulus of training and get fitter and stronger without eating excess amounts, which will be stored as fat.

You could write a book about this, and many people have, but a good approach is to eat at least five portions of fruit and veg per day, eat protein, carbohydrates and fats at each main meal, and spread the calories you eat over the whole day, with three equal-sized main meals and two snacks, but don't increase the total calories to include the snacks.

So, start off doing that and if you aren't recovering from training and are losing weight you need to eat more. If you are recovering from training and putting weight on, try eating a little less.

Drinking enough is simple – if your urine isn't very pale yellow or clear you aren't drinking enough water. Tea and coffee are OK in moderation, and so is alcohol in perhaps more moderation, but they don't rehydrate you like water does so they shouldn't replace it. Plus, alcohol turns to fat, so cutting down on booze should speed up fat loss, provided you don't replace its calories.

On the subject of losing weight, cycling is easier if you are lean, but we aren't racing in this book. It's not about performance, it's about enjoyment, so don't worry about being whippet-thin. Lose some weight if you can, and training for and riding 100 miles is a great way of doing

it, but don't get hung up about it. You'll enjoy 100 miles more if you are fit, strong and heavy, than if you are unfit, weak and thin.

Fuelling your training, and your 100-mile rides, starts before you set off. Your last meal before a training session should be a normal balanced meal you'd take at the same time any other day.

It's best to eat nothing during an intense one-hour session because one of the major adaptations they stimulate, an increase in the number of special cells in muscles fibres where fuel is processed to produce energy, is enhanced by low blood sugar. You can and should drink water during a short session, especially if you sweat a lot.

You should drink throughout long rides, either water or a dilute energy drink. Eat after one hour of a long ride and eat small amounts of solid food or gels every 30 to 60 minutes after that. Eat sugary stuff while riding, either cakes or sports-nutrition products, and always take more food with you than you think you'll need.

Fuelling a 100-mile ride starts the evening before, when you should enjoy a big meal but not so big that you feel uncomfortable, with plenty of carbohydrates in it. Eat a normal breakfast before the ride, with extra carbs if you can, and eat and drink regularly throughout the ride. There are a lot of well-researched and carefully prepared sports-nutrition products on the market. Use them to fuel your training and riding if you like them, but normal food such as cakes and biscuits, even light sandwiches, work very well. And one of the joys of cycling is stopping at a cafe for something to eat and drink.

Above: **Eating and drinking while riding should be practised in training until you can do it smoothly and without taking your eyes off the road ahead. Keep one hand on the rear brake lever so you can control your speed if necessary.**

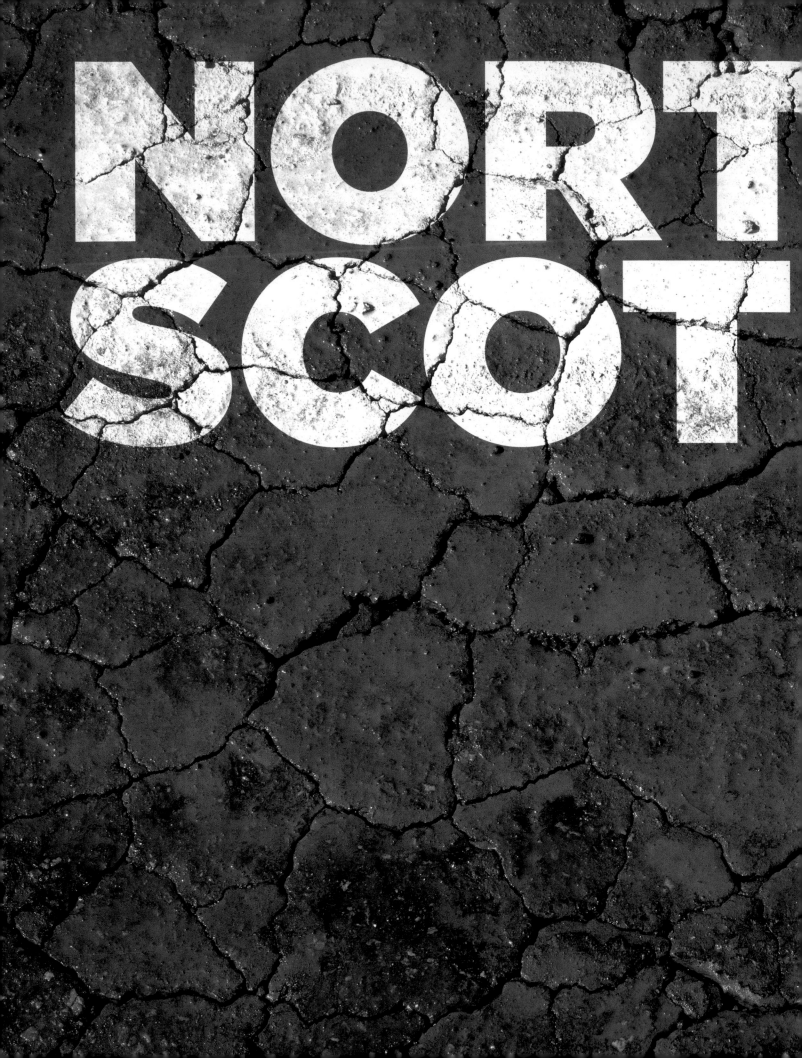

CAPE WRATH

RIDE FACTS

Rating
Rock hard

Total climbing
1740 metres

Killer climbs
Meall na Moine
and Bealach nam
Meirleach

There couldn't be a more inspiring ride to open this book. It visits the lonely north-western tip of Britain, and follows an age-old cycling tradition before passing majestic mountains, jewelled lochs and finally reaching the open sea. You will have it almost all to yourself, as few people live here, and even fewer visit. This is the closest place to wilderness in the whole of the British Isles.

Not many rides start by taking a ferry, but this one does. The road to Cape Wrath starts on the west bank of the Kyle of Durness, and you start on the east. It's the only road to the Cape, and the ferry is the only way to reach it. The ferry service is tide and weather dependent, and details can be found on www.capewrathferry.co.uk.

Long before the mountain bike was invented, adventurous cyclists would ride the 22 miles of rough track to Cape

Wrath and back to become part of the Cape Wrath Fellowship. The road is much improved, but the wistful, wild experience remains. Even the name is romantic. There are only two capes in the UK, this one and Cape Cornwall, 99 rides away.

Back in Keoldale you head south-west on the only road there is to begin the Meall na Moine climb. It's not steep but it's four miles long and climbs between some very old mountains. You are in the oldest part of Britain, which has a geology dating from 3500 million years ago and is as old as anywhere on the planet. The mountains' rounded, worn-down shape really shows their age. Two of the highest are Foinaven and Arkle, which you see to your left on the descent to Rhiconich.

At Laxford Bridge the direction switches to the south-east, still on the A383 and following the River Laxford

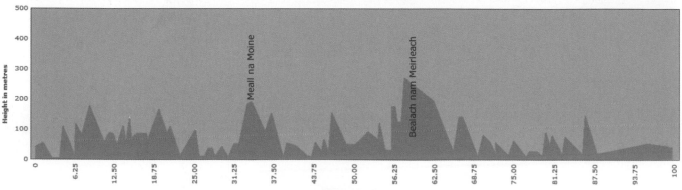

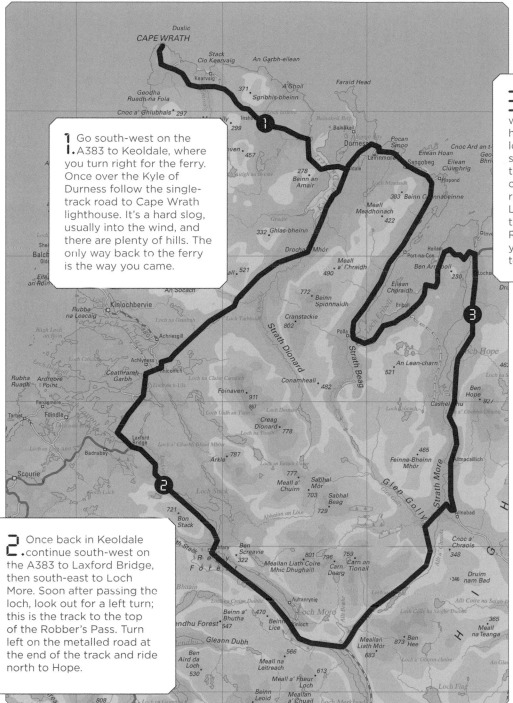

1. Go south-west on the A383 to Keoldale, where you turn right for the ferry. Once over the Kyle of Durness follow the single-track road to Cape Wrath lighthouse. It's a hard slog, usually into the wind, and there are plenty of hills. The only way back to the ferry is the way you came.

2. Once back in Keoldale continue south-west on the A383 to Laxford Bridge, then south-east to Loch More. Soon after passing the loch, look out for a left turn; this is the track to the top of the Robber's Pass. Turn left on the metalled road at the end of the track and ride north to Hope.

3. Turn left and ride west towards Loch Eriboll, watch for the sharp left-hander on the banks of the loch that has a steep climb straight after it. Ride around the loch to Rispond and the coast – as with most of this ride there's only one road. Loch Eriboll is a sea loch that opens into the sea at Rispond. Keep the sea on your right shoulder and return to Durness.

START + FINISH:
Durness

GETTING THERE:
Durness is in Sutherland, on the north coast of Scotland, and you can only get there by road. Take the A9 north from Inverness, then the A386 at Tain to Lairg; there, head north on the A386, then west on the A383. Inverness to Durness is 123 miles, and it's remote.

BIKE SHOP: **Bikes of Inverness, 39/41 Grant Street, Inverness**

CAFE: **Coco Mountain in Balnakeil, which is part of Durness and right next to the sea, serves sophisticated coffee, tea and hot chocolate, and is also a drop-dead gorgeous chocolatier.**

LOCAL DELICACY: **Chanterelle mushrooms**

inland past Ben Stack to Loch More. This is the start of the next climb, the formidable Bealach nam Meirleach, or the 'Robber's Pass' in English.

This is the wildest and loneliest place in this wild and lonely ride. The road is made from hard-packed stone, and it can be muddy in places. It's an old drove road through what used to be forest. There are still some patches of trees today, but it's mostly open moorland.

Just beyond the summit, which is at 266 metres, you pass a series of mountain lochs, then descend by following a stream, the Allt a' Chraois, on its noisy journey down through the Gabernuisgach estate.

You eventually reach a metalled road in Strath More and head due north along a flat-bottomed valley, where Strathmore River meanders lazily towards the sea. First, though, the river runs into Loch Hope, while you ride along its right bank to Hope village. There's a loop south and north around Loch Eriboll to the final leg, west along the undulating coast road back to Durness.

BEN ARMINE FOREST

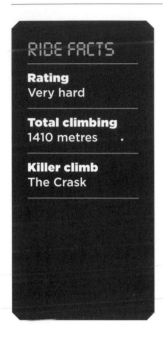

RIDE FACTS

Rating
Very hard

Total climbing
1410 metres

Killer climb
The Crask

'NOTHING CAN DETRACT FROM THE BEAUTY OF THIS RIDE'

This is another committing ride. Once you set off on long rides this far north there are few shortcuts; get halfway around and it's as difficult to go back as it is to continue. That's why all the rides in Northern Scotland are rated hard or above. They are for fit, experienced cyclists. If you don't match that description yet, get a few 100-mile rides in other areas under your wheels, and then come up here and have a go.

You must come prepared. This is a ride of lochs, streams and rivers; the map is suffused with wriggly blue veins of water. It rains a lot here. It can be blue skies by the coast, and lashing down on the back of this circuit.

If you have the experience, don't let my grim warnings put you off; nothing can detract from the beauty of this ride. The opening leg is stunning, with the sea on one side, all grey and majestic, and craggy cliffs and heather-clad mountains on the other.

You are riding part of the 'End to End', Land's End to John O'Groats, or vice versa, so you might have company, but you'll leave them at Helmsdale to enter Strath Ullie. Now the riding gets serious as the route goes up and down, but always gaining more height than it loses. It's hard going, and just to make it harder the mountains, now on both sides, funnel wind down the valley in an attempt to blow you backwards

The scenery changes with height, opening out as the route shifts into the valley of the River Helmsdale, then past

Loch Badanloch. At last there's a summit to this arduous leg, with incredible views of forests dotting the hillsides as far as the eye can see.

The forests are coniferous today, where they used to be broadleaf trees. The Highland Clearances ended the natural scenery when small self-sufficient farmers called crofters were moved out, with force in some cases, by landowners who wanted to farm sheep for more profit. It changed the Highlands socially, and it changed how they look.

Syre is the northerly turn of this ride, from where you head south through the Naver Forest, then past Loch Naver to Altnaharra. The Met Office has a weather station here that holds the record for the lowest temperature ever recorded in the UK, minus 27 degrees, in February 1995. It's also the start of this route's hardest climb, the Crask. Dig in; there's a pub on top.

The descent is straight and fast, but it can be wet and slippery because it runs beneath a lot of trees. The long downhill ends at Loch Shin, the largest loch in Sutherland, with Lairg at the south-east outlet, where the River Shin emerges.

Lairg is the crossroads of the north. Not only do major road routes intersect here, but the railway, the Far North Line, has a station in Lairg. The last ride section is tough. It starts on a main road but there is a hilly loop of tiny lanes before reaching Loch Brora and then the coast, where you started 100 miles ago.

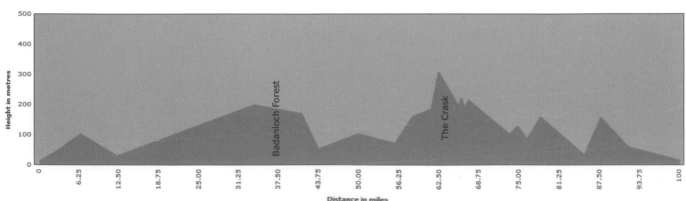

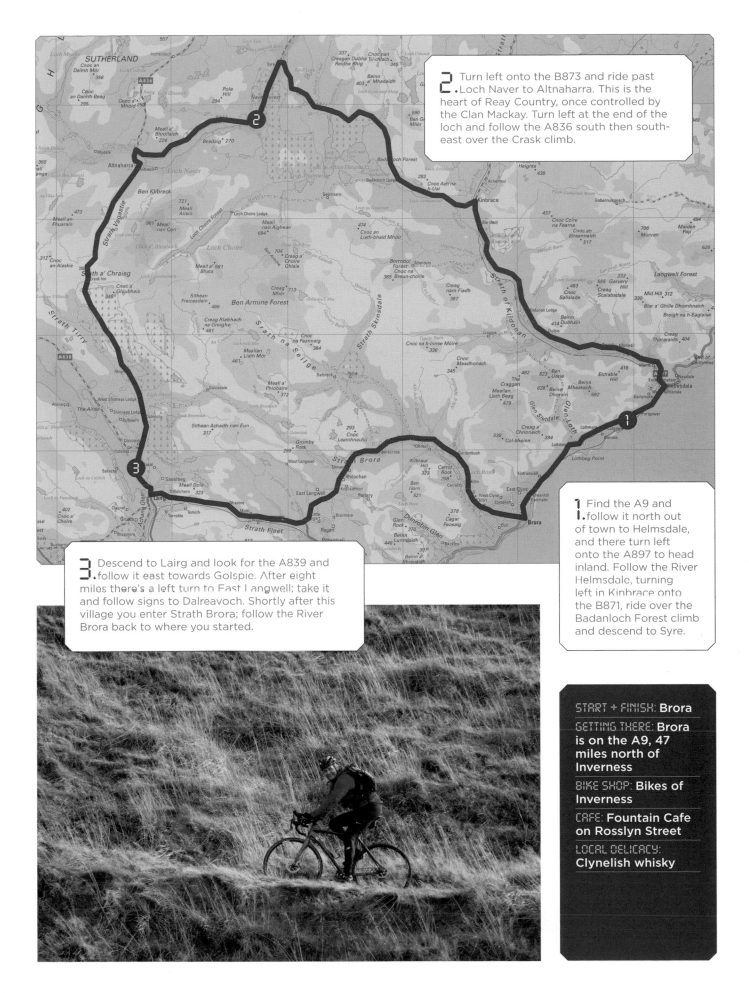

2. Turn left onto the B873 and ride past Loch Naver to Altnaharra. This is the heart of Reay Country, once controlled by the Clan Mackay. Turn left at the end of the loch and follow the A836 south then south-east over the Crask climb.

3. Descend to Lairg and look for the A839 and follow it east towards Golspie. After eight miles there's a left turn to East Langwell; take it and follow signs to Dalreavoch. Shortly after this village you enter Strath Brora; follow the River Brora back to where you started.

1. Find the A9 and follow it north out of town to Helmsdale, and there turn left onto the A897 to head inland. Follow the River Helmsdale, turning left in Kinbrace onto the B871, ride over the Badanloch Forest climb and descend to Syre.

START + FINISH: Brora

GETTING THERE: Brora is on the A9, 47 miles north of Inverness

BIKE SHOP: Bikes of Inverness

CAFE: Fountain Cafe on Rosslyn Street

LOCAL DELICACY: Clynelish whisky

LOCH NESS

NORTHERN SCOTLAND

RIDE FACTS

Rating
Hard

Total climbing
1600 metres

Killer climbs
General Wade's
Military Road,
Tom Bailgeann
and Ashie Moor

'YOUR MIND IS PREY TO ALL KINDS OF THOUGHTS AS YOU RIDE ALONG THE DARK, TREE-COVERED LOCH ROAD'

Riding a whole circuit of Loch Ness, with its dark waters and mysterious monster, is a thrill, but add a trip into the mountains surrounding it and you've got a classic route. It's also a route of two halves: the first is undulating, the second much hillier.

The ride starts in Inverness, which in Gaelic means 'at the mouth of the River Ness', close to the Caledonian Canal. You'll see the canal again in another 57 miles, at the other end of Loch Ness. It uses the Great Glen, a rift valley that cuts the Highlands in half, stringing together several lochs to provide a waterway right across Scotland.

Out of Inverness you are in The Aird, a lowland area of forest south of the Beauly Firth. It's a gentle start but things get more serious with a climb up Strathglass, then away from it into Glen Urquhart, and the descent to Drumnadrochit and Loch Ness.

Although Loch Lomond has a larger surface area, Loch Ness is greater in volume, so it is the largest inland mass of water in Scotland. It is 22.6 miles long but only 1.7 miles wide at the most. Its volume comes from being incredibly deep: 122 metres on average and 227 metres at its deepest. Deep enough to hide a mystery, and the Loch Ness Monster is a mystery.

There have been several sightings of the monster, affectionately known as Nessie, over many years, although fewer recently. Some pictures, too, but none that provides credible evidence of a monster lurking in the deep, dark waters of the loch.

But still your mind is prey to all kinds of thoughts as you ride along the dark, tree-covered loch road. Gaze across the water and the surface can suddenly break, creating ripples for no apparent reason. Is it the monster? No, it's a local weather effect caused by air blown off high mountains hitting icy water.

You turn at Fort Augustus on the south-west shore of the loch, cross the Caledonian Canal again and begin to climb away from the loch. This is General

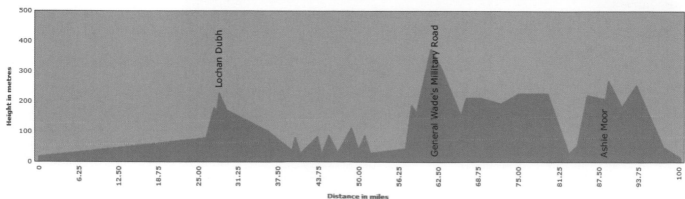

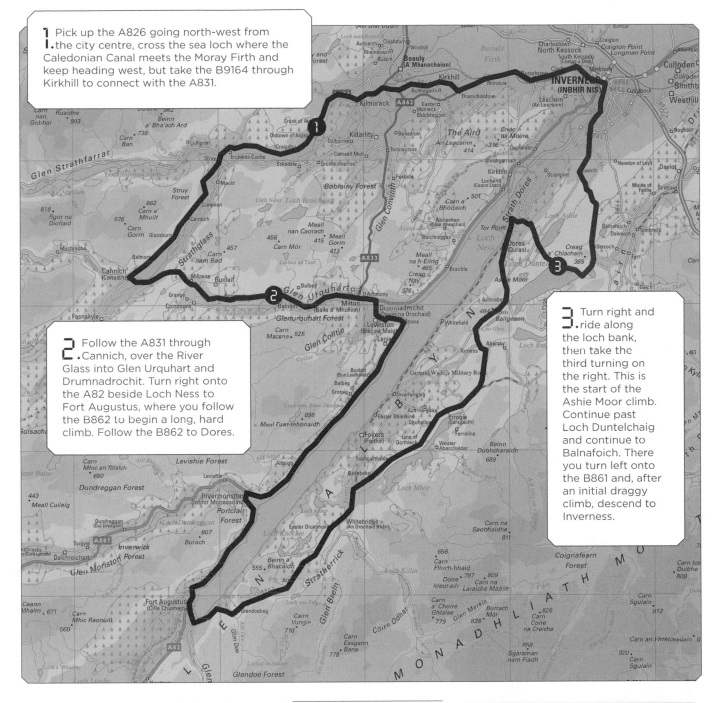

1. Pick up the A826 going north-west from the city centre, cross the sea loch where the Caledonian Canal meets the Moray Firth and keep heading west, but take the B9164 through Kirkhill to connect with the A831.

2. Follow the A831 through Cannich, over the River Glass into Glen Urquhart and Drumnadrochit. Turn right onto the A82 beside Loch Ness to Fort Augustus, where you follow the B862 to begin a long, hard climb. Follow the B862 to Dores.

3. Turn right and ride along the loch bank, then take the third turning on the right. This is the start of the Ashie Moor climb. Continue past Loch Duntelchaig and continue to Balnafoich. There you turn left onto the B861 and, after an initial draggy climb, descend to Inverness.

Wade's Military Road and the first of three tough climbs in quick succession. There are military roads throughout Scotland, built by the English during their eighteenth-century occupation to connect their garrisons.

A short descent leads to a shelf along the northern edge of the Monadhliath mountains. This is a magnificent mountain treat, where you pass a series of rivers and high lochs, before leaving it to drop down to the low road by Loch Ness. After this exhilarating descent, with its incredible views, you have one more climb, Ashie Moor, before a final swoop down to Inverness.

'YOUR MIND IS PREY TO ALL KINDS OF THOUGHTS AS YOU RIDE ALONG THE DARK, TREE-COVERED LOCH ROAD'

START + FINISH: Inverness

GETTING THERE: Inverness is on the A9, 96 miles north of Perth. It has a rail link with the rest of the UK through Edinburgh. You can fly to Edinburgh or Aberdeen and reach Inverness by road or rail.

BIKE SHOP: Bikes of Inverness

CAFE: Velocity, which combines a cafe with a bike workshop

LOCAL DELICACY: Venison

NORTHERN SCOTLAND

SKYE

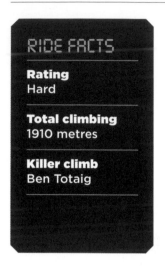

RIDE FACTS

Rating
Hard

Total climbing
1910 metres

Killer climb
Ben Totaig

'A LONG DESCENT INTO PORTREE AT THE END OF WHAT HAS BEEN A MAGICAL DAY'

Riding around an island is something every cyclist should do. Any coastal ride is a delight, but this takes in three of Skye's four peninsulas and is full of wonder. And Skye's coastal scenery of cliffs and arches, stacks and small islands – wild to the west, calmer in the east – provides an extra dimension.

The ride starts in Skye's largest town, Portree, and it begins with a climb. This takes you to Loch Fada, which sits in a trough between two groups of hills running parallel to the coast. They block any view of the sea until you reach the adjoining Loch Leathan, where the Sound of Raasay and Raasay island can be seen.

The view inland is no less impressive. The Storr towers 719 metres above you, a huge rocky peak with a cliff-like summit that was created by the UK's largest landslip. The curious rocky pinnacles jutting out in front of the summit are evidence of further earth movement.

The road closes on the sea as you ride north along the Trotternish peninsula, passing an area of cliffs where the sea has blasted out large holes to form spectacular arches. It's hard riding, but the route north has slightly easier stretches, especially past Staffin Bay, where huge fossilised dinosaur footprints have been found in the rocks.

From Staffin Bay the route goes a little further north, then crosses the top of the peninsula. The next section, south to Uig, is the easiest on the route. Take your time to appreciate the views across the

Little Minch towards the wild, wet and wonderful island of North Uist.

Uig is quite wonderful, too. It's where the North Uist ferry sails from a pier that juts out into Uig Bay. The coast is flatter here, marked by small shingle beaches, and the place names could have been lifted from Tolkien: Earlish, Hinnisdal Bridge and the wonderful Loch Snizort Beag, which separates the Trotternish and Vaternish peninsulas.

You cross the southern edge of Vaternish to Dunvegan, a village where the Giant MacAskill Museum is run by Peter MacAskill, father of death-defying street-trials cyclist Danny MacAskill. The museum is dedicated to the life of Angus Mor MacAskill, a real-life giant also known as Black Angus. He was born on South Harris and was two metres 36 centimetres tall (7ft 9in) and weighed 230 kg – that's over 36 stones. He became famous as a circus strongman, and is reputed to have been able to lift up and carry a horse.

And you'll feel like you've carried a horse after the next leg to Meanish Pier at Milovaig, out and back along the never-ending undulations of the Duirinish peninsula, before the last sea leg along Loch Bracadale to Bracadale village.

This is where the only inland leg of the ride starts, made up of a long climb, with the massive Cuillin Hills looming over the southern horizon, then a long descent into Portree at the end of what has been a magical day.

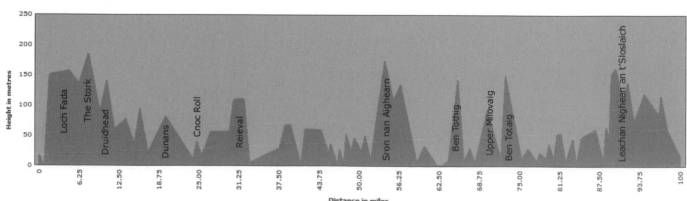

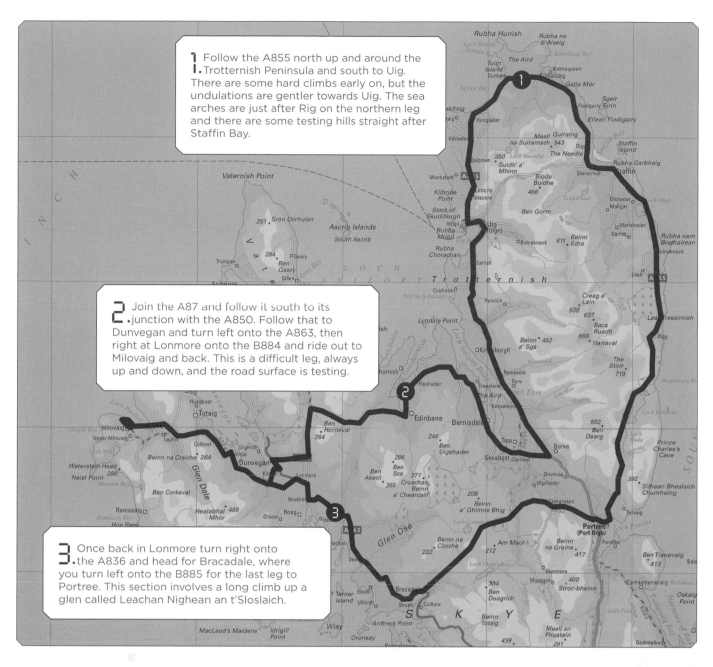

1. Follow the A855 north up and around the Trotternish Peninsula and south to Uig. There are some hard climbs early on, but the undulations are gentler towards Uig. The sea arches are just after Rig on the northern leg and there are some testing hills straight after Staffin Bay.

2. Join the A87 and follow it south to its junction with the A850. Follow that to Dunvegan and turn left onto the A863, then right at Lonmore onto the B884 and ride out to Milovaig and back. This is a difficult leg, always up and down, and the road surface is testing.

3. Once back in Lonmore turn right onto the A836 and head for Bracadale, where you turn left onto the B885 for the last leg to Portree. This section involves a long climb up a glen called Leachan Nighean an t'Sloslaich.

START + FINISH: Portree

GETTING THERE: Portree is on the A87, 37 miles north-west of the Skye Bridge, which is Skye's connection with the mainland across the Kyle of Lochalsh. Citybus has a service from Glasgow to Portree and there's a rail line to Plockton on the mainland side of the bridge, from where there is a bus service.

BIKE SHOP: Island Cycles, The Green

CAFE: Cafe Arriba on the Brae Quay

LOCAL DELICACY: Fresh langoustines

CAIRNGORM

There's a Tour de France mountain stage feel to this ride because there's a full-scale mountain at the end of it. It also meanders around the Spey Valley, tracing ribbons of water through open meadows and lush forests. The ride is also slightly over 100 miles – sorry.

You start in Aviemore, home of Scottish skiing; so yes, this is a ride for the summer. Head north-east on a small road next to the A9 to Carrbridge then follow the River Dunlain east to where it joins the Spey.

In true mountain-stage fashion the first bit of riding is a gentle prelude to what follows. It changes as you cross the Spey and begin the day's first long climb from 200 metres in Grantown to over 450 metres on the summit six miles later.

There's a short but steep descent to a bridge, then a very steep climb away from it before you sweep downhill through the Bridge of Brown to where a beautiful loop of Strath Avon and Glenlivet begins. Breathe deeply as you pass the Glenlivet whisky distillery; it will give you strength and inspiration.

The loop goes around two mountains, Carn Liath and Carn Daimh, and ends in Tomintoul, where the infamous Tomintoul

'THERE'S A TOUR DE FRANCE MOUNTAIN STAGE FEEL TO THIS RIDE BECAUSE THERE'S A FULL-SCALE MOUNTAIN AT THE END OF IT'

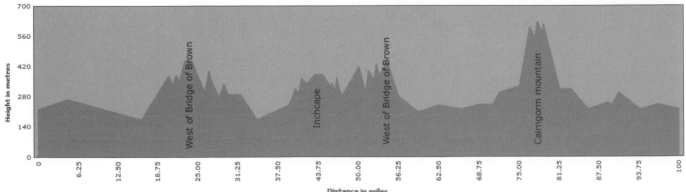

Height in metres

700 · 560 · 420 · 280 · 140 · 0

West of Bridge of Brown · Inchcape · West of Bridge of Brown · Cairngorm mountain

0 · 6.25 · 12.50 · 18.75 · 25.00 · 31.25 · 37.50 · 43.75 · 50.00 · 56.25 · 62.50 · 68.75 · 75.00 · 81.25 · 87.50 · 93.75 · 100

Distance in miles

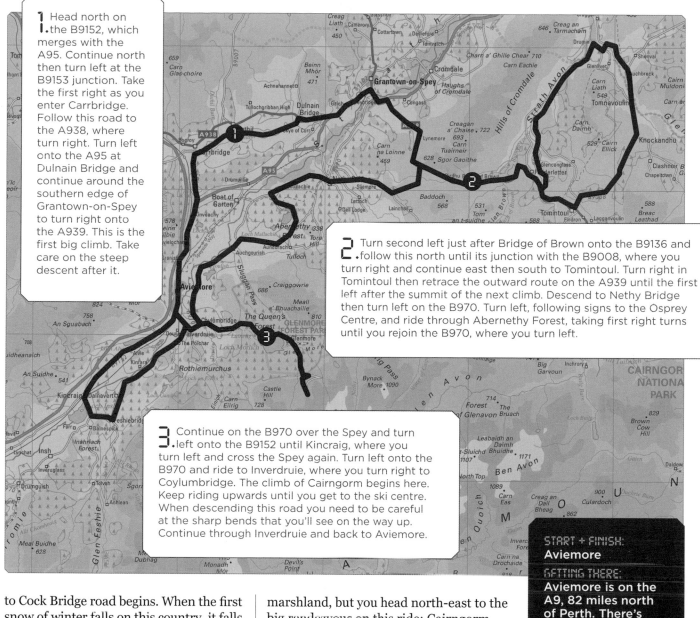

1. Head north on the B9152, which merges with the A95. Continue north then turn left at the B9153 junction. Take the first right as you enter Carrbridge. Follow this road to the A938, where turn right. Turn left onto the A95 at Dulnain Bridge and continue around the southern edge of Grantown-on-Spey to turn right onto the A939. This is the first big climb. Take care on the steep descent after it.

2. Turn second left just after Bridge of Brown onto the B9136 and follow this north until its junction with the B9008, where you turn right and continue east then south to Tomintoul. Turn right in Tomintoul then retrace the outward route on the A939 until the first left after the summit of the next climb. Descend to Nethy Bridge then turn left on the B970. Turn left, following signs to the Osprey Centre, and ride through Abernethy Forest, taking first right turns until you rejoin the B970, where you turn left.

3. Continue on the B970 over the Spey and turn left onto the B9152 until Kincraig, where you turn left and cross the Spey again. Turn left onto the B970 and ride to Inverdruie, where you turn right to Coylumbridge. The climb of Cairngorm begins here. Keep riding upwards until you get to the ski centre. When descending this road you need to be careful at the sharp bends that you'll see on the way up. Continue through Inverdruie and back to Aviemore.

to Cock Bridge road begins. When the first snow of winter falls on this country, it falls on this road and it's often blocked. It's high and exposed and called the Lecht, but happily you don't go that way.

After retracing part of the first climb you then descend to the Spey by another route through Abernethy Forest. Owned by the RSPB, it's gorgeous and is home to many birds, some of them quite rare, like the Scottish crossbill, black grouse and osprey. There are also wild cats here, a very rare sight in the UK.

Eventually you cross the River Spey, which is a salmon river and, like all salmon rivers, looks dark, deep, mysterious and slightly threatening. You ride upstream then cross again at the first bridge south-west of Aviemore, which spans the place where the river flows out of Loch Insh. South-west of that the Insh Nature Reserve occupies a wide area of

marshland, but you head north-east to the big rendezvous on this ride: Cairngorm.

The summit of Cairngorm stands at 1245 metres, but the road ends below that at the beginning of the ski lifts, 650 metres above sea level. The road climb is 7.5 miles long, gaining 413 metres at an average gradient of 3.5 per cent. The last four miles are the killer, though. From the water-sports centre on Loch Morlich the climb gets quite hard, but once you break clear of the Queen's Forest it's brutal. The final two miles climb at 7.5 per cent average with several steeper sections within that. There is a race up this climb. The best time for the measured 10 kilometres is just under 30 minutes, achieved in 2011. To all intents the ride ends at the top, because you can freewheel almost all the way back to Aviemore. Enjoy the rush, and the view, but be careful on the tight bends.

START + FINISH:
Aviemore

GETTING THERE:
Aviemore is on the A9, 82 miles north of Perth. There's a rail link through Perth and Stirling with Glasgow and Edinburgh.

BIKE SHOP:
Mike's Bikes

CAFE: Cafe Bleu

LOCAL DELICACY: The Hot Chocolate Mountain served in the Ptarmigan Restaurant, located at the end of the funicular railway above the ski station. At 1077 metres it's the highest restaurant in the UK.

MOIDART

RIDE FACTS

Rating
Very hard

Total climbing
2300 metres

Killer climb
Taob Dubh

'YOU WON'T EVER FORGET THE VIEWS OF BEN NEVIS GETTING CLOSER AS YOU RIDE'

Jason Macintyre was a talented racing cyclist from Fort William. He was good enough to ride the Tour de France, but stayed in Scotland to help care for his handicapped daughter. Still, he was a national champion, and I came here in 2008 to interview him and take photographs on his favourite ride, which he called the Glen Uig Loop. Five months later he was killed in a road accident while training here. This is Jason's ride.

It starts in Fort William right under Britain's highest mountain, Ben Nevis, and after ten miles requires a short ferry crossing of the Corran Narrows. From there the ride just keeps getting better and better.

Stately mountains are reflected in Loch Linnhe, then fade slowly and disappear as you enter the fortress hills of Kingair Loch. They signal the start of the ride's hardest climb, Taob Dubh. It's not hard in absolute terms, but it's just one of many on this ride. Pace yourself, because afterwards the hills come thick and fast.

Up and down to Loch Sunart, then to the south-west tip of Loch Shiel, and you've reached halfway. There's no going back now. Jason reckoned this ride was character-building, because once you're halfway you're committed to the finish. It certainly became part of who he was, and it gave him some of the steely determination that enabled him to compete at so high a level without the advantages of other top racers.

You climb to Captain Robinson's Cairn and descend past the Seven Men of Moidart. This refers to seven beech trees that were planted here because it's said to be where Bonnie Prince Charlie landed with seven companions on his return from exile in 1745, although there's a question mark over that. Only four of the seven beeches remain.

Hills, headlands and loch shores are a repeating pattern until you reach Glen Uig and its village, and the most beautiful view of this incredible ride. Look north-west from Glenuig and the sea is studded with islands – Eigg, Muck, Rum, Canna – and on the horizon you can just see the Cuillin Hills of Skye.

It's remote here; access by road was only made in 1966, and mains electricity didn't reach the tiny settlement until 1983. Yet there have been people here for thousands of years. The Gulf Stream passes nearby, making the climate milder than it should be this far north. The land was productive until the Highland Clearances changed it, and transport was by horseback and by sea and loch.

You join the A830 'Road to the Isles' at Lochailort and head east back to Fort William. Glenfinnan is just over one third of the way back. This is where Bonnie Prince Charlie raised his standard and began his fight to win back the Scottish throne for his father, James Stuart, and make Scotland Scottish once more – a fight which ended eight months later at the Battle of Culloden. A huge and noble tower marks the spot.

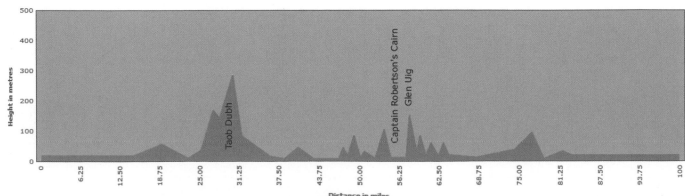

Distance in miles

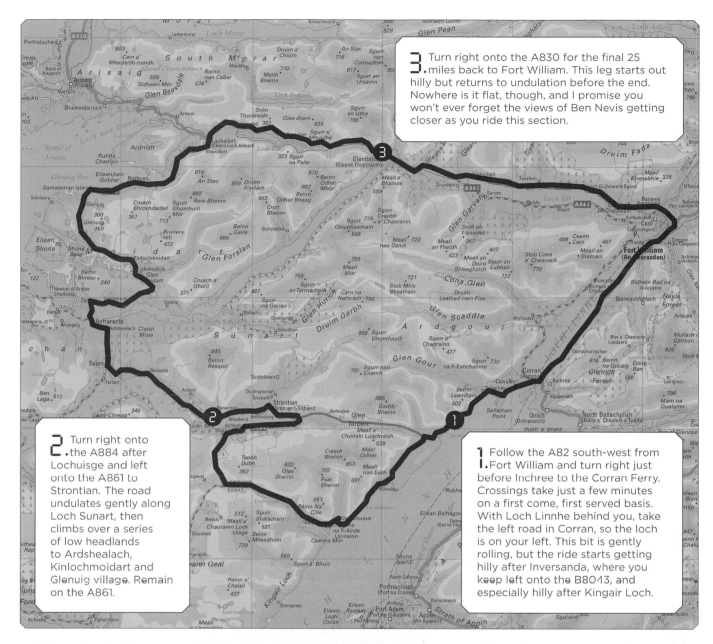

3. Turn right onto the A830 for the final 25 miles back to Fort William. This leg starts out hilly but returns to undulation before the end. Nowhere is it flat, though, and I promise you won't ever forget the views of Ben Nevis getting closer as you ride this section.

2. Turn right onto the A884 after Lochuisge and left onto the A861 to Strontian. The road undulates gently along Loch Sunart, then climbs over a series of low headlands to Ardshealach, Kinlochmoidart and Glenuig village. Remain on the A861.

1. Follow the A82 south-west from Fort William and turn right just before Inchree to the Corran Ferry. Crossings take just a few minutes on a first come, first served basis. With Loch Linnhe behind you, take the left road in Corran, so the loch is on your left. This bit is gently rolling, but the ride starts getting hilly after Inversanda, where you keep left onto the B8043, and especially hilly after Kingair Loch.

START + FINISH: Fort William

GETTING THERE: Fort William is on the A82, 95 miles north of Glasgow. There is also a rail link with Glasgow.

BIKE SHOP: Nevis Cycles, 4 & 6 Lochy Crescent, Inverlochy

CAFE: JJ's Cafe in Lochybridge is on the Road to the Isles, so you see it as you finish the ride.

LOCAL DELICACY: Smoked salmon

GLENCOE

RIDE FACTS

Rating
Very hard

Total climbing
2200 metres

Killer climb
Glencoe

I would include this ride just for the glory of cycling in Glencoe. Even if the other 87 miles were a flat, dull, concrete dual carriageway, this one would still be worth riding; but they aren't. Wild, watery moors, quiet glens, muscular mountains and even the sea all feature in this epic ride.

It starts in South Ballachulish with a gentle ride around Loch Leven. This is a sea loch with anything but gentle tides, and its narrow entrance sees fierce currents in spring. Surprisingly, given today's tranquil setting, the area has a history of heavy industry. There was a huge aluminium smelter at the head of the loch at the start of the last century, and ships chugged up and down it all day, taking away raw aluminium.

The loch is bordered by huge mountains, creating a striking contrast, but be prepared to be awed by what comes next. You leave the loch shore and swing through a complete 180 degrees at Glencoe village and begin to climb the Pass of Glencoe. It's huge, one of the few climbs in the UK that has the feel of a European mountain pass. The road wriggles up a long, deep, U-shaped valley, dwarfed by giant, dark peaks. It's the height difference that gives Glencoe such scale. The road reaches 300 metres, but the mountains are all over 900, and some as high as 1000 metres.

The pass climbs from sea level, then suddenly opens onto the wild and vast expanse of Rannoch Moor. A formidable place in rough weather, the moor is utterly beautiful when the sun picks out the ribbons and splashes of water that make up almost half of its area.

Rannoch Moor really is an anomaly on the ride, being wide, windy and open. You encounter more mountains as you cross it and descend to Bridge of Orchy, then on down Glen Orchy, following its river, one of the finest stretches of white water in the country.

The glen opens up in Strath of Orchy as the route joins the aptly named Loch Awe. This leads to the Pass of Brander, scene in 1308 of a terrible battle in the Scottish Civil War. The pass takes you to Loch Etive, and Connel, where you cross the loch by a bridge and head north. If you do this ride in spring you could witness the Falls of

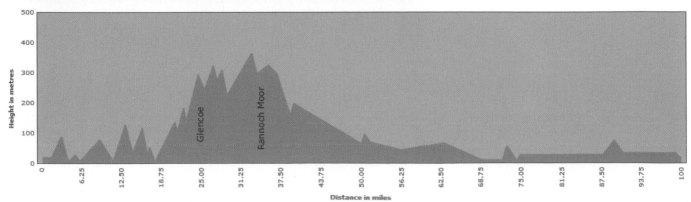

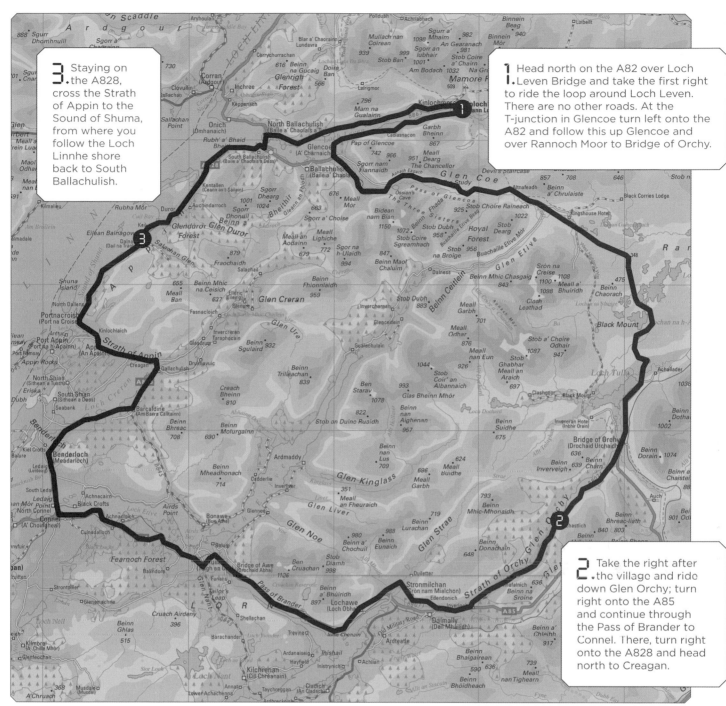

3. Staying on the A828, cross the Strath of Appin to the Sound of Shuma, from where you follow the Loch Linnhe shore back to South Ballachulish.

1. Head north on the A82 over Loch Leven Bridge and take the first right to ride the loop around Loch Leven. There are no other roads. At the T-junction in Glencoe turn left onto the A82 and follow this up Glencoe and over Rannoch Moor to Bridge of Orchy.

2. Take the right after the village and ride down Glen Orchy; turn right onto the A85 and continue through the Pass of Brander to Connel. There, turn right onto the A828 and head north to Creagan.

Lora going on right underneath you.

It's a tidal race created when the Firth of Lorn empties so quickly with the pull of the receding tide that it falls below the waters of Loch Etive. This empties over a rocky shelf, causing rapids, which change into a succession of big waves when the tide rushes back into the loch.

There's a short glimpse of the sea as you ride past Ardmucknish Bay, after which the route crosses the Benderloch peninsula to Loch Creran, the Strath of Appin and Loch Linnhe, and finishes with an undulating ride back to South Ballachulish.

'WILD, WATERY MOORS, QUIET GLENS, MUSCULAR MOUNTAINS AND EVEN THE SEA ALL FEATURE IN THIS EPIC RIDE'

START + FINISH: South Ballachulish

GETTING THERE: South Ballachulish is on the A82, 13 miles south of Fort William. Its only rail contact is at Fort William, from where buses travel to South Ballachulish and Glencoe.

BIKE SHOP: CrankItUpGear in Glencoe

CAFE: Quarry Cafe at the Ballachulish visitor centre

LOCAL DELICACY: Tablet cake

GRAMPIAN MOUNTAINS

RIDE FACTS

Rating
Hard

Total climbing
1770 metres

Killer climb
The Lecht

'THIS RIDE INVOLVES CLIMBING THE HIGHEST MAIN ROAD IN BRITAIN, THE LECHT, AND A LOT MORE BESIDES'

This ride involves climbing the highest main road in Britain, the Lecht, and a lot more besides. It's a ride of contrasts, exploring the Cairngorm mountains of Braemar and the low-lying lushness of the Cromar, places that lie at either end of Royal Deeside. It's also a great place for cycling because local businesses are making special efforts to attract cyclists there.

Deeside is 'Royal' because of Balmoral, and you ride past the Queen's castle after the first leg of the ride, which goes from Ballater up to the Spittal of Glenmuick and back. The mountain on your right is Lochnagar. It's a formidable sight, with its steep sides rising out of Loch Muick and its 1155-metre peak. However, it looks even more impressive when you ride west and see the huge corrie, or hollow, formed by a glacier, scooped out of its north side with a 300-metre rock wall behind it.

You turn left short of Ballater but get a great view of the perfect conical mountain just behind the town, called Craigendaroch. Loch Muick and all of the next section lie within the Balmoral Estate, and you get a fine view of the castle on this B-road where it bends sharp right to follow the River Dee. King Robert II of Scotland had a hunting lodge here back in the 14th century, but Queen Victoria and Prince Albert bought the Balmoral Estate for the British royal family in 1851 and then built the current castle there.

Ride past the castle's front gates and up the Dee valley to Braemar, where the annual Gathering is one of the highlights of the Highland Games circuit. Cycle races, run off on grass tracks on a handicap basis, where the slower riders start with a lead, are a big part of the modern Highland Games. Braemar is another turning point on this ride,

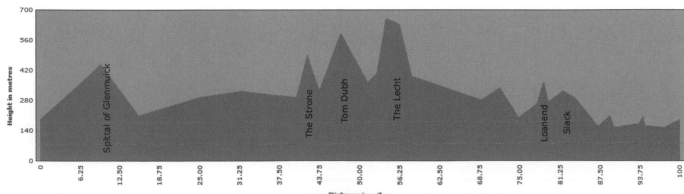

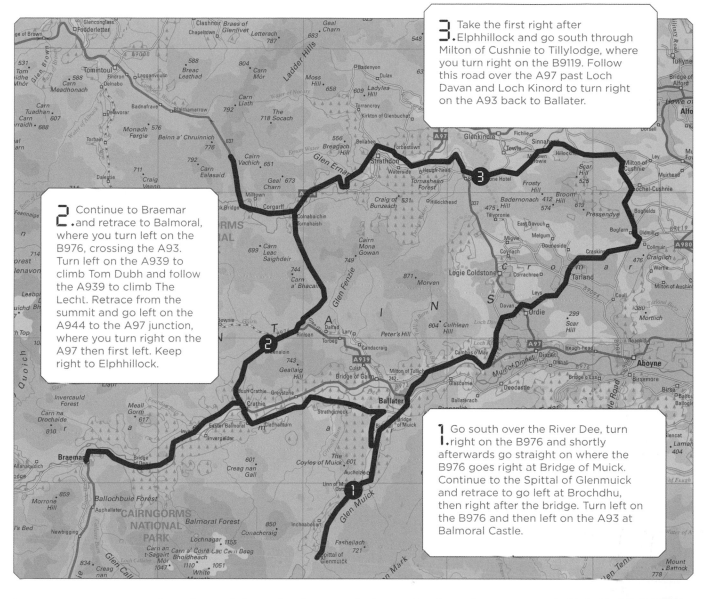

3. Take the first right after Elphhillock and go south through Milton of Cushnie to Tillylodge, where you turn right on the B9119. Follow this road over the A97 past Loch Davan and Loch Kinord to turn right on the A93 back to Ballater.

2. Continue to Braemar and retrace to Balmoral, where you turn left on the B976, crossing the A93. Turn left on the A939 to climb Tom Dubh and follow the A939 to climb The Lecht. Retrace from the summit and go left on the A944 to the A97 junction, where you turn right on the A97 then first left. Keep right to Elphhillock.

1. Go south over the River Dee, turn right on the B976 and shortly afterwards go straight on where the B976 goes right at Bridge of Muick. Continue to the Spittal of Glenmuick and retrace to go left at Brochdhu, then right after the bridge. Turn left on the B976 and then left on the A93 at Balmoral Castle.

because you retrace to Balmoral, turn left and start climbing.

Most of the uphill in this ride is packed into the next 18 miles. First you climb the Old Military Road over The Strone. It starts in a tranquil, tree-lined setting but soon tracks up a fenceless path through wild moorland, where the sheep look like stones and the stones look like sheep, and the only thing to distinguish between them is movement.

The climb of Tom Dubh is hard and straight and leads to the Don valley, where there's an interlude of woodland and gentler terrain until Cock Bridge, and the start of the Lecht. The first kilometre is the hardest as it rises 144 metres in that distance, so has a 14.4 per cent gradient. The road then goes downhill for 500 metres before rearing up ahead for the next dead-straight mile at a near 8 per cent average, and with two steeper kicks within

that just to make it extra hard. Catch a headwind on this bit – and you often do – and it's purgatory. The last section is a short ride down, then up to the ski station, which is the official summit.

The view from the top is fairly barren. The Lecht is a hill to ride simply because it's the highest. Now turn around and descend to the Don again and follow it to Heugh-head, where you begin a circuit of the Cromar.

There are still mountains here, but they are smaller in scale and more isolated. The Cromar, in between them, is green and pleasant, and stone circles and traces of hut circles near Tarland are evidence of human life going back 4000 years. Look out for red squirrels as you ride through the forests, and for the cycle-route signs after Lochs Davan and Kinord, because it makes a nice alternative to the main road route to Ballater.

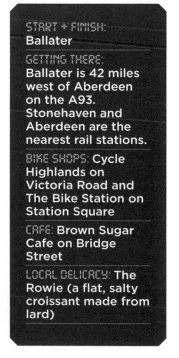

START + FINISH: **Ballater**

GETTING THERE: **Ballater is 42 miles west of Aberdeen on the A93. Stonehaven and Aberdeen are the nearest rail stations.**

BIKE SHOPS: **Cycle Highlands on Victoria Road and The Bike Station on Station Square**

CAFE: **Brown Sugar Cafe on Bridge Street**

LOCAL DELICACY: **The Rowie (a flat, salty croissant made from lard)**

PERTH AND KINROSS

RIDE FACTS

Rating
Hard

Total climbing
1850 metres

Killer climb
A' Chrois

This is a ride of glens and lochs in a beautiful mountain setting. It starts in Aberfeldy, which is a bit of a literary heavyweight because it inspired the Robbie Burns poem 'The Birks of Aberfeldy' and its finest house is owned by J. K. Rowling, the Harry Potter author. The house is called Killiechassie House and it's on the banks of the River Tay on the opposite side to the main part of Aberfeldy.

The Birks of Abefeldy are the birch trees that line Urlar Burn, a stream you cross just as you leave town on the first leg of this ride, and before tackling the slope to Glen Cochill. Burns was inspired by the Urlar's steep valley and the trees that line it, and by the Falls of Moness a little further upstream.

You can only reach the falls on foot, so press on up the main road to a viewpoint on a sharp right bend about half a mile from the summit. It's worth stopping here to look back over the Tay valley and at the mountains beyond.

A long downhill section leads to the entrance of Glen Quaich, where you leave the main road to ride past lonely Loch Freuchie and begin a long and very steep climb that passes between the summits of A' Chrois and Meall a' Chroire Chreagaig mountains. It leads to an equally steep descent, which twists and turns a lot near the end, calling for extreme care.

The descent ends on the south bank of Loch Tay, which you follow from end to end from Kenmore to Killin. Back in the Iron Age people lived on the lochs here

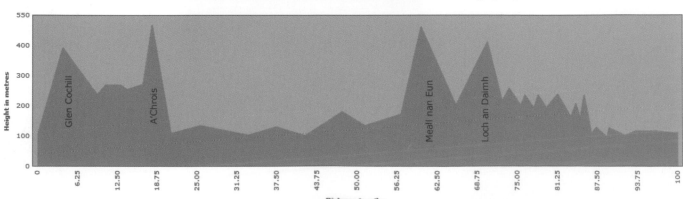

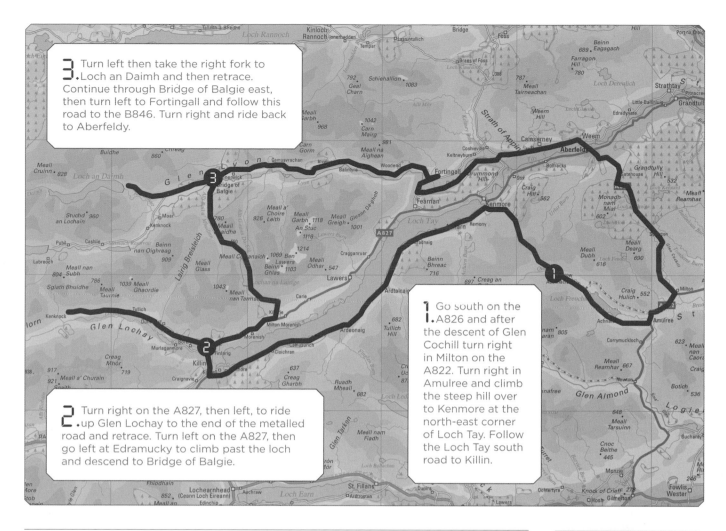

3. Turn left then take the right fork to Loch an Daimh and then retrace. Continue through Bridge of Balgie east, then turn left to Fortingall and follow this road to the B846. Turn right and ride back to Aberfeldy.

1. Go south on the A826 and after the descent of Glen Cochill turn right in Milton on the A822. Turn right in Amulree and climb the steep hill over to Kenmore at the north-east corner of Loch Tay. Follow the Loch Tay south road to Killin.

2. Turn right on the A827, then left, to ride up Glen Lochay to the end of the metalled road and retrace. Turn left on the A827, then go left at Edramucky to climb past the loch and descend to Bridge of Balgie.

'THIS IS A RIDE OF GLENS AND LOCHS IN A BEAUTIFUL MOUNTAIN SETTING'

in small wooden stockades built on piles, called crannogs. There was one on Loch Freuchie, and the remains of 23 crannogs have been found in Loch Tay. One of them was reconstructed, and a Crannog Centre created; it's by the water just after you start out on the south loch road.

Loch Tay is immense, 14 miles long, but on the north side the ride twice turns away from it. The first time is to ride up Glen Lochay as far as the metalled road goes, and back; the next is to scale the pass between some of the mountains that line Loch Tay's north side. The highest, Ben Lawers, is the tenth highest mountain in Britain at 1214 metres, and is just east of this road. If visibility is fine you should see it as you ride along the Loch Tay road.

From Bridge of Balgie an out-and-back leg leads to another lonely loch in Glen Lyon, before following the River Lyon east around the back of the Ben Lawers massif, past the Tay Forest Park to the Appin of Dull. It sounds a terrible place, but it's not. Appin is an old word for abbey and Dull is a pretty village that lies just above the wide, flat floodplain formed by the Tay where it flows out of Loch Tay. The people of Dull have a great sense of humour – in 2012 they invited the Oregon town of Boring to twin with them, and Boring accepted.

This wider opening in the mountains has probably been lived in for a long time because evidence of Stone Age markings has been found on rocks around the Appin of Dull. The valley leads back to Aberfeldy, where it closes up again, explaining why people chose to live here. It's an area that outsiders would have found hard to discover.

START + FINISH:
Aberfeldy

GETTING THERE:
Aberfeldy is 33 miles north-west of Perth and reached via the A9 and A827.

BIKE SHOP: Escape Route in nearby Pitlochry is a well-stocked and very competent shop.

CAFE: The Watermill Bookshop in Kenmore has a cafe and is also a very interesting place to visit.

LOCAL DELICACY:
Perthshire ham

NORTHERN SCOTLAND

LOCH LOMOND AND THE TROSSACHS

'THE ROAD CLIMBS SLOWLY UPWARDS UNTIL YOU BREAK CLEAR OF THE FOREST AND DESCEND TO LOCH ARKLET'

The most satisfying rides are loops, but occasionally the land doesn't lend itself to one, and that's especially true in the mountains. A loop of Loch Lomond and the Trossachs wouldn't do the area justice, so this ride has two out-and-back legs in order to reveal its secrets and its full beauty.

It starts in Drymen, which looks like a rural outpost but is surprisingly close to Glasgow. The first leg is to a ferry pier under Ben Lomond and back, riding a quiet road that rises and falls next to Loch Lomond and is part of the West Highland Way cycle route. I'm not sure if this is the high road or the low road, but the banks of Loch Lomond are certainly bonny.

Back in Drymen there's a tough climb through Garadhban Forest called Bat a' Charchel, before a long descent through the much larger Loch Ard Forest, where there are some great mountain-bike trails. You're heading for Aberfoyle.

This is Rob Roy country. Rob Roy McGregor was born by the side of Loch

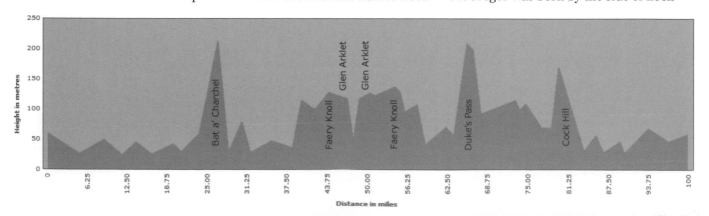

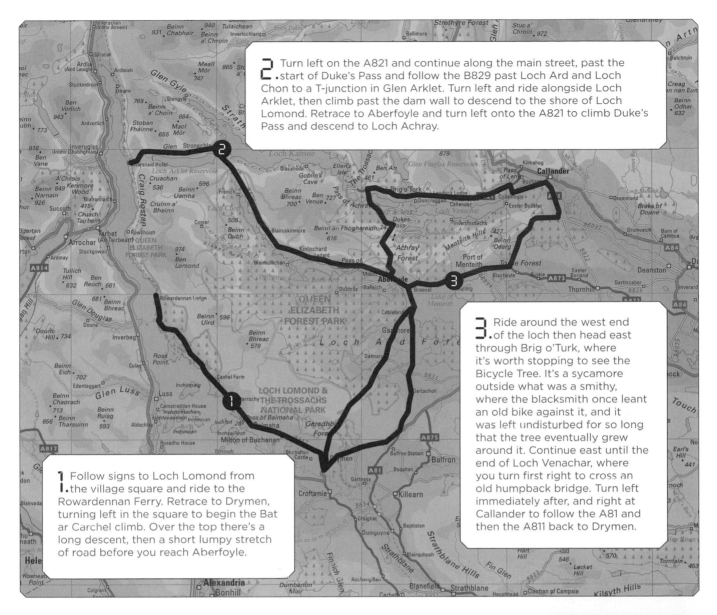

2. Turn left on the A821 and continue along the main street, past the start of Duke's Pass and follow the B829 past Loch Ard and Loch Chon to a T-junction in Glen Arklet. Turn left and ride alongside Loch Arklet, then climb past the dam wall to descend to the shore of Loch Lomond. Retrace to Aberfoyle and turn left onto the A821 to climb Duke's Pass and descend to Loch Achray.

3. Ride around the west end of the loch then head east through Brig o'Turk, where it's worth stopping to see the Bicycle Tree. It's a sycamore outside what was a smithy, where the blacksmith once leant an old bike against it, and it was left undisturbed for so long that the tree eventually grew around it. Continue east until the end of Loch Venachar, where you turn first right to cross an old humpback bridge. Turn left immediately after, and right at Callander to follow the A81 and then the A811 back to Drymen.

1. Follow signs to Loch Lomond from the village square and ride to the Rowardennan Ferry. Retrace to Drymen, turning left in the square to begin the Bat ar Carchel climb. Over the top there's a long descent, then a short lumpy stretch of road before you reach Aberfoyle.

Katrine, just over the Duke's Pass from Aberfoyle, and was a Scottish 18th-century Robin Hood. He was a real person, and his legend was set forever when Sir Walter Scott published the book *Rob Roy* in 1817. It's been adapted into two films, most recently with Liam Neeson in the title role.

Duke's Pass comes later. Aberfoyle is the start of the second out-and-back leg of this ride, a wonderful section along a deep, forested valley, where Loch Ard and Loch Chon lie. The road climbs slowly upwards until you break clear of the forest and descend to Loch Arklet.

This is remote. It lies in its own glen between Loch Katrine and Loch Lomond, and that's your turnaround point. It's a quiet place, a secret one, too, a place where Rob Roy used to hide and where the authorities built a garrison to flush him out.

Back in Aberfoyle the theme turns from folk legend to cycling ones. The next section follows the route of Scotland's oldest bike race: the Tour of the Trossachs time trial. It has been won by the best Scottish racers, including the Tour de France King of the Mountains Robert Millar and the world record holder Graeme Obree. The key to the whole race is the Duke's Pass, and it's a stunning place. From the summit you see into the heart of the Trossachs, across to the summits of Ben Venue and Ben Ledi, and down into Lochs Achray and Venachar.

They are where the ride goes, around Loch Achray and along its north shore, then the north shore of Loch Venachar and through Brig o'Turk to Callander. The race route continues past the Lake of Menteith to Braeval, and then you shoot south for the start of the last leg back to Drymen.

START + FINISH:
Drymen

GETTING THERE:
Drymen is 22 miles north of Glasgow using the A809 and A811. There's no rail link but there is a bus service.

BIKE SHOP: **Lomond Activities**

CAFE: **The Pottery Cafe in the village square**

LOCAL DELICACY:
Harviestoun Schiehallion draught beer

KNAPDALE

Knapdale isn't the obvious choice for a bike ride. It's a lonely, weather-beaten extension to Scotland, hanging down between the mainland and Jura, and separated from both by either sea or sea loch. A narrow waist of land connects Knapdale to Argyll in the north, and an even narrower neck connects it to Kintyre in the south. In fact it's a struggle to find 100 miles of road on Kintyre, but I managed, just, with a bit of repetition and a short loop in Argyll to start with. However, it's well worth visiting because cycling in Knapdale is a joy on so many levels.

On this compact ride not only do you start and finish at Lochgilphead but you also pass through it en route. It's one of the quietest county towns you'll ever visit, but Lochgilphead made worldwide news in 2012 when a local nine-year-old's school writing project went viral. She is Martha Payne and her blog is called Never Seconds. In it she describes her school meals in the manner of a restaurant critic. The local council banned it at first, but retreated in the face of criticism and Martha raised over £100,000 for charity.

The Argyll loop is nothing like the rest of the ride. It's a circuit of Moine Mhor, a pan-flat wetland of open ponds and mossy hummocks. You reach it by a bridge over the River Add and the Crinan Canal, which was built to provide a direct, navigable link between the Inner Hebrides and Glasgow via the River Clyde, without sailing right around Kintyre.

This part of Scotland is where the Clyde Puffers plied their trade. They were tiny steam ships that carried any cargo they could get from Glasgow to the isolated communities of Argyll, Kintyre and the Western Isles. Their crews and captains were colourful characters, and their lives are immortalised in the fictional Para Handy books written by a Glasgow journalist called Neil Munro.

The attraction of this ride becomes clear on the section down to Danna Island, which is at the end of a 12-mile finger of land pointing south-west into the Sound of Jura. It's an exciting journey, with a band of rocky hills on one side and Loch Sween on the other. Time it right and you can ride on Danna, which is cut off by the high tide.

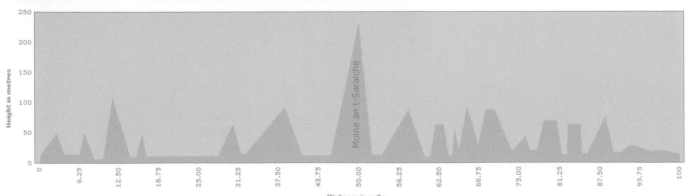

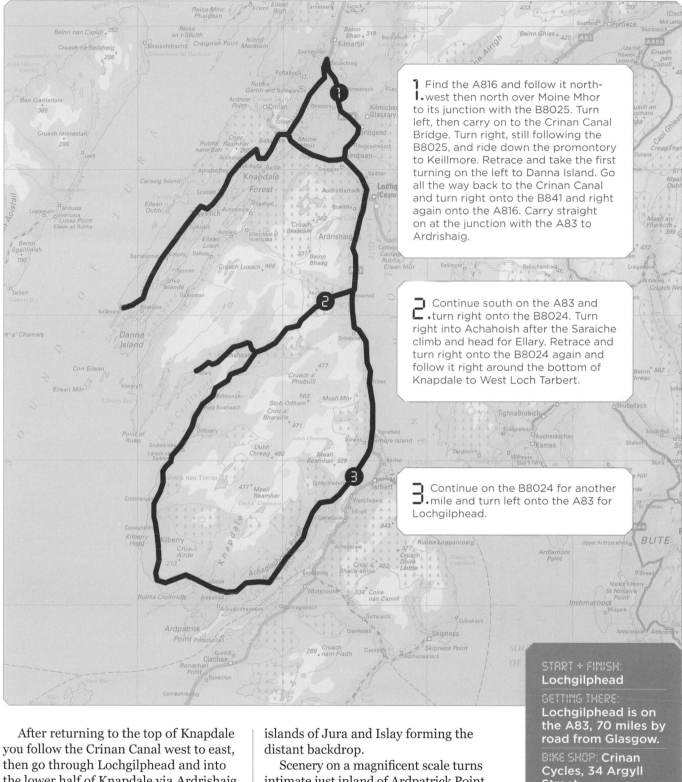

1. Find the A816 and follow it north-west then north over Moine Mhor to its junction with the B8025. Turn left, then carry on to the Crinan Canal Bridge. Turn right, still following the B8025, and ride down the promontory to Keillmore. Retrace and take the first turning on the left to Danna Island. Go all the way back to the Crinan Canal and turn right onto the B841 and right again onto the A816. Carry straight on at the junction with the A83 to Ardrishaig.

2. Continue south on the A83 and turn right onto the B8024. Turn right into Achahoish after the Saraiche climb and head for Ellary. Retrace and turn right onto the B8024 again and follow it right around the bottom of Knapdale to West Loch Tarbert.

3. Continue on the B8024 for another mile and turn left onto the A83 for Lochgilphead.

After returning to the top of Knapdale you follow the Crinan Canal west to east, then go through Lochgilphead and into the lower half of Knapdale via Ardrishaig and the edge of Loch Fyne.

Striking inland you climb the only long hill, Moine an t-Saraiche, which just about scrapes the 200-metre contour after three miles of climbing from sea level. You return to the sea on the other side at Loch Caolisport, where a fascinating ride around the Knapdale coast begins. Sea loch becomes open sea, with the bulky

islands of Jura and Islay forming the distant backdrop.

Scenery on a magnificent scale turns intimate just inland of Ardpatrick Point as you swing through 180 degrees and onto the banks of West Loch Tarbert to begin the run for home. Loch Fyne is your company for the final leg, with the Isle of Bute behind you and the mainland immediately across the loch. The road runs right next to the rocky shore, squeezed there by a chain of peaks of which Sliabh Gaoil is the highest at 562 metres.

START + FINISH:
Lochgilphead

GETTING THERE:
Lochgilphead is on the A83, 70 miles by road from Glasgow.

BIKE SHOP: Crinan Cycles, 34 Argyll Street

CAFE: Argyll Cafe, 25 Argyll Street

LOCAL DELICACY:
Loch Fyne kippers

SOUTHERN SCOTLAND

THE LAMMERMUIRS

RIDE FACTS

Rating
Hard

Total climbing
1600 metres

Killer climb
Wanside Rig

'IT'S A LONELY LANDSCAPE BUT A HAUNTING ONE, TOO'

The Lammermuir Hills have the look of English moorland rather than Scottish mountain. They aren't high; Meikle Says Law at 532 metres is the roof of the Lammermuirs, or Lammermoor as the area was known. They share a landscape with neighbouring Northumberland. Even the hills' suffixes, Law and Rig, are just as common south of the border.

Start in Duns, birthplace of 1963 and 1965 Formula 1 champion Jim Clark, and head west across the southern edge of the Lammermuirs to Lauderdale and the Royal Burgh of Lauder. It's a pretty place but a busy one, because the A68 runs straight up Lauderdale to Edinburgh. You quickly

leave it behind, though, as you climb over Lauder Common and descend to much more peaceful Stow.

Stow is on the banks of Gala Water, an attractive river that winds through a steep-sided valley to join the Tweed between Galashiels and Melrose. And Gala Water keeps you company for the next few miles as you climb steadily up its valley, then that of its tributary, Armet Water, for a long and winding climb to the edge of Fala Moor.

After a short descent the next part of the ride undulates through pleasant farmland to Gifford, where Scotland's great reformer John Knox was born. So

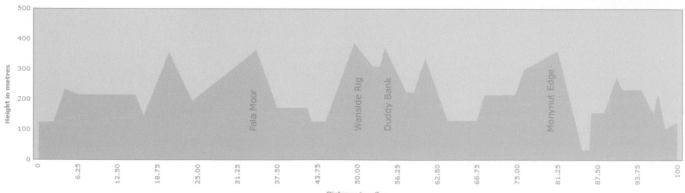

Height in metres

500
400
300
200
100
0

Fala Moor

Wanside Rig

Duddy Bank

Monynut Edge

0   6.25   12.50   18.75   25.00   31.25   37.50   43.75   50.00   56.25   62.50   68.75   75.00   81.25   87.50   93.75   100

Distance in miles

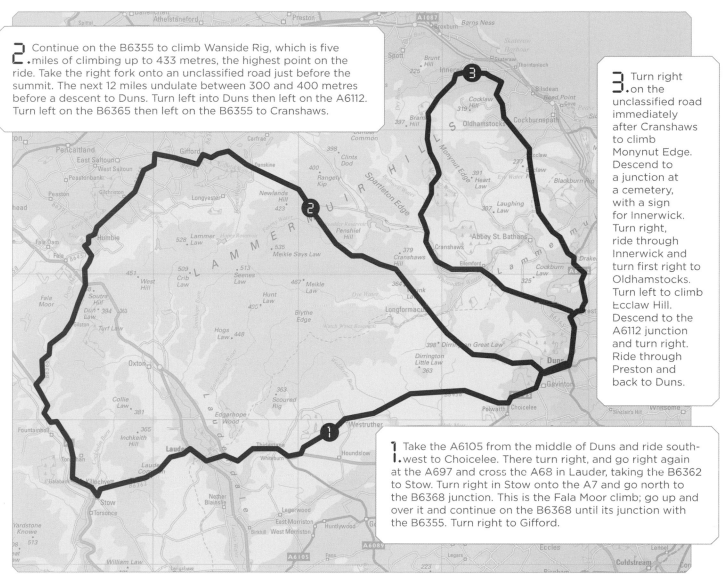

2. Continue on the B6355 to climb Wanside Rig, which is five miles of climbing up to 433 metres, the highest point on the ride. Take the right fork onto an unclassified road just before the summit. The next 12 miles undulate between 300 and 400 metres before a descent to Duns. Turn left into Duns then left on the A6112. Turn left on the B6365 then left on the B6355 to Cranshaws.

3. Turn right on the unclassified road immediately after Cranshaws to climb Monynut Edge. Descend to a junction at a cemetery, with a sign for Innerwick. Turn right, ride through Innerwick and turn first right to Oldhamstocks. Turn left to climb Ecclaw Hill. Descend to the A6112 junction and turn right. Ride through Preston and back to Duns.

1. Take the A6105 from the middle of Duns and ride south-west to Choicelee. There turn right, and go right again at the A697 and cross the A68 in Lauder, taking the B6362 to Stow. Turn right in Stow onto the A7 and go north to the B6368 junction. This is the Fala Moor climb; go up and over it and continue on the B6368 until its junction with the B6355. Turn right to Gifford.

far you've skirted the Lammermuirs, going from their south to their north side; now you climb into them. There's a drag out of town through Yester Woods, with the once dramatic Yester Castle on your right, then you descend sharply before just as sharply beginning to climb again.

A tough and exposed slog takes you to Wanside Rig and into the heart of the Lammermuirs. Now you see them for what they are, a huge horizon of subtly shaded moorland, topped by hundreds of little peaks and under vast and often changing sky.

Duddy Bank is hard, and the wind can be your best friend or worst enemy here. Whatever its direction, you will feel it; there's nothing, and certainly no trees, to stop it. It's a lonely landscape but a haunting one, too, a place for thinking big thoughts. The only place of any size is Longformacus, where Gaetano Donizetti

set his opera *Lucia di Lammermoor*, based on Sir Walter Scott's *The Bride of Lammermoor*.

The ride continues in character again to Duns, where a loop of the Lammermuirs' eastern fringe starts. This traces the Whiteadder valley (yes, there's a Blackadder south of Duns, too) up to Monynut Edge, and it's a spectacular experience. You climb up the face of a steep valley cut by the tumbling Gowt Burn, through a pass at the top, then plunge down to Innerwick to catch a glimpse of the North Sea.

Inland you face a little more climbing. Ecclaw Hill is tough, but it's the last big climb of the day as the rest of the ride is mostly downhill to Preston; then there's a little climb back to Duns. It's a good ride, a different ride for Scotland, and one that prepares you for the changes south of the border.

START + FINISH:
Duns

GETTING THERE:
Duns is on the A6105, 15 miles west of Berwick-upon-Tweed and the A1. Berwick is on the East Coast main rail line, with a bus link to Duns.

BIKE SHOP:
Border Bikes

CAFE: Cedar Cafe

LOCAL DELICACY:
Hoardweel Farm Organics Berkshire pork

SOUTHERN SCOTLAND

ETTRICK FOREST

RIDE FACTS

Rating
Hard

Total climbing
2095 metres

Killer climb
Devil's Beef Tub

'IT'S SO QUIET AND PEACEFUL THAT TIME SEEMS SUSPENDED HERE'

All of this ride is beautiful, but one part stands out. Locals call it Talla, a high-sided valley with a pale-blue lake at the bottom, surrounded by green and purple hills. It's so quiet and peaceful that time, or at least normal time, seems suspended here.

The start is in bustling Peebles, not far south of Edinburgh, and the ride is based on a circuit that keen Edinburgh cyclists have ridden for years. It begins by the River Tweed, and follows it downstream

to Innerleithen on a back road that mimics the meanders. You leave the river, only to meet its source later and follow it back to Peebles.

Leaving the Tweed at Traquair brings on the first climb, a long pull up Paddock Burn to the base of Mountbenger Law, where after a short descent you enter the Yarrow valley. Yarrow Water tumbles down bare hillsides today, most of the area having become pasture land hundreds of years

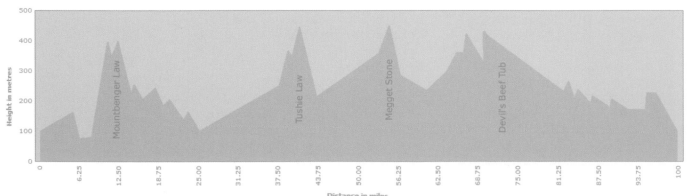

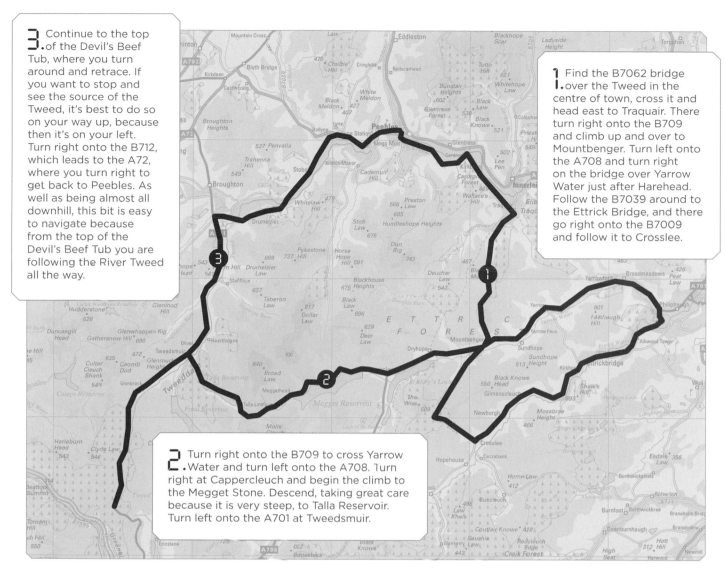

3. Continue to the top of the Devil's Beef Tub, where you turn around and retrace. If you want to stop and see the source of the Tweed, it's best to do so on your way up, because then it's on your left. Turn right onto the B712, which leads to the A72, where you turn right to get back to Peebles. As well as being almost all downhill, this bit is easy to navigate because from the top of the Devil's Beef Tub you are following the River Tweed all the way.

1. Find the B7062 bridge over the Tweed in the centre of town, cross it and head east to Traquair. There turn right onto the B709 and climb up and over to Mountbenger. Turn left onto the A708 and turn right on the bridge over Yarrow Water just after Harehead. Follow the B7039 around to the Ettrick Bridge, and there go right onto the B7009 and follow it to Crosslee.

2. Turn right onto the B709 to cross Yarrow Water and turn left onto the A708. Turn right at Cappercleuch and begin the climb to the Megget Stone. Descend, taking great care because it is very steep, to Talla Reservoir. Turn left onto the A701 at Tweedsmuir.

---

ago, but once this was in the heart of Ettrick Forest.

It's an area with literary connections. The poet James Hogg, known as 'the Ettrick Shepherd', farmed in the area, and David Balfour, the hero of Robert Louis Stevenson's book *Kidnapped* came from a fictional village in the forest. Ettrick still inspires writers today, such as Alice Munro, and you can see why.

Yarrow Water joins Ettrick Water near Selkirk, and they both join the Tweed further downstream, but you head in the opposite direction, up the Ettrick valley, then over a shoulder of Turner Cleuch Law and back to the Yarrow, close to where it flows out of St Mary's Loch. The route then runs along the north side of the loch, leaving it at Cappercleuch to climb towards Talla.

You climb past Megget Reservoir and get your first glimpse of Talla at the Megget Stone, and it feels like discovering a lost world. There's an exhilarating

plunge down a steep descent and within seconds you are in the valley bottom. There's something slightly magical about Talla. Maybe it's the quiet, or the unique green in the grass, or a faint purple in the grey rock. It has them all.

The valley ends as Talla's stream flows into the Tweed, now a much noisier river than the stately and older one you left back in Innerleithen. This is also the beginning of the Devil's Beef Tub climb.

It's long but not too steep, and it's wild and exposed, too. You pass the source of the Tweed, marked by a stone before the summit, from where you look down into the Devil's Beef Tub itself. It's a huge natural hollow in the mountainside, where the 17th-century Border Reivers used to hide their rustled cattle.

The summit is your turning place, where you can ready yourself for a long descent. First by the way you came, and then, still mostly downhill, following the Tweed all the way back to Peebles.

START + FINISH:
Peebles

GETTING THERE:
Peebles is 23 miles south of Edinburgh by the A703 and A701. There's no rail link but a good bus service from Edinburgh.

BIKE SHOP: Alpine Bikes in Innerleithen

CAFE: Cocoa Black near Cuddy Bridge

LOCAL DELICACY: Clootie dumplings

TEVIOTDALE, ESKDALE AND LIDDESDALE

RIDE FACTS

Rating
Very hard

Total climbing
1990 metres

Killer climb
Note o' the Gate

'THE TREES CUT OUT THE WIND AND BUFFER ALMOST ALL SOUNDS'

Craik, Eskdalemuir, Newcastleton and Wauchope – this is the Tour of Forests. Apart from a few stretches of open countryside, it's green, sometimes mysterious and sometimes very dark. It's a ride for sunny days, when the leaves sparkle and shadows dance; on other days this will be a ride for profound thoughts and silent contemplation.

Hawick is the place to start. It's the capital of Scottish knitwear and it's big rugby union country. Bill McLaren, 'the voice of rugby', came from Hawick. The town is in the middle of Teviotdale, and this ride explores the Teviot watershed and beyond.

It begins with a tough climb to the summit at Bellendean Rig; ten miles gone, 90 to go. The view is huge; Craik Forest is on your left, Hawick behind, and in front the twin peaks of Cacra Hill (471 metres) and Annelshope Hill (434 metres). You descend with the run of Rankle Burn then swing south-west into the Upper Ettrick valley and towards a deeper encounter with Craik Forest.

The road runs up a small river valley. The forests cover acres of hills dissected by noisy burns and fast-flowing rivers. Many of the burns are salmon spawning grounds, and if you time your visit well you could catch a silvery flash as the fish negotiate the rocky sections.

Look out for the seismological station just as you leave the forest and enter Eskdalemuir, although anything as dramatic as an earthquake will be the last thing on your mind. The peace and tranquillity of this ride are incredible. The trees cut out the wind and buffer almost all sounds except for those of the birds that live among them. You'll pass the Samye Ling Buddhist Centre, the first in the western world, in a clearing in Eskdalemuir Forest. There's nowhere more suitable.

Follow the White Esk for a while as it flows south through Castle O'er Forest to join the Black Esk. The route does the same later, but first you cut a corner by climbing Shaw Rigg. Then the Black and White join to form a single Esk, and the road follows its valley bottom until a short sharp climb just before Langholm. This is the historic home of the Armstrong clan. First man on the moon Neil Armstrong had roots here, and he was made a freeman of the town.

Leaving Langholm you also leave Eskdale to take on the lumpy ride into Liddesdale and begin a long haul up the valley. On one side is a forest, on the other the dark, denuded shape of Arnton Fell and Saughtree Fell.

Saughtree village is where the ride's hardest climb, Note o' the Gate, begins. It's five miles long and wriggles its way up to 376 metres through Wauchope Forest. You might see black grouse here or goshawks. Wauchope is the last forest of the day; now there's just a loop into the main Teviot valley to go before a little sting in the tail: a steep climb called Crumhaugh Hill that is right at the entrance to Hawick.

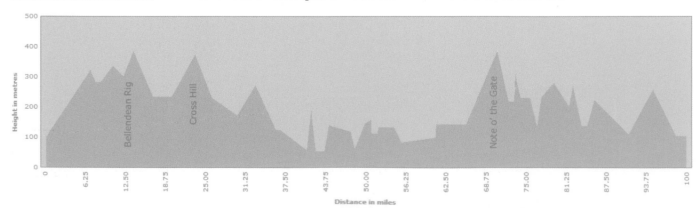

Height in metres / Bellendean Rig / Cross Hill / Note o' the Gate / Distance in miles

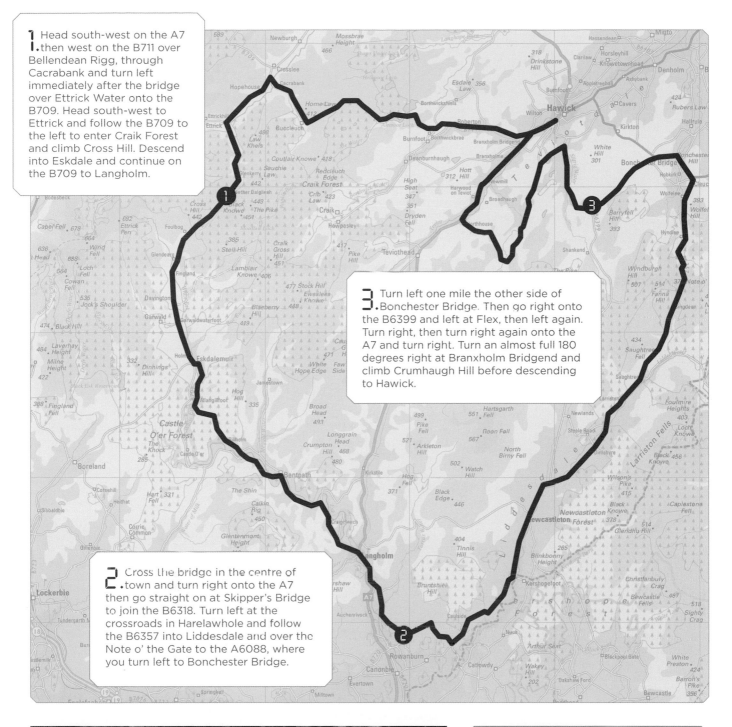

1. Head south-west on the A7 then west on the B711 over Bellendean Rigg, through Cacrabank and turn left immediately after the bridge over Ettrick Water onto the B709. Head south-west to Ettrick and follow the B709 to the left to enter Craik Forest and climb Cross Hill. Descend into Eskdale and continue on the B709 to Langholm.

3. Turn left one mile the other side of Bonchester Bridge. Then go right onto the B6399 and left at Flex, then left again. Turn right, then turn right again onto the A7 and turn right. Turn an almost full 180 degrees right at Branxholm Bridgend and climb Crumhaugh Hill before descending to Hawick.

2. Cross the bridge in the centre of town and turn right onto the A7 then go straight on at Skipper's Bridge to join the B6318. Turn left at the crossroads in Harelawhole and follow the B6357 into Liddesdale and over the Note o' the Gate to the A6088, where you turn left to Bonchester Bridge.

START + FINISH: Hawick

GETTING THERE: Hawick is on the A7, 49 miles north of Carlisle. There's no rail line to Hawick but there's a regular bus service from Edinburgh, and the London (Victoria) to Edinburgh coach service stops in Hawick.

BIKE SHOP: Borders Cycles

CAFE: The Damascus Drum on Silver Street

LOCAL DELICACY: Tea-smoked Borders lamb

SOUTH AYRSHIRE

RIDE FACTS

Rating
Hard

Total climbing
1400 metres

Killer climb
Nick of the
Balloch Pass

Starting in Girvan, with most of the first half flat and all the second half hilly, this ride explores the South Ayrshire coast and interior: the cliffs, hills and forests of a sparsely populated part of Britain that is great for cycling. And South Ayrshire has a rich cycling history. The Girvan Three Day was until recently one of the top races in the country, and the innovative world-record breaker Graeme Obree lives just north of this route. It includes some of his training roads.

The ride begins with a trip down the undulating A77 coast road to Ballantrae. It's a splendid ride with great views over the Firth of Clyde to Arran. On a clear day you can see the Mull of Kintyre and the tiny island of Ailsa Craig, or Paddy's Milestone as it's known locally because it's on the way to Ireland. Take care, though, because the A77 is the link between Glasgow and the ferry port of Stranraer, so it's much used by heavy-goods vehicles.

The busy bit only lasts ten miles;

you are soon into quieter country, following the River Stinchar north-east to Pinwherry, then south-east through Barrhill, after which the road climbs over Dornal Hill and you slip into Galloway. There's a long descent to Bargrennan, where the ride changes from scenic to spectacular.

The huge Glentrool Forest, draped over a range of hills, continues for miles in every direction. You ride through it up Glen Trool past the 7stanes mountain-bike centre to the loch and back, then on to the foot of the Nick of the Balloch Pass, which is so good I've made you climb it twice. Well, the last part of it anyway. It's a long pull from Glentrool village; you don't break through the tree line until very close to the summit at 390 metres, and it's a spectacular if very lonely place to be.

The descent takes you over Witches Bridge and you go through North Balloch. Then you begin a loop made up of a delightful little road that wanders between

'ON A CLEAR DAY YOU CAN SEE THE MULL OF KINTYRE AND THE TINY ISLAND OF AILSA CRAIG'

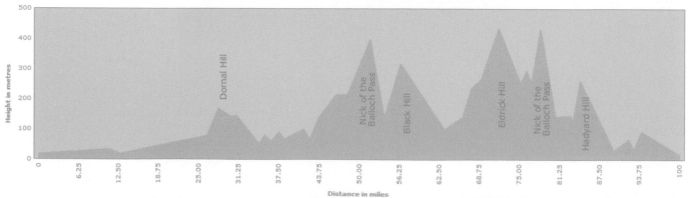

Height in metres

500
400
300
200
100
0

Dornal Hill
Nick of the Balloch Pass
Black Hill
Eldrick Hill
Nick of the Balloch Pass
Hadyard Hill

0   6.25   12.50   18.75   25.00   31.25   37.50   43.75   50.00   56.25   62.50   68.75   75.00   81.25   87.50   93.75   100

Distance in miles

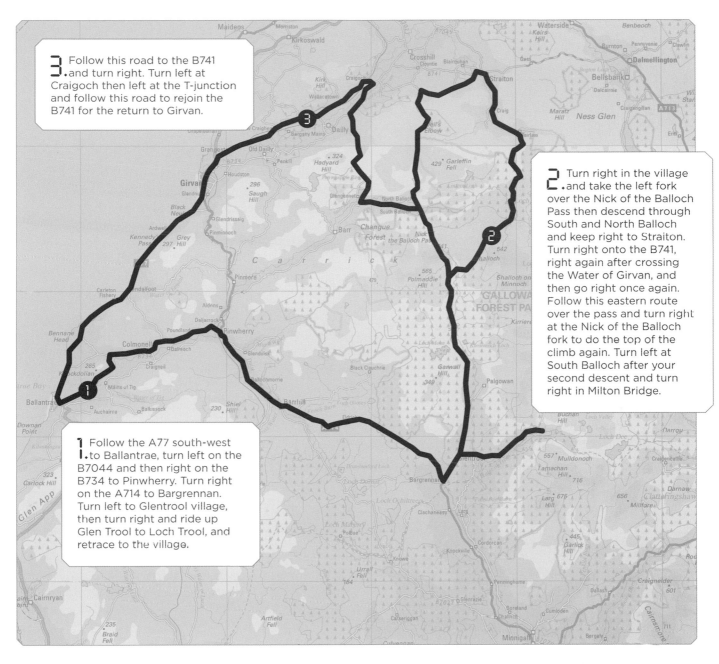

3. Follow this road to the B741 and turn right. Turn left at Craigoch then left at the T-junction and follow this road to rejoin the B741 for the return to Girvan.

2. Turn right in the village and take the left fork over the Nick of the Balloch Pass then descend through South and North Balloch and keep right to Straiton. Turn right onto the B741, right again after crossing the Water of Girvan, and then go right once again. Follow this eastern route over the pass and turn right at the Nick of the Balloch fork to do the top of the climb again. Turn left at South Balloch after your second descent and turn right in Milton Bridge.

1. Follow the A77 south-west to Ballantrae, turn left on the B7044 and then right on the B734 to Pinwherry. Turn right on the A714 to Bargrennan. Turn left to Glentrool village, then turn right and ride up Glen Trool to Loch Trool, and retrace to the village.

the hills to Straiton, from where it follows a lovely winding river called the Water of Girvan upstream until a waterfall splashes into it.

This signals the start of the pass between Eldrick Hill and Shalloch, which tops out at 433 metres, with a descent that joins the ascent of Nick of the Balloch — not too far from its summit, thankfully. Up and over you go again, only this time turning left at South Balloch to ride with the flow of the River Stinchar.

After a few idyllic miles the route leaves the river and heads north towards Maybole. Graeme Obree lives just a bit further north of here, but he often trains on the roads you've just ridden. Obree turned cycling upside down when he

broke the world hour record in 1993, something that had previously been the preserve of top Tour de France racers.

Amazingly, Obree beat the world's best by riding a radically designed bike that he had made himself and he was fuelled by jam sandwiches. He did it again in 1994, and he won two world titles. He was offered a place in a big team but they couldn't accommodate his singular ways, or his principles. He was way ahead of his time and would probably make a fortune if he broke those records today, but when Obree was at his best there wasn't an Obree-shaped space in the cycling world. That's a sobering thought to take along the final stretch to Girvan.

START + FINISH: Girvan

GETTING THERE: Girvan is on the A77, 19 miles south of Ayr and has a rail link with Glasgow.

BIKE SHOP: Carrick Cycles on Main Street in Ayr is the nearest.

CAFE: Maly's on Dalrymple Street

LOCAL DELICACY: Square sausage

LOWTHER HILLS

RIDE FACTS

Rating
Hard

Total climbing
2000 metres

Killer climb
Mennock Pass

The Lowther Hills are an area of rounded peaks and lush green valleys bordered by Clydesdale in the north, Nithsdale in the west and the upper Tweed to the east. Their southern flank is covered by the Forest of Ae.

This ride criss-crosses the Lowthers, using the three passes that cut through the range: the Dalveen, the Mennock and the Crawick. It also visits the Forest of Ae, which mountain-bikers know as part of the 7stanes mountain-bike project. Naturalists know it for red squirrels. The smaller of Britain's two squirrels, the indigenous red has been pushed into small protected areas like this by its grey and much bigger cousin from America.

The Ae loop from Thornhill is a nice warm-up for the Dalveen Pass. This is the longest of the Lowther passes, and the side you climb starts in Carronbridge. It's 7.5 miles up a valley created by Carron Water, which is a strange-looking valley

because it goes from narrow to wide and back to narrow again.

The descent is fun. It's fairly straight and provides a great rush of speed, but go carefully at the sharp bend just before Elvanfoot. That's where the next climb starts, one of the two eastern ascents of the Mennock Pass. This one climbs the Elvan Water valley, after which you turn short of the Mennock summit at Leadhills and descend what is the alternative way over the Mennock from the east. This is a much narrower valley and it leads to Abington and Clydesdale, where the ageless peace you've experienced so far is shattered by the noisy M74.

Luckily the noise is gone in a few minutes. Just follow Duneaton Water to Crawfordjohn, which is where curling stones are made. Next you enter Crawick, the lowest of the Lowther passes. It's hardly a climb from this side. The road gently undulates to Crawick Moss, then descends with a bit more gusto to Crawick village in Nithsdale.

This was an important artery for Scotland in the days before motorways, which explains why the next town, Sanquhar, grew here. Its strange name sounds more like Afghanistan than Scotland, but Sanquhar comes from a Gaelic word meaning old seat. Robbie Burns was a regular visitor to the town, and curling is big here. Sanquhar has one of the oldest curling societies in the world.

The west side of the Mennock Pass starts two miles further down the road.

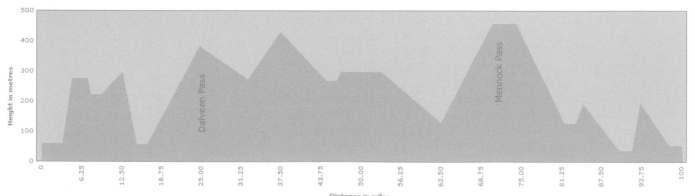

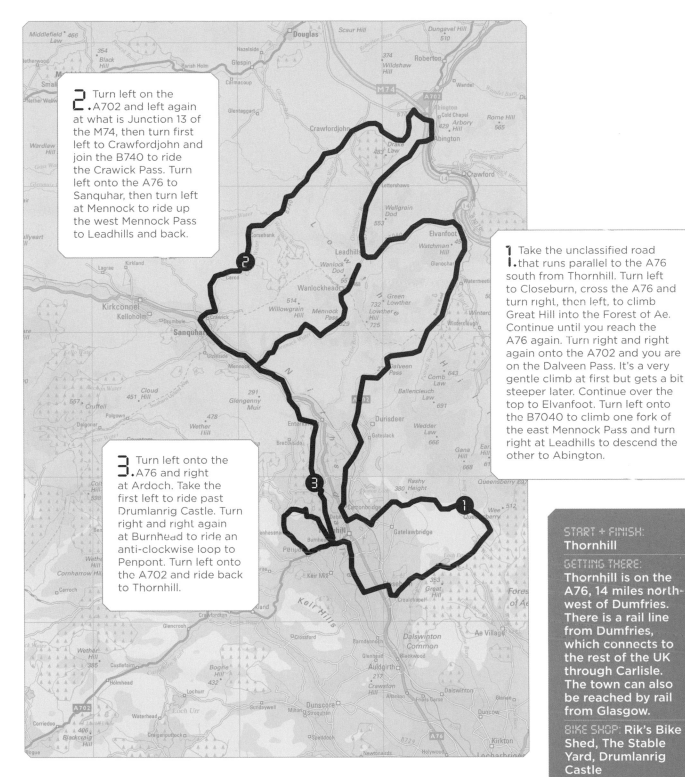

2. Turn left on the A702 and left again at what is Junction 13 of the M74, then turn first left to Crawfordjohn and join the B740 to ride the Crawick Pass. Turn left onto the A76 to Sanquhar, then turn left at Mennock to ride up the west Mennock Pass to Leadhills and back.

1. Take the unclassified road that runs parallel to the A76 south from Thornhill. Turn left to Closeburn, cross the A76 and turn right, then left, to climb Great Hill into the Forest of Ae. Continue until you reach the A76 again. Turn right and right again onto the A702 and you are on the Dalveen Pass. It's a very gentle climb at first but gets a bit steeper later. Continue over the top to Elvanfoot. Turn left onto the B7040 to climb one fork of the east Mennock Pass and turn right at Leadhills to descend the other to Abington.

3. Turn left onto the A76 and right at Ardoch. Take the first left to ride past Drumlanrig Castle. Turn right and right again at Burnhead to ride an anti-clockwise loop to Penpont. Turn left onto the A702 and ride back to Thornhill.

START + FINISH:
Thornhill

GETTING THERE:
Thornhill is on the A76, 14 miles north-west of Dumfries. There is a rail line from Dumfries, which connects to the rest of the UK through Carlisle. The town can also be reached by rail from Glasgow.

BIKE SHOP: Rik's Bike Shed, The Stable Yard, Drumlanrig Castle

CAFE: Drumlanrig Cafe at the castle is used to cyclists because of the mountain-bike centre there.

LOCAL DELICACY: Galloway beef

It's your second ascent, but this time you go all the way to the top. It really is a beautiful climb that winds upwards between glorious hills that become bigger as you approach Wanlockhead and the summit.

This is Scotland's highest village, at a very respectable 489 metres. It has a wild feel, but push on to Leadhills and it gets even wilder. This used to be a busy mining village and the evidence of mining can still be seen all around. It's the coldest place in Britain with a year-round average temperature of 6.81 degrees Celsius.

The descent is wonderful, and so is the trip to Drumlanrig Castle that rounds off this ride. It's called the Pink Palace, because of the unusual sandstone in which it was built, and the roads around it are a delight. This detour was added to make up the 100 miles, but is one worth doing in its own right.

GALLOWAY

'THE ARTISTS CAME FOR THE GENTLE LIGHT AND THE GENTLE WEATHER, BROUGHT TO GALLOWAY BY THE GULF STREAM'

Galloway is an often overlooked part of Scotland. It's a lower part, and a more benign part, particularly so for cycling, but it's no less beautiful than the rest. This ride is typical Galloway; you visit estuaries, cross rivers and see the sea, but most of it is in Galloway's beautiful forested hills, with an occasional glimpse of a craggy mountain to remind you that this is Scotland.

Castle Douglas, named for the Earls of Douglas but a town since Roman times, is the best place to start. It nestles in the lumpy countryside just behind the Galloway coast. The route heads north,

following Ure Water almost to its source, where lumpy becomes hilly.

You climb over the brilliantly named Green Top of Drunwhirn and descend to New Galloway. Famous for the Kite Trail, referring to the elegant, fork-tailed birds of prey you see circling overhead, New Galloway is also the home of the Scottish Alternative Games, held in August each year. Sports include hurling the curling stone, tractor pulling and snail racing. There's a buskers' bandstand, too.

They ought to put a cycling hill climb in the programme, because a long one faces you straight out of town, over the side of

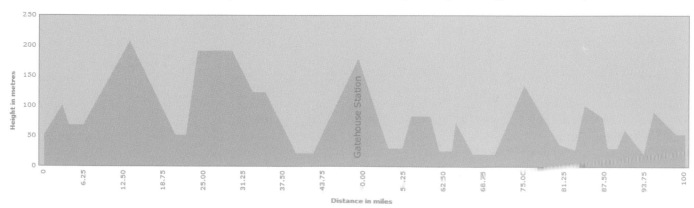

Height in metres — 250, 200, 150, 100, 50

Gatehouse Station

Distance in miles — 0, 6.25, 12.50, 18.75, 25.00, 31.25, 37.50, 43.75, 0.00, 5.25, 62.50, 68.75, 75.00, 81.25, 87.50, 93.75, 100

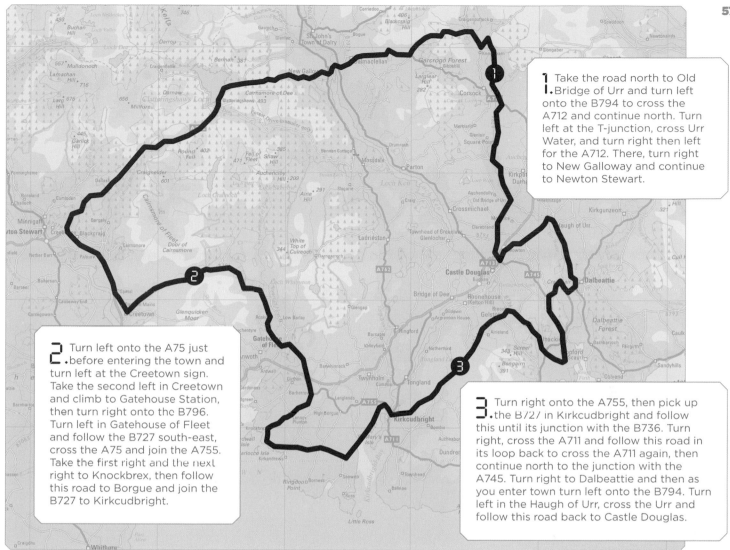

1. Take the road north to Old Bridge of Urr and turn left onto the B794 to cross the A712 and continue north. Turn left at the T-junction, cross Urr Water, and turn right then left for the A712. There, turn right to New Galloway and continue to Newton Stewart.

2. Turn left onto the A75 just before entering the town and turn left at the Creetown sign. Take the second left in Creetown and climb to Gatehouse Station, then turn right onto the B796. Turn left in Gatehouse of Fleet and follow the B727 south-east, cross the A75 and join the A755. Take the first right and the next right to Knockbrex, then follow this road to Borgue and join the B727 to Kirkcudbright.

3. Turn right onto the A755, then pick up the B727 in Kirkcudbright and follow this until its junction with the B736. Turn right, cross the A711 and follow this road in its loop back to cross the A711 again, then continue north to the junction with the A745. Turn right to Dalbeattie and then as you enter town turn left onto the B794. Turn left in the Haugh of Urr, cross the Urr and follow this road back to Castle Douglas.

Cairnsmore to Clatteringshaws Loch. This was created by damming the River Dee and is part of a broader hydro-electric scheme. It looks incredible, a lonely lake in the middle of a huge forest. The forest undulates into the distance, with just an occasional bare top peeking out above the 300-metre contour.

You're now on the Queen's Drive, a stretch of the A712 named to commemorate the Queen's Silver Jubilee in 1977. It leads to Newton Stewart, where you change direction to follow the River Cree downstream almost to Creetown, where another longish climb begins.

This climbs a valley carved by Moneypool Burn, where there is also a disused railway line, up to Gatehouse Station. From here you drop down into the Fleet valley and follow it to Gatehouse of Fleet. You're in a lumpy part again, where chains of similar-sized oval hills line up perpendicular to the coast. This is the north side of the Solway Firth, and you can see the mountains of Cumbria over the water, if it's not raining. On very fine days you can even see the Isle of Man.

A quick loop around the edge of Wigtown Bay, with the Islands of Fleet just offshore, takes you to Kirkcudbright, a town famous for associations with several Scottish artists and as one of the locations for the 1973 horror film *The Wicker Man*. The artists came for the gentle light and the gentle weather, brought to Galloway by the Gulf Stream. It's so gentle that palm trees grow here, especially further west.

The scenery changes again as you climb inland, away from town, and into an area of low mountains that forms the western edge of Dalbeattie Forest. You plunge down towards Orchardton Bay, just catching a glimpse of the sea, then ride up the Urr estuary to the Haugh of Urr before taking the military road back to Castle Douglas.

START + FINISH:
Castle Douglas

GETTING THERE:
Castle Douglas is 57 miles west of Carlisle on the A75. There's no rail line, but there is a rail link to Dumfries from Glasgow and Carlisle, and Dumfries is just 15 miles away with bus links.

BIKE SHOP: Castle Douglas Cycles on Church Street

CAFE: Design Cafe on King Street

LOCAL DELICACY:
Smoked seafood

NORT
EAST
ENGL
ENGL

THE CHEVIOTS

RIDE FACTS

Rating
Hard

Total climbing
1400 metres

Killer climb
Coquetdale

The wild and wonderful Cheviot Hills straddle the eastern half of the Scottish border but lie mostly in England, in the long, lonely county of Northumberland This is the true north, the furthest north in England you can go, and the Cheviots are a vast tract of gaunt, empty hills dissected by secret river valleys.

Alnwick is the place to start; its magnificent castle was home to the powerful medieval Earls of Northumberland. The first leg takes you to Rothbury, where another powerful dynasty made its home. Lord Armstrong, born in Newcastle in 1810, became one of the greatest industrialists of the Victorian age, making armaments and building warships on the Tyne. The house he built in Rothbury is called Cragside, and Armstrong used water from the lakes behind it to create hydro-electricity, which he used to power incandescent lamps. It was the first house in the world to be lit that way, and it's now owned by the National Trust.

Rothbury is on the banks of the River Coquet, and the ride follows the Coquet almost to its source, 21 miles away. Nearly all of this section is uphill, but it's a fantastic experience. The road gets narrower and quieter as you ascend, winding around the hills that the river couldn't wash out of its way. Most of the climb is easy but there are some steep bits, especially near Fulhope.

'THE CHEVIOTS ARE A VAST TRACT OF GAUNT, EMPTY HILLS DISSECTED BY SECRET RIVER VALLEYS'

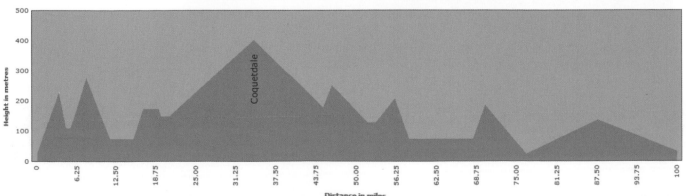

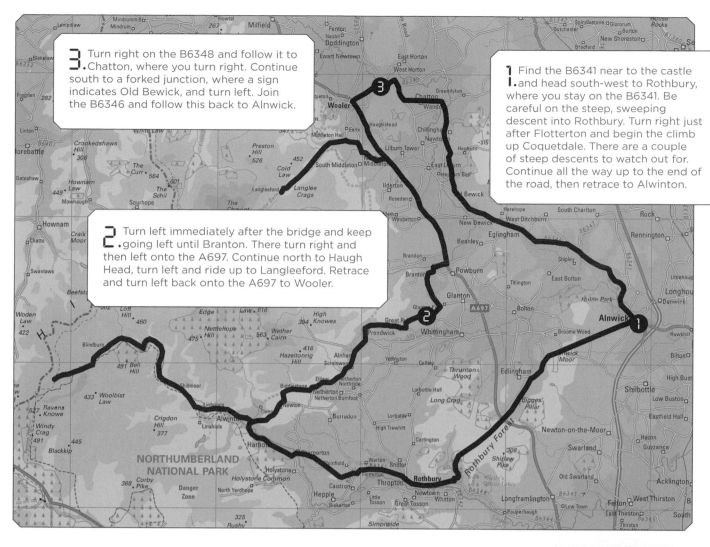

3. Turn right on the B6348 and follow it to Chatton, where you turn right. Continue south to a forked junction, where a sign indicates Old Bewick, and turn left. Join the B6346 and follow this back to Alnwick.

1. Find the B6341 near to the castle and head south-west to Rothbury, where you stay on the B6341. Be careful on the steep, sweeping descent into Rothbury. Turn right just after Flotterton and begin the climb up Coquetdale. There are a couple of steep descents to watch out for. Continue all the way up to the end of the road, then retrace to Alwinton.

2. Turn left immediately after the bridge and keep going left until Branton. There turn right and then left onto the A697. Continue north to Haugh Head, turn left and ride up to Langleeford. Retrace and turn left back onto the A697 to Wooler.

Eventually you come to the end of the road at Chew Green, the site of a Roman camp called Ad Fines. It's next to an older road, one that ran south-east to York. The camp is nearly 400 metres above sea level, 800 metres from the Scottish border, and a wilder, emptier place would be hard to find.

What a Roman soldier must have thought looking out over these barren fells on a bleak January day 2000 years ago, I cannot imagine, but I love it. Northumberland is one of England's undiscovered gems, and a fantastic place for cycling. You'll agree during the descent of Coquetdale and be totally converted by the road that spears north-east out of the dale and follows the southern edges of the Cheviots to Powburn.

There's a stretch of main road after that, north to near Wooler and the start of the second set-piece climb of the day, the Cheviot — well, as far up the Cheviot as you can get by road. Follow Harthope Burn as far as the metalled road goes and

ride back down again. There's a drive at the end of the road, but it leads to a secluded house, Langleeford Hope, and is designated as a footpath so bikes aren't allowed on it.

Riding up a road to a dead end and back is one of the cathartic things cyclists do to pay homage to a place. In this case it's Northumberland's highest mountain. It's only 815 metres, and not much more than a dome of higher land in high country, but the Cheviot still means a lot to a lot of people. None more than the Pennine Way walkers, because the Cheviot is the last hill on the south-to-north route.

Once back on the main road you leave the Northumberland National Park in Wooler and enter a different Northumberland for the ride back to Alnwick. There are no more cathartic acts, no more significant climbs. This is a lower, less wild and slightly more populated Northumberland; a softer end to what is a hard ride.

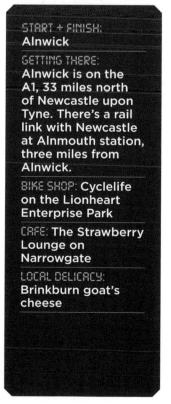

START + FINISH:
Alnwick

GETTING THERE:
Alnwick is on the A1, 33 miles north of Newcastle upon Tyne. There's a rail link with Newcastle at Alnmouth station, three miles from Alnwick.

BIKE SHOP: **Cyclelife on the Lionheart Enterprise Park**

CAFE: **The Strawberry Lounge on Narrowgate**

LOCAL DELICACY: **Brinkburn goat's cheese**

UPPER TYNE VALLEY

NORTH-EAST ENGLAND

RIDE FACTS

Rating
Hard

Total climbing
1800 metres

Killer climb
Willyshaw Rigg

'THE ROUTE GOES AS FAR AS THE ROAD GOES, UNDULATING GENTLY INTO THE MIDDLE OF THE FOREST'

They call it the Coaly Tyne, but that only applies to the river from Newcastle, where back in 1530 some canny merchants won the right to ship every scrap of coal from the whole of the north-east through the city. It's where the saying 'taking coals to Newcastle' comes from. The coal industry is gone now and the lower Tyne is clean, while the upper Tyne is still as unspoilt as it always was.

The Tyne starts life as two rivers, the South and North Tyne, which meet just above Hexham, where this ride starts. The town is dominated by its abbey, and was a significant staging post in the low-level passage through the Pennines between Carlisle and Newcastle. This was created by the Tyne flowing east and the River Irthing flowing west.

This is another ride that starts with a climb, but as compensation all of the tough work is over by halfway. There's a haul of over six miles up the south side of the South Tyne valley, then a switchback descent into the Allen valley. This leads to a longer pull to the ride's highest point on Willyshaw Rigg at 470 metres.

The climb tops out above England's highest town, but you avoid Alston's busy streets by following a steep but narrow descent into the South Tyne valley. You trace the valley floor north on an undulating road before coming to what is probably the hardest section of the ride.

The hills around Featherstone Castle aren't long but they are very steep, and five come in quick succession before a short

stretch of the A69. They all have an average gradient of at least 10 per cent, and a couple have stretches more than twice as steep.

You now meet Hadrian's Wall, which was built from AD 122 to mark the northern limit of the Roman Empire. It stretches from the Solway Firth in the west to Wallsend in the east, and much of it is still visible. It will be your ride partner for a long time, after a brief visit to somewhere very special.

Wark Forest is vast, remote and an oasis of peace. The route goes as far as the road goes, undulating gently into the middle of the forest. At first it seems an unremarkable place, hardly worth the effort, but Wark holds many secrets, notably the Irthing Gorge and its waterfalls, where peregrine falcons nest, and the derelict Blue Streak rocket site.

You get back into contact with Hadrian's Wall at Gilsland and follow it for the next 18 miles before striking off into the North Tyne valley to Bellingham. Pronounced Bellingjum by the locals, this is a stopping place on the Pennine Way, so you'll find plenty of cafes there if you are flagging a bit.

The journey back to Hexham follows the east bank of the North Tyne, crossing Hadrian's Wall again at Low Brunton, where you can just see the remains of a Roman bridge. Take a few deep breaths now, because there's a steep hill called Hill End to come. The good news is that from the top you can freewheel almost all the way to the finish.

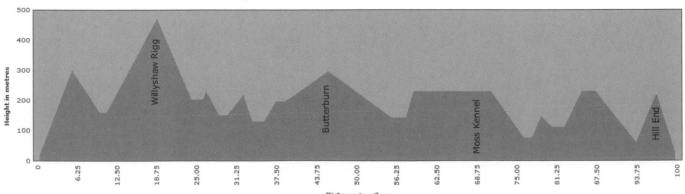

3. Turn right to Townhead, then left on the B6320. Stay on this road right to the centre of Bellingham. Turn right to Redesmouth and right just after Redesmouth to Birtley. Turn left after Birtley then left at the next T-junction. Turn right just after Barrasford and right onto the A6079. Turn left at Low Brunton onto the B6318. Turn right at Milecastle 25, then take the next right and third left to follow signs back to Hexham.

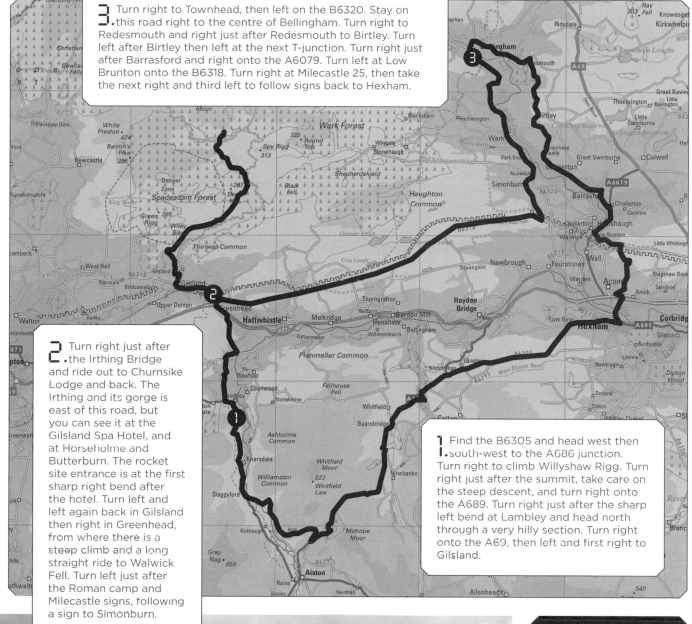

2. Turn right just after the Irthing Bridge and ride out to Churnsike Lodge and back. The Irthing and its gorge is east of this road, but you can see it at the Gilsland Spa Hotel, and at Horseholme and Butterburn. The rocket site entrance is at the first sharp right bend after the hotel. Turn left and left again back in Gilsland then right in Greenhead, from where there is a steep climb and a long straight ride to Walwick Fell. Turn left just after the Roman camp and Milecastle signs, following a sign to Simonburn.

1. Find the B6305 and head west then south-west to the A686 junction. Turn right to climb Willyshaw Rigg. Turn right just after the summit, take care on the steep descent, and turn right onto the A689. Turn right just after the sharp left bend at Lambley and head north through a very hilly section. Turn right onto the A69, then left and first right to Gilsland.

START + FINISH:
Hexham

GETTING THERE:
Hexham is next to the A69, 22 miles west of Newcastle city centre. There's a regular rail and bus link with Newcastle, too.

BIKE SHOP: The Bike Shop, St Mary's Chare

CAFE: Mrs Miggin's Coffee House, St Mary's Wynd

LOCAL DELICACY: Pease pudding

WEARDALE

RIDE FACTS

Rating
Very hard

Total climbing
3000 metres

Killer climb
Crawleyside

'THIS IS HARD CYCLING, BUT THE ROADS ARE QUIET AND THE VIEWS ARE STUNNING'

The year 2012 saw a British racer wearing the rainbow jersey as world road champion and another Briton winning the world's biggest road race, the Tour de France, but there has never been a big professional road race held regularly in this country. We've hosted the world championships a couple of times and had sections of the Tour de France here, but we haven't got a Classic, a major single-day road race. We could have one; we have the terrain to make a Classic, and it's in Weardale. There was a race here once, the Vaux Grand Prix, and it attracted some really big names during the 1960s and 1970s. Its route could stand comparison with any of the major races in the world today. You'll see why when you've ridden this one.

The ride starts and finishes where the Vaux GP started and finished, in Wolsingham, the gateway to Weardale. You do five miles to settle in, and then the climbing begins. Crawleyside gets the killer climb tag, but the choice is marginal because the hills here are all fearsome. Crawleyside wins because its first two bends are very tough, and its overall height gain is big.

The Durham Fells are like this; steep at first and with wide, rounded tops. They are bare and high. This is hard cycling,

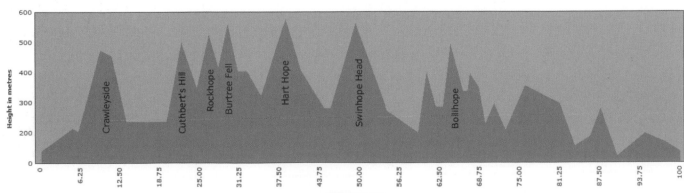

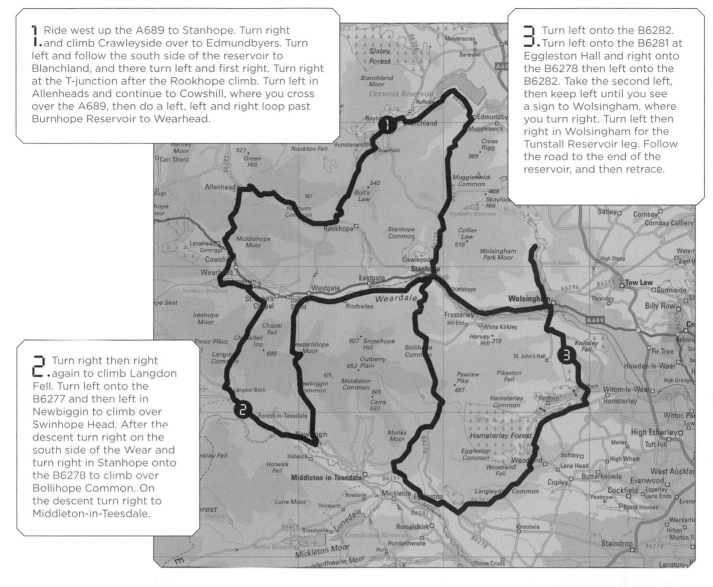

1. Ride west up the A689 to Stanhope. Turn right and climb Crawleyside over to Edmundbyers. Turn left and follow the south side of the reservoir to Blanchland, and there turn left and first right. Turn right at the T-junction after the Rookhope climb. Turn left in Allenheads and continue to Cowshill, where you cross over the A689, then do a left, left and right loop past Burnhope Reservoir to Wearhead.

3. Turn left onto the B6282. Turn left onto the B6281 at Eggleston Hall and right onto the B6278 then left onto the B6282. Take the second left, then keep left until you see a sign to Wolsingham, where you turn right. Turn left then right in Wolsingham for the Tunstall Reservoir leg. Follow the road to the end of the reservoir, and then retrace.

2. Turn right then right again to climb Langdon Fell. Turn left onto the B6277 and then left in Newbiggin to climb over Swinhope Head. After the descent turn right on the south side of the Wear and turn right in Stanhope onto the B6278 to climb over Bollihope Common. On the descent turn right to Middleton-in-Teesdale.

but the roads are quiet and the views are stunning. The route is softer in the valleys, but hard climbs are never far away.

The section past the reservoir at Edmundbyers is typical. It leads to Cuthbert's Hill, a long drag up to 507 metres that's followed by a head-spinning descent to Rookhope Burn and the next climb. The pattern is set: long, hard climbs are followed by steep descents, like the one down to Allenheads, the highest village in England.

Burtree Fell is next, then the giant Langdon Fell, the highest hill on the route at 637 metres and one of the highest metalled roads in Britain. It takes you across Langdon Common to a long, straight descent into Teesdale, where the downhill theme continues past High Force. This is not the highest waterfall in England, as some claim, but the sight of the River Tees crashing down a rock face in a single 21.5-metre drop is still impressive.

Swinhope Head is the next climb, another 600-metre effort through barren moorland, with a tricky descent back into Weardale. You follow the south bank of the river to Stanhope and the start of the last major climb.

The Bollihope Common climb starts with a leg-breaking pitch of 12 per cent, but quickly eases to a long, twisting drag before plunging down into picturesque Middleton-in-Teesdale. This is the busiest section of the ride, as you pass through a series of villages before the trek up along the edge of Hamsterley Forest and back to Wolsingham.

The final leg is added on to bring the ride to 100 miles. It's just out to Tunstall Reservoir and back and is only there to make up the numbers. In fact there's no need to feel guilty if you don't do it, because you've already completed one of the most demanding rides in this book.

They've got to bring that race back here.

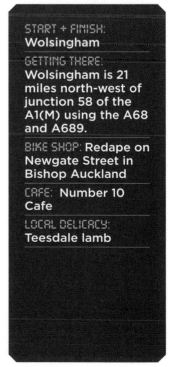

START + FINISH:
Wolsingham

GETTING THERE:
Wolsingham is 21 miles north-west of junction 58 of the A1(M) using the A68 and A689.

BIKE SHOP: Redape on Newgate Street in Bishop Auckland

CAFE: Number 10 Cafe

LOCAL DELICACY: Teesdale lamb

STAINMORE AND SWALEDALE

RIDE FACTS

Rating
Very hard

Total climbing
2200 metres

Killer climb
Lamps Moss

This ride straddles the Pennine spine of Britain and visits two unique areas: wild and empty Stainmore, and the two most northerly of the Yorkshire Dales, Swaledale and Arkengarthdale. It has some tough climbs, and it visits Britain's highest pub.

Richmond is a great town with every amenity for lovers of the outdoors. It's a stage town in the Coast to Coast walk, and it's on several famous cycling routes. It's also close to the Yorkshire Dales, an area that has always attracted adventurous cyclists. The route starts with a quiet amble into the Tees Valley.

The landscape changes through Staindrop as you head into the hills. Shot Moss is a long uphill drag that starts as soon as you cross the River Lune in Mickleton. The vast upland area on your right is the Lune Forest, although there's hardly a tree to be seen. It's one of several old forest sites in the area, reflecting a massively changed landscape.

You soon drop down the other side into Brough, which is the western entrance to the Stainmore Gap. As well as being narrower here, the Pennines are lower, thus creating a gap. The A66, still a very important road route, runs through it, and the gap creates some separation between the Northern Fells and the Yorkshire Dales.

That's where you're heading next, after riding through Kirkby Stephen, where the Midland Room at the railway station is a brilliant cyclists' cafe. Stock up, because the ride out of town is up the hardest hill on the route. It goes up Lamps Moss to Birkdale Common and the source of Birkdale Beck, which joins with Great Sled Dale and Whitsundale Beck just above Keld to form the River Swale.

Swaledale is the most northerly of the better-known dales, but you climb out of it and over to what is actually the most northerly, Arkengarthdale, passing the legendary Tan Hill Inn on the way. This lonely building is the highest pub in Britain, at 528 metres; it has a bleak-looking exterior but a very lively interior.

You descend into Arkengarthdale, where you can still see some evidence of the extensive lead mining that took place there. Then there's a short pass between Reeth Low Moor and Reeth High Moor back into Swaledale.

It's a narrow valley with steep sides but a flat bottom, and if you ride here in the spring the meadows are a blaze

'IF YOU RIDE HERE IN THE SPRING THE MEADOWS ARE A BLAZE OF WILDFLOWERS'

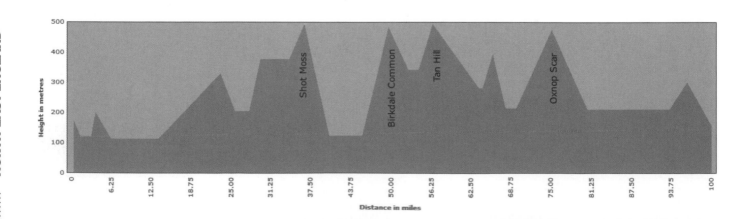

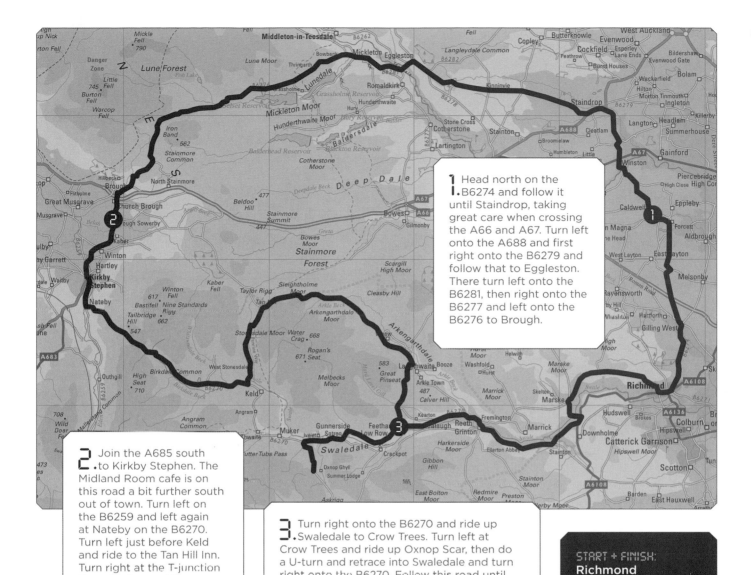

1. Head north on the B6274 and follow it until Staindrop, taking great care when crossing the A66 and A67. Turn left onto the A688 and first right onto the B6279 and follow that to Eggleston. There turn left onto the B6281, then right onto the B6277 and left onto the B6276 to Brough.

2. Join the A685 south to Kirkby Stephen. The Midland Room cafe is on this road a bit further south out of town. Turn left on the B6259 and left again at Nateby on the B6270. Turn left just before Keld and ride to the Tan Hill Inn. Turn right at the T-junction there to descend to Arkengarthdale. Turn right just before Langthwaite and ride to Feetham.

3. Turn right onto the B6270 and ride up Swaledale to Crow Trees. Turn left at Crow Trees and ride up Oxnop Scar, then do a U-turn and retrace into Swaledale and turn right onto the B6270. Follow this road until the A6108 junction and turn left, then left again. Turn right in Marske, from where you have to climb a last, cheeky little hill before descending into Richmond.

of wildflowers; and you will see lambs belonging to the distinctive round-horned Swaledale sheep.

I sent the route up and down Oxnop Scar because if you carry on just past the summit there is a beautiful view into Wensleydale. The top of Oxnop is a great place to stop and imagine what the dale looked like when lead mining thrived here. If you look hard you can link up the scars of old mines, just as they would once have been linked by tracks and roadways. It was totally different from today, a noisy world of fires used for smelting, which is where many of the forests went: into ugly spoil heaps and dammed-up rivers and becks. It's something to think about on the ride back to Richmond.

START + FINISH:
Richmond

GETTING THERE:
Richmond is seven miles from the Catterick exit of the A1 and four from the Scotch Corner exit. Nearest rail link is to Northallerton 13 miles away.

BIKE SHOP: Arthur Caygill Cycles on the Gallowfields Trading Estate, Richmond

CAFE: Dales Bike Centre, Fremington, near Reeth and about seven miles west of Richmond

LOCAL DELICACY: Swaledale cheese

CLEVELAND HILLS

RIDE FACTS

Rating
Hard

Total climbing
1800 metres

Killer climb
Bransdale

The Cleveland Hills are the other side of the more famous North Yorkshire Moors. They form a rolling-topped, steep-sided plateau, but unlike their North Yorkshire cousins the Cleveland Hills are less well known and much quieter. Up here you won't be competing with as many cars out for a spin, even during the summer.

Stokesley sits at the base of the hills, close to their major attractions but in the gently undulating Leven valley, so you can ease yourself into the ride. You enter the Cleveland Hills via the Hambleton Hills at their western edge, a smaller limestone fringe to the darker Jurassic block behind.

The climb onto Osmotherley Moor is short but steep, because the western edge of these hills is almost a cliff face, created during the Ice Age by a glacier that pushed down between these hills and the Pennines towards the Vale of York. The steep-hill theme continues for another 12 miles to Rievaulx, and its magnificent Cistercian abbey.

Technically the ride borrows a bit of the North Yorkshire Moors now, with a loop up and down Bransdale, to its twin peaks on either side of a tiny village called Cockayne. This part of the ride is beautiful and remote; the nearest village to Cockayne is Chop Gate, three miles away over the moors but 22 miles by road.

Chop Gate is in the true Cleveland Hills and you head back there after returning to Helmsley. This is great cycling country, and some of the best races in the UK are

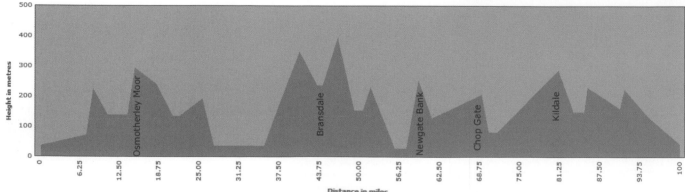

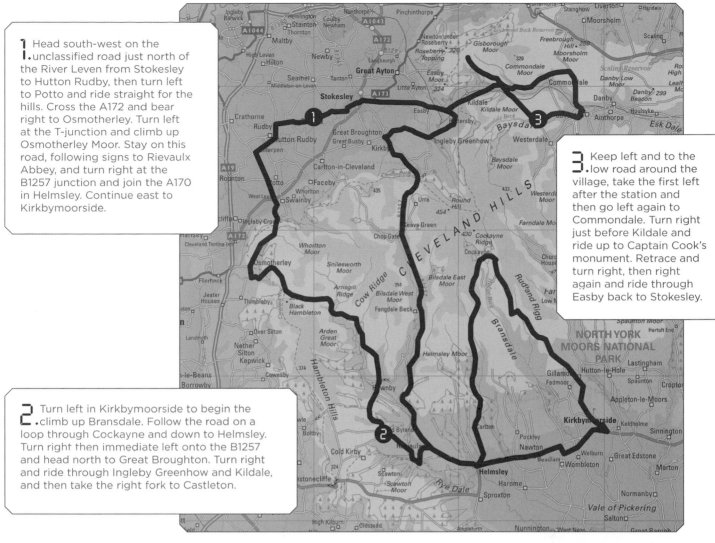

1. Head south-west on the unclassified road just north of the River Leven from Stokesley to Hutton Rudby, then turn left to Potto and ride straight for the hills. Cross the A172 and bear right to Osmotherley. Turn left at the T-junction and climb up Osmotherley Moor. Stay on this road, following signs to Rievaulx Abbey, and turn right at the B1257 junction and join the A170 in Helmsley. Continue east to Kirkbymoorside.

3. Keep left and to the low road around the village, take the first left after the station and then go left again to Commondale. Turn right just before Kildale and ride up to Captain Cook's monument. Retrace and turn right, then right again and ride through Easby back to Stokesley.

2. Turn left in Kirkbymoorside to begin the climb up Bransdale. Follow the road on a loop through Cockayne and down to Helmsley. Turn right then immediate left onto the B1257 and head north to Great Broughton. Turn right and ride through Ingleby Greenhow and Kildale, and then take the right fork to Castleton.

'THIS IS GREAT CYCLING COUNTRY, AND SOME OF THE BEST RACES IN THE UK ARE HELD IN THE AREA'

held in the area. The hills race tough but never too long, and road surfaces are generally good, too.

As you climb out of Helmsley, Newgate Bank will test your legs; then there's a steadier climb after Chop Gate. The descent leads back to Stokesley, which is a temptation, but you head east instead towards Kildale and the last major climb. It takes you to Castleton, a small town at the confluence of the rivers that form the Esk, which winds its way to Whitby and into the North Sea.

The steep up-and-down theme continues back towards Kildale for the final act of the ride, a look at the monument to Teesside's most famous son, Captain Cook. James Cook was born in Marton, which is now part of Middlesbrough, and he grew up in Great Ayton, where the route goes next. Cook was the first European to reach the eastern coast of Australia, and he is responsible for mapping places as far apart as New Zealand, Hawaii and Newfoundland.

Roseberry Topping is another remarkable hill to be seen on the last part of the ride. Conical in shape, it's an outlier of the North Yorkshire Moors, and it stands out for miles, dominating the ride back to Stokesley.

START + FINISH:
Stokesley

GETTING THERE:
Stokesley is on the A712 nine miles south of Middlesbrough.

BIKE SHOP:
Westbrook Cycles

CAFE: **Howards Eatery**

LOCAL DELICACY:
Yorkshire ham

NORTH YORKSHIRE MOORS

RIDE FACTS

Rating
Very hard

Total climbing
2200 metres

Killer climb
Rosedale Chimney

This is a ride with everything: super-steep climbs, wild moors, forests and sea. The North Yorkshire Moors are subtly different from the Cleveland Hills. The block that forms them both is deeply dissected in the North Yorkshire Moors, and the overall altitude dips down towards the coast.

You will also meet one of hardest hills in Britain, Rosedale Chimney, but at least you get it over with quickly because it's not far from the start in Pickering. Ten miles away to be exact, ten miles of steady riding up Rosedale, left at Rosedale Abbey, across the River Seven and there

it is: just under one and half kilometres of 12.5 per cent average gradient with some head- and wheel-spinning bits of 33 per cent thrown in.

Your eyes will water. Rosedale Chimney is an old favourite of international races like the Tour of Britain and the Milk Race, but riding up it has long been a rite of passage for northern club racers. Among them there's long been talk about who can climb the Chimney using only their big chainring. Many have tried but few succeed. Don't try it, though, at least not now. You've got another 90 miles to go, with many more steep hills. Some of them are big named climbs and others, especially on the coastal section, anonymous little heartbreakers.

You need your strength soon enough to climb out of Farndale, where in spring a blanket of daffodils awaits. Blakey Ridge leads to the head of Rosedale, where you descend to the abbey again, then ride up the other side of it to Northdale Rigg. This isn't as notorious as the Chimney, but it doesn't feel any easier. It is at least shorter.

The Rigg is the last of the really hard climbs, but there are many more hills to come as the route rattles around the Esk Valley while following it down to the sea at Whitby. I always find this town fascinating, but at the same time a bit scary. It is certainly beautiful, and the tiny, tiered streets and theatre-like setting of the harbour are spectacular. But then there are the dark ruins of the abbey, and the links with Bram Stoker and his

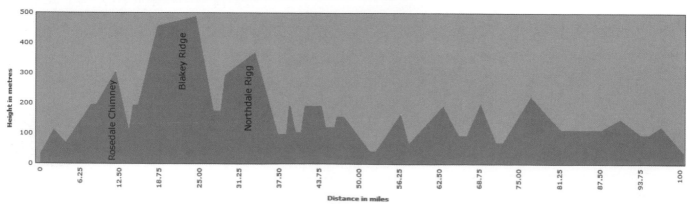

Height in metres

Rosedale Chimney

Blakey Ridge

Northdale Rigg

500
400
300
200
100
0

0 6.25 12.50 18.75 25.00 31.25 37.50 43.75 50.00 56.25 62.50 68.75 75.00 81.25 87.50 93.75 100

Distance in miles

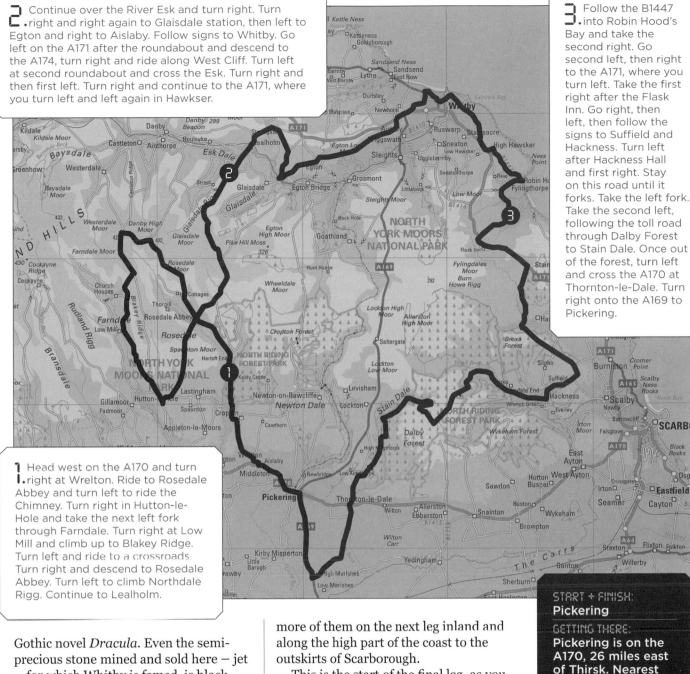

2. Continue over the River Esk and turn right. Turn right and right again to Glaisdale station, then left to Egton and right to Aislaby. Follow signs to Whitby. Go left on the A171 after the roundabout and descend to the A174, turn right and ride along West Cliff. Turn left at second roundabout and cross the Esk. Turn right and then first left. Turn right and continue to the A171, where you turn left and left again in Hawkser.

3. Follow the B1447 into Robin Hood's Bay and take the second right. Go second left, then right to the A171, where you turn left. Take the first right after the Flask Inn. Go right, then left, then follow the signs to Suffield and Hackness. Turn left after Hackness Hall and first right. Stay on this road until it forks. Take the left fork. Take the second left, following the toll road through Dalby Forest to Stain Dale. Once out of the forest, turn left and cross the A170 at Thornton-le-Dale. Turn right onto the A169 to Pickering.

1. Head west on the A170 and turn right at Wrelton. Ride to Rosedale Abbey and turn left to ride the Chimney. Turn right in Hutton-le-Hole and take the next left fork through Farndale. Turn right at Low Mill and climb up to Blakey Ridge. Turn left and ride to a crossroads. Turn right and descend to Rosedale Abbey. Turn left to climb Northdale Rigg. Continue to Lealholm.

Gothic novel *Dracula*. Even the semi-precious stone mined and sold here — jet — for which Whitby is famed, is black. The weather doesn't help much, either; Whitby seems to trap sea fogs and cold, clammy winds between its cliffs, even on warm summer days.

The place exerts a pull, and so does gravity; you really feel it as you try to leave through the steep streets of tiny cottages. In contrast Robin Hood's Bay is far more open, brighter and quite welcoming, even if the hills are just as steep, and there are

more of them on the next leg inland and along the high part of the coast to the outskirts of Scarborough.

This is the start of the final leg, as you turn into Dalby Forest, location of the National Mountain Bike Centre. There are more climbs, particularly through Staindale, which is a delightful place, a forest planted with oak, ash and other broadleaf trees, as well as Scots pines. It's a nice decompression before the encore: a little addition across the River Rye and Derwent's flood plain to get to the magic 100.

'THERE ARE MANY MORE HILLS TO COME AS THE ROUTE RATTLES AROUND THE ESK VALLEY'

START + FINISH:
Pickering

GETTING THERE:
Pickering is on the A170, 26 miles east of Thirsk. Nearest national rail link is at Malton, which connects with York, seven miles south.

BIKE SHOP: **Pickering Cycle Centre in the Market Place**

CAFE: **Cedarbarn Cafe on Thornton Road**

LOCAL DELICACY:
Scarborough Shearling (moorland-reared lamb, which feeds on heather and wild bilberry)

YORKSHIRE DALES

RIDE FACTS

Rating
Very hard

Total climbing
1900 metres

Killer climb
Fleet Moss

'TEN DALES, SEVEN MAJOR CLIMBS AND ONE OF THE BEST DAYS YOU COULD HAVE ON A BIKE'

This is a glorious ride but it's a hard one. I've avoided the main roads so you see the Dales as they really are: a place where natural beauty springs through every blade of grass and can be seen in every rocky corner. Main roads use gaps and valleys, so avoiding them means hills, not just the famous set-piece climbs like this ride's killer, Fleet Moss, but lots of lesser ups and downs along the way.

The ride starts in Kettlewell in upper Wharfedale, but the route quickly switches into Littondale before climbing Chapel Fell and descending to Malham, where Airedale begins. The River Aire's source is Janet's Foss, but it's quickly augmented by Malham Beck, flowing out from under Malham Cove, where it once crashed down the 80-metre cliff face.

The Yorkshire Dales are largely limestone, so it's a porous country where streams and rivers play hide and seek as they sink then emerge miles downstream when they hit impermeable rock. It means there's another dimension here, a subterranean one of potholes and caves carved out by water, while many of the valleys were created, like Malham Cove, when the ground was still frozen after the last Ice Age. The rivers that carved them sank when ice held in the rock below thawed.

There's a short stretch of the A65 after Settle, with a diversion through Austwick, and then you reach Ingleton under mighty Ingleborough. This is one of the Three Peaks: Whernside, Ingleborough and Pen-y-ghent, major landmarks that form a challenge to walkers and to competitors in the Three Peaks fell race or the Three Peaks cyclo-cross.

Dale leads to dale; the ride goes from Kingsdale to Dentdale, birthplace of Adam Sedgwick, one of the fathers of geology. He grew up surrounded by the earth's history laid bare in the hillsides here. Then there's the climb of Newby Head Moss, and down Widdale for the briefest dip into Wensleydale.

Hawes is where Fleet Moss starts. It's the longest and hardest climb on this route, 350 metres gained in six kilometres to 589 metres, the highest point of the ride. One of the great days of Yorkshire cycling happened here in 1987, when local hero Sid Barras, who still cycles in the Dales nearly every day, led the Tour of Britain up Fleet Moss, with Tour de France King of the Mountains Steven Rooks the only racer strong enough to follow him.

Fleet Moss leads to Langstrothdale, with its succession of Viking village names, then to Hubberholme, where J. B. Priestley is buried. After that it's over Kidstones and into Bishopdale. Another short run down Wensleydale leads to the last climb to Hunter's Stone, which is at the top of Coverdale. And that's it: ten dales, seven major climbs and one of the best days you could have on a bike.

The Dales have secluded villages, isolated farms and green hills punctuated

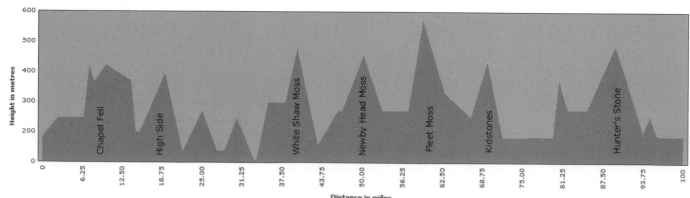

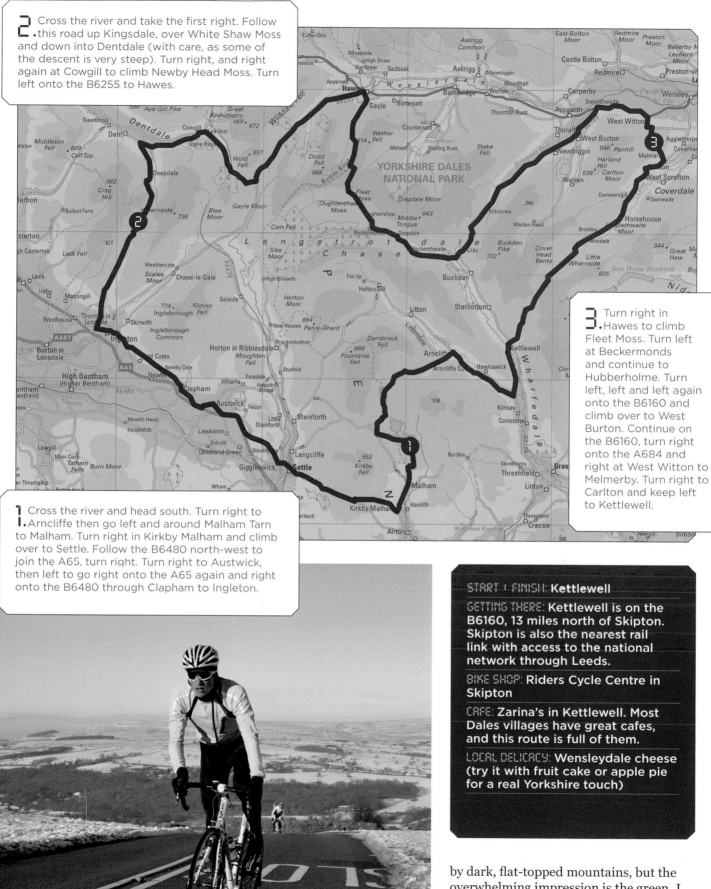

2. Cross the river and take the first right. Follow this road up Kingsdale, over White Shaw Moss and down into Dentdale (with care, as some of the descent is very steep). Turn right, and right again at Cowgill to climb Newby Head Moss. Turn left onto the B6255 to Hawes.

3. Turn right in Hawes to climb Fleet Moss. Turn left at Beckermonds and continue to Hubberholme. Turn left, left and left again onto the B6160 and climb over to West Burton. Continue on the B6160, turn right onto the A684 and right at West Witton to Melmerby. Turn right to Carlton and keep left to Kettlewell.

1. Cross the river and head south. Turn right to Arncliffe then go left and around Malham Tarn to Malham. Turn right in Kirkby Malham and climb over to Settle. Follow the B6480 north-west to join the A65, turn right. Turn right to Austwick, then left to go right onto the A65 again and right onto the B6480 through Clapham to Ingleton.

START | FINISH: Kettlewell

GETTING THERE: Kettlewell is on the B6160, 13 miles north of Skipton. Skipton is also the nearest rail link with access to the national network through Leeds.

BIKE SHOP: Riders Cycle Centre in Skipton

CAFE: Zarina's in Kettlewell. Most Dales villages have great cafes, and this route is full of them.

LOCAL DELICACY: Wensleydale cheese (try it with fruit cake or apple pie for a real Yorkshire touch)

by dark, flat-topped mountains, but the overwhelming impression is the green. I can't work out if it's a trick of the light or the underlying stone, but no green is quite as green as Yorkshire Dales green. You'll remember it for ever.

EMMERDALE

Please drive carefully through our village

VALE OF YORK

RIDE FACTS

Rating
Easy/medium

Total climbing
700 metres

Killer climb
Yearsley Moor

The Vale of York is a wide-open plain north of York and between the Yorkshire Dales, which is part of the Pennine massif, and the North Yorkshire Moors and Wolds. It was once a huge lake, after retreating ice left millions of tonnes of debris in two sets of low hills called moraines. The moraines ran from east to west, damming all rivers to the north and filling the whole lowland area with water.

The moraines were eventually eroded and the lakes dispersed, leaving today's fertile plain, which this ride explores, along with two upland areas, the Howardian Hills and the edges of the Hambleton Hills a bit further north. It's a great place to ride 100 miles, with lots of quiet lanes and just a few testing drags, most of which are done with early on.

Start in Haxby, just north of York, then cross the River Derwent and loosely follow the gap it's made through to Malton. This is a lovely old town that has been an important centre since Roman times. It's also where Charles Dickens wrote *A Christmas Carol*. It occupies a once strategic gap between the Wolds and the Howardian Hills, which are where you go next.

They form a long, undulating ridge on which sits Castle Howard. This beautiful stately home became familiar through the TV series *Brideshead Revisited* and has been the setting for several films since. You pass behind the house and cross its near five-mile long, dead-straight approach road, which is an amazing sight

as it rolls off in two tree-lined directions.

The Howardians give way to the Hambleton Hills at Ampleforth. These are the hills that curl around the western edge of the North Yorkshire Moors. They make for a lumpy ride, and are great bike-racing country. The 2012 British national road

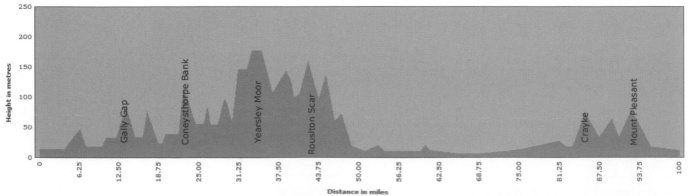

Height in metres — Distance in miles

(Labels on elevation profile: Gally Gap, Coneysthorpe Bank, Yearsley Moor, Rousliton Scar, Crayke, Mount Pleasant)

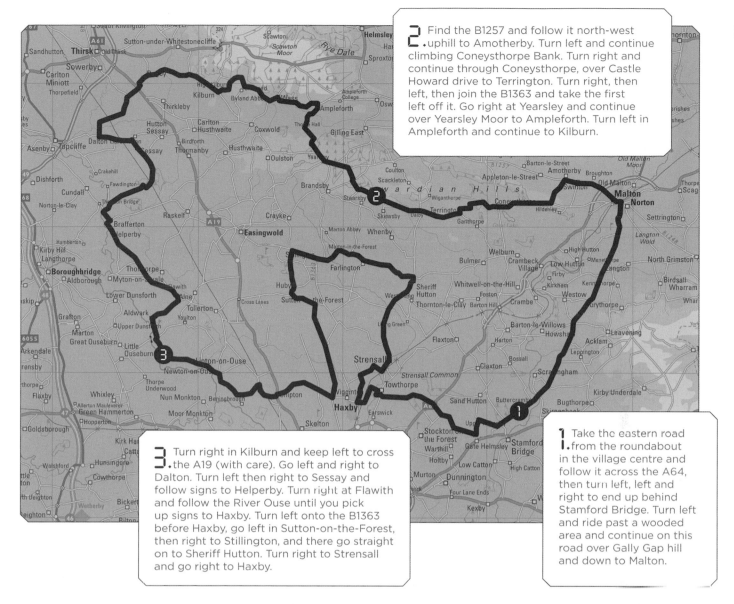

2. Find the B1257 and follow it north-west uphill to Amotherby. Turn left and continue climbing Coneysthorpe Bank. Turn right and continue through Coneysthorpe, over Castle Howard drive to Terrington. Turn right, then left, then join the B1363 and take the first left off it. Go right at Yearsley and continue over Yearsley Moor to Ampleforth. Turn left in Ampleforth and continue to Kilburn.

1. Take the eastern road from the roundabout in the village centre and follow it across the A64, then turn left, left and right to end up behind Stamford Bridge. Turn left and ride past a wooded area and continue on this road over Gally Gap hill and down to Malton.

3. Turn right in Kilburn and keep left to cross the A19 (with care). Go left and right to Dalton. Turn left then right to Sessay and follow signs to Helperby. Turn right at Flawith and follow the River Ouse until you pick up signs to Haxby. Turn left onto the B1363 before Haxby, go left in Sutton-on-the-Forest, then right to Stillington, and there go straight on to Sheriff Hutton. Turn right to Strensall and go right to Haxby.

'IT'S A GREAT PLACE TO RIDE 100 MILES, WITH LOTS OF QUIET LANES AND JUST A FEW TESTING DRAGS'

race championships were held here, on a circuit based on Ampleforth.

Ampleforth to Kilburn is a quite testing stretch of road with no flat. Flat riding comes after you descend into the Vale of Mowbray, a smaller, more undulating lowland area just north of the Vale of York.

If you look back at the hills, just above Kilburn you'll see the Hambletons' white corallian limestone revealed in the shape of a giant horse, created in 1857 by the local schoolteacher, John Hodgson. You can see it all the way from the A1, and in my childhood it seemed to mark the gateway to the north as we drove from South Yorkshire to visit relatives in Durham.

The rest of this ride rattles gently alongside the River Ure until the tiny Ouse Gill Beck joins it at Cuddy Shaw Reach, when it miraculously becomes the River Ouse. The route then breaks away towards Haxby, where I've added a loop around the heart of the Vale of York to make up the distance.

The Vale's quiet brick and pantile villages are glorious places, and the whole area, which used to be the Forest of Galtres and loved by royal hunters, is full of history. Battles were fought here, and even today this ride can end with a bang as close to the finish you pass Strensall Barracks firing range.

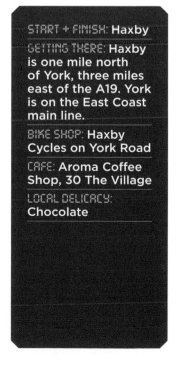

START + FINISH: Haxby

GETTING THERE: Haxby is one mile north of York, three miles east of the A19. York is on the East Coast main line.

BIKE SHOP: Haxby Cycles on York Road

CAFE: Aroma Coffee Shop, 30 The Village

LOCAL DELICACY: Chocolate

YORKSHIRE WOLDS

'THE YORKSHIRE WOLDS ARE A BRIGHT AND COLOURFUL GEM, AND THIS RIDE SHOWS THEM AT THEIR BEST'

The Wolds are a chalk upland, with all the characteristics of chalk-upland landscape: bright green grass, few trees and open views under a wide sky. They are hilly but nowhere near as high or intimidating as their neighbours, the North Yorkshire Moors.

Beverley isn't actually in the Wolds; it's on a flat plain east of them called Holderness. But I've started the ride here because it allows you to follow the whole arc of hills, south to east, see where they meet the coast, then ride back on relatively flat roads. This would be a good choice of ride if you've already done a couple of flatter 100-milers and want to try something more challenging, but don't feel ready for the really hard ones yet.

First you climb the east side of the Wolds, the easy side. Then you get some idea of the steeper western side on the climb out of Pocklington. Look left after the left turn close to the top and you see right across the Vale of York towards the Yorkshire Dales, and on a clear day it's possible to see the Emley Moor TV mast in the central Pennines.

The road goes around the edge of Warter Wold and tops out at 206 metres. This isn't far from the highest point of the Wolds, Garrowby Hill (242 metres), which is about five miles to the north. The route runs to the east of there, but where possible follows the top of the western edge to provide a succession of great views.

The Wolds escarpment rises steeply out of the Vale of York in the west and out of the Vale of Pickering in the north, forming an upland arc that dips eastwards, except where the Wolds meet the coast. There they have been weathered into dazzling white cliffs.

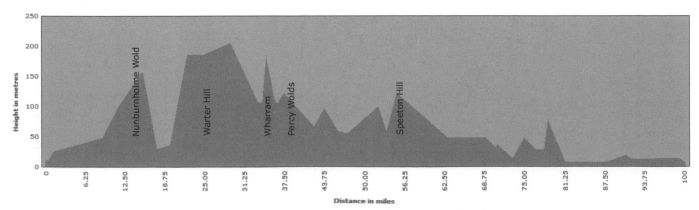

Height in metres | Distance in miles

Nunburnholme Wold, Warter Hill, Wharram, Percy Wolds, Speeton Hill

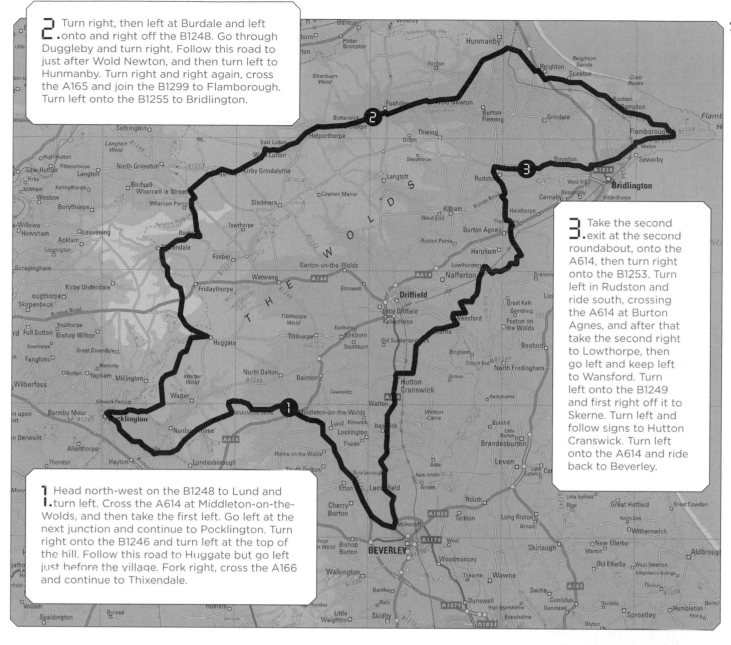

2. Turn right, then left at Burdale and left onto and right off the B1248. Go through Duggleby and turn right. Follow this road to just after Wold Newton, and then turn left to Hunmanby. Turn right and right again, cross the A165 and join the B1299 to Flamborough. Turn left onto the B1255 to Bridlington.

3. Take the second exit at the second roundabout, onto the A614, then turn right onto the B1253. Turn left in Rudston and ride south, crossing the A614 at Burton Agnes, and after that take the second right to Lowthorpe, then go left and keep left to Wansford. Turn left onto the B1249 and first right off it to Skerne. Turn left and follow signs to Hutton Cranswick. Turn left onto the A614 and ride back to Beverley.

1. Head north-west on the B1248 to Lund and turn left. Cross the A614 at Middleton-on-the-Wolds, and then take the first left. Go left at the next junction and continue to Pocklington. Turn right onto the B1246 and turn left at the top of the hill. Follow this road to Huggate but go left just before the village. Fork right, cross the A166 and continue to Thixendale.

I've tried to stay on top of the Wolds all the way, but hills are inevitable because there are so many valleys. They weren't created by water, though. There is very little surface water on the Wolds. The valleys were created by glaciers during the Ice Age, and the absence of water causes the area's 'upside-down farming'.

Streams and rivers only run above ground in the lower valley bottoms, where the chalk has been eroded to reveal an impermeable layer of rock. That's why in the Wolds animals graze in the valley bottoms and crops grow on the hillsides and on the tops, whereas it's usually the other way around.

Nowhere are the Wolds more spectacular than at Flamborough Head. You approach from the north-west through Hunmanby, where there are fantastic views out over the sea, which is 100 metres, and almost directly, below you. The cliffs are incredible, especially at Flamborough, where they rival Dover's more famous white cliffs.

After skirting the holiday town of Bridlington and heading inland, you leave the Wolds, and by now I think you'll agree that they have a special charm. It's one that inspired the artist David Hockney. His paintings brought the Wolds to national attention in March 2012 with an exhibition called *The Bigger Picture*. Hockney's bright depictions of secret places aren't exaggerations; the Yorkshire Wolds are a bright and colourful gem, and this ride shows them at their best.

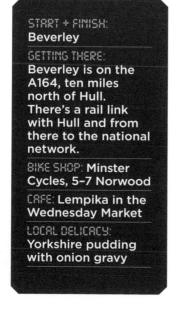

START + FINISH: Beverley

GETTING THERE: Beverley is on the A164, ten miles north of Hull. There's a rail link with Hull and from there to the national network.

BIKE SHOP: Minster Cycles, 5–7 Norwood

CAFE: Lempika in the Wednesday Market

LOCAL DELICACY: Yorkshire pudding with onion gravy

CENTRAL PENNINES

'IT'S THE END OF A RIDE THROUGH OLD INDUSTRIAL TOWNS AND WILD MOORS IN HIGH PLACES'

This is a ride through gaunt countryside where the grass grows lank and yellow and the hilltops are called scars or edges. It's serious country, it has seen a lot, and some of the things it has seen have left their mark on its face. It's a country with worry lines and crow's feet; even the sheep aren't soft and woolly. They have long, straggly fleeces and a demonic look in their eye.

It may not be pretty, but the central Pennines have great bone structure, like the faded beauty of a former film star. It's a hilly ride, and a convoluted one, set in a narrow upland band and surrounded by some of the biggest cities in the north.

It starts in Haworth, home of the Brontës, and straightaway it climbs onto the moors that haunted the literary sisters. This is where Emily Brontë set *Wuthering Heights* in her mind's eye; Cathy and Heathcliff ran to each other up here along the Brontë Way that accompanies you to the top of Combe Hill.

You've climbed from Yorkshire into Lancashire, and the rest of this ride flits between the counties that meet along this Pennine spine of England. The next climb, Widdop Moor, goes back to Yorkshire, to Hebden Bridge, where you skirt the town and the edge of the Calder Valley.

This is a phoenix place. After the woollen industry died it was almost dead and depopulated, but during the 1970s properties were bought for a song by hippies. They built a cooperative life and an alternative economy in these hills, and

now Hebden Bridge is a very desirable place to live, and a slight whiff of the Summer of Love still lingers on.

Climbing on the shoulders of the Calder Valley takes you past Coal Clough Wind Farm and back into Lancashire. The Rossendale climb leads to Todmorden Moor, and then to the only respite on this ride, a 12-mile stretch by the Rochdale Canal to Littleborough and a series of towns and villages whose names read like a poem to the north: Denshaw, Delph, Dobcross and Diggle.

Most of the Todmorden to Marsden stretch is main road. It can be busy in places, so take care, but the trans-Pennine M62 takes a lot of traffic away, making the old A62 Standedge climb a great place to ride. You cross the Huddersfield Narrow Canal in Marsden, ride along its waterfront, then begin a tough hill that leads to Buckstones Moss. It's the cumulative effect of these two hills that gives Buckstones its killer-climb tag.

Buckstones looks spectacular, too, especially where a hairpin junction leads onto the descent past Scammonden Dam and over the M62 bridge. The Little House on the Prairie, the farmhouse that the motorway splits to avoid, is below you on the left. The descent ends in Ripponden, then Blackstone Edge leads up then down to Cragg Vale and the Calder Valley for the final climb.

Cock Hill is nearly four miles long, with well over 300 metres gained. It takes

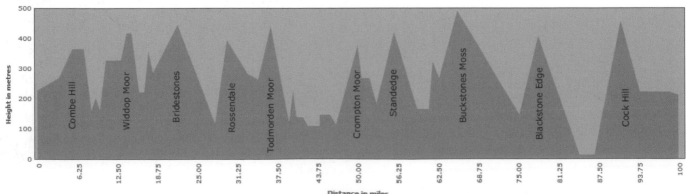

1. Head west out of Haworth following the Brontë Way signs. Turn left at Laneshawbridge to Trawden. Go straight on, then turn left at Clarion House. Keep left, climb Widdop Moor and descend to Slack, where you turn right. Turn right at Blackshaw Head and left at Mereclough. Descend to the A646 and turn right. Turn left onto the A671 and follow this to Bacup.

2. Turn left on the A681 to Todmorden and turn right onto the A6033. Follow this to Littleborough, then turn left, signposted Milnrow, onto the B6225 past Hollingworth Lake. Turn left onto the A633 and go under the M62. Turn left onto the A640 and right in Denshaw onto the A6052. Turn left in Delph onto the A62 and follow it to Marsden.

3. Turn left to cross the River Colne and Huddersfield Canal. Turn right and ride alongside the canal. Then take the first left that goes under a rail bridge. Climb the hill by keeping left, then go right at the top to Pole Moor. Turn left onto the A640. Turn next right onto the B6114. Turn left to Ripponden, then left onto the A58. Turn right at the top of the climb onto the B6138. Turn left in Mytholmroyd onto the A646 and turn right in Hebden Bridge onto the A6033 and follow this to Haworth.

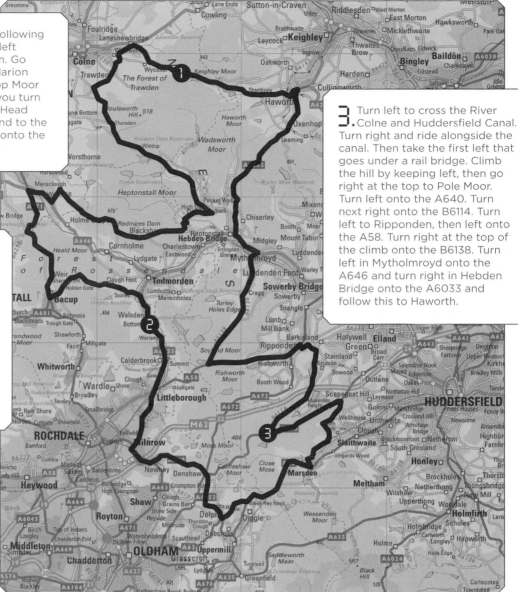

you from pretty town streets up onto wild moors and eventually back to Haworth. It's the end of a ride that links wool with cotton, Yorkshire with Lancashire, through old industrial towns and wild moors in high places.

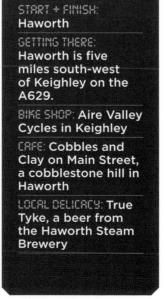

START + FINISH: **Haworth**

GETTING THERE: **Haworth is five miles south-west of Keighley on the A629.**

BIKE SHOP: **Aire Valley Cycles in Keighley**

CAFE: **Cobbles and Clay on Main Street, a cobblestone hill in Haworth**

LOCAL DELICACY: **True Tyke, a beer from the Haworth Steam Brewery**

HIGH PEAK

RIDE FACTS

Rating
Very hard

Total climbing
2500 metres

Killer climb
The Strines

So many great British cyclists live or have lived around this ride, especially since British Cycling moved its headquarters to Manchester, and this is where they train. The route is a tour of the High Peak, a deeply dissected plateau that is full of hard climbs and wide open spaces. It's a challenging ride, tough enough for a Tour de France racer, but a very rewarding one.

The killer climb is different from other rides because it's not one climb but a series of them, known locally as the Strines, and it's right at the start of the ride. It sounds a bit harsh, but you'll thank me later; nobody wants to do the Strines on tired legs. You ride down and up three steep, V-shaped valleys on the eastern edge of the High Peak plateau, and the climbs get longer and harder as you go. There's a cafe at the end in Langsett; you might need refuelling already and there's a long way to go.

The wild and wonderful Holme Moss comes next, an iconic climb in British bike-racing history. Lots of races have climbed the two and a half miles that take you to 529 metres, the highest point of the ride. The plunge down to Woodhead is fast and makes a stark contrast. The Strines are scattered with fairy-tale woods and tinkling streams, and Holme Moss's ascent is green and pleasant, but the descent shows why the High Peak is sometimes called the Dark Peak.

It is dark and mysterious, and the moors have chilling and very northern names, like Bleaklow and Shining Clough, but it has long attracted the

'THE DESCENT SHOWS WHY THE HIGH PEAK IS SOMETIMES CALLED THE DARK PEAK'

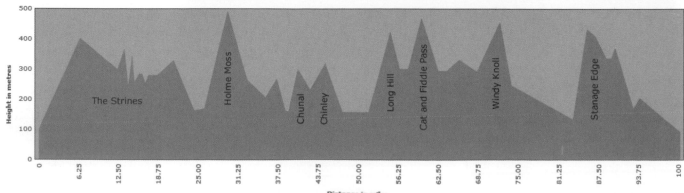

2. Join the A624 in Glossop and carry straight on over Chunal, through Hayfield and over Chinley Head to Chinley and turn right onto the B6062, left onto the A6 and right onto the A5004 and Whaley Bridge. Continue to the top of Long Hill and turn right. Turn left after Errwood Reservoir and go right then left at the top of the Goyt valley climb, which takes you to the Cat and Fiddle Pass (A537). Turn left and left again and descend to Buxton.

1. Start on the B6076 in Stannington and go left at the top of the hill. Turn right onto the A57 and take the first right. Follow this road north, keeping left to Langsett and the end of the Strines. Turn left on the A616, then go straight on at the roundabout. Descend to New Mill and turn left to Holmfirth. Turn right then left in the town centre onto the A6024 and follow this over Holme Moss. Turn right onto the A628 at Woodhead, then left at Crowden on the B6105 to Glossop.

hearts and minds of those who live around it. Hayfield is where the Mass Trespass took place in 1932, when a group from the Manchester area walked onto Kinder Scout in defiance of local landowners. Some of them were imprisoned, but their actions that day led to the introduction of laws that now enshrine our right to roam.

The route works steadily west as it goes south, through Chinley then up Long Hill before descending to a quick change of scenery in the lovely Goyt valley. This is an alternative way up another famous cycling climb, the Cat and Fiddle Pass, which connects Macclesfield with Buxton, the highest market town in England.

The section from Buxton to Windy Knoll is actually part of the White Peak. This is limestone country, and contrasts sharply with the usual dark gritstone character of this ride, which returns at Mam Tor. This is sometimes called the shivering mountain, because it has a face so unstable that the main road over it crumbled away.

Mam Tor guards the right-hand side of a rocky cutting, which you thread through and descend to the Vale of Edale. This deep valley has a forgotten-valley feel; it's a place that's not on the way to anywhere, so it's one of the High Peak's better-kept secrets.

3. Pick up the A6 north, direction Chapel-en-le-Frith, out of Buxton. Turn right onto the A623 after Dove Holes and go straight on the unclassified road in Sparrowpit. Keep left after the top of the next climb, which is also the top of Winnats Pass and take the second right to Edale. Follow the valley road east to Hope. Turn left onto the A6187 and go left at the sharp right bend on this road in Hathersage. Go over Stanage Edge and turn left in Ringinglow. Keep left until the second T-junction, where you go right. Turn left towards Rivelin, cross the A57 (with care), then go right, back to Stannington.

The last climb in a long day begins in Hathersage. Stanage Edge is a rock-climbing Mecca and there's usually someone to be seen climbing up its vertical walls like a bright-coloured spider. From the top you ride downhill almost all the way to the finish on the western edge of Sheffield.

START + FINISH:
Stannington

GETTING THERE:
Stannington is a Sheffield suburb that has the High Peak on its doorstep.

BIKE SHOP: **Langsett Cycles on Infirmary Road in Sheffield**

CAFE: **Bank View Cafe in Langsett**

LOCAL DELICACY: **High Peak honey**

NORTH LINCOLNSHIRE

RIDE FACTS

Rating
Easy

Total climbing
350 metres

Killer climb
None, but wind can be a factor

'CROSS THE DON AT MOORENDS AND YOU ENTER A LANDSCAPE OF SOFT MISTS AND POLLARDED WILLOWS'

There's a lot of the Netherlands in this low-lying part of Britain, and some of it was actually created by a Dutchman. Cornelius Vermuyden was a 17th-century engineer, an expert in reclaiming land from sea and marsh. He was contracted to drain much of this area and create the flat, fertile and in places beguiling land that it is today.

There are echoes of the Low Countries throughout the ride: banked flood defences, laser-straight canals and quaint drawbridges that allow barges and road transport to work in harmony, as well as some of the older architecture. The start is in Brigg, a market town at the foot of the Lincolnshire Wolds. It undulates north over the Wolds foothills through a series of pretty villages to South Ferriby, where you do a hard left to ride along the south bank of the mighty River Humber. Read's Island is on your right. It was once occupied by a farm, but that has gone, as has half of the island, washed away by the 2008 floods that badly affected this region.

You climb onto the northern tip of the Lincoln Ridge, then at Alkborough the route turns south into the Trent valley. The ancient village overlooks Trent Falls, the confluence of the Trent and the Ouse, at which point they form the Humber. This isn't a dramatic waterfall, but at times of high tide a distinct wave called the Trent Aegir forms here to flow upstream.

After crossing the Trent at Gunness, you follow it north before turning hard left again at the River Ouse. You see a lot of Vermuyden's work here. He was

contracted by King Charles I to drain Hatfield Chase, a massive and still largely empty area south of Goole.

Goole is still a busy place, but was once a very important port. With access via the Ouse and Humber to the North Sea, it stands at the end of the Aire and Calder Navigation and the River Don, which was straightened by Vermuyden for its final few miles and called the Dutch River. Through these waterways Goole was linked to Yorkshire's coalmining heartland. Coal went out through Goole and pit props came in. The old timber pond, where the wood for props was off-loaded before being pulled inland, is now a marina.

Cross the Don at Moorends and you enter a landscape of soft mists and pollarded willows. It's more like Holland's neighbour, the Belgian province of Flanders. Its tiny linear villages of old brick houses, along with its dykes, ditches and drawbridges, give this little area north of Doncaster an atmosphere all of its own.

You leave it at Stainforth, an old mining village, and ride through Hatfield and then into something that looks extremely Dutch. A long straight road runs to the Isle of Axholme, which really was an island before Vermuyden's work.

The final leg goes north then east to cross the Trent at Gunness again and you skirt the southern edge of Scunthorpe before heading back to Brigg. Scunthorpe is a large town for this area, having grown with its large steelworks, but work there is vastly reduced today.

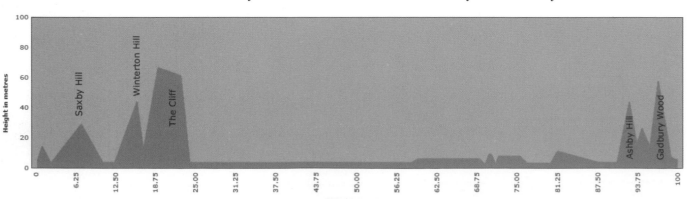

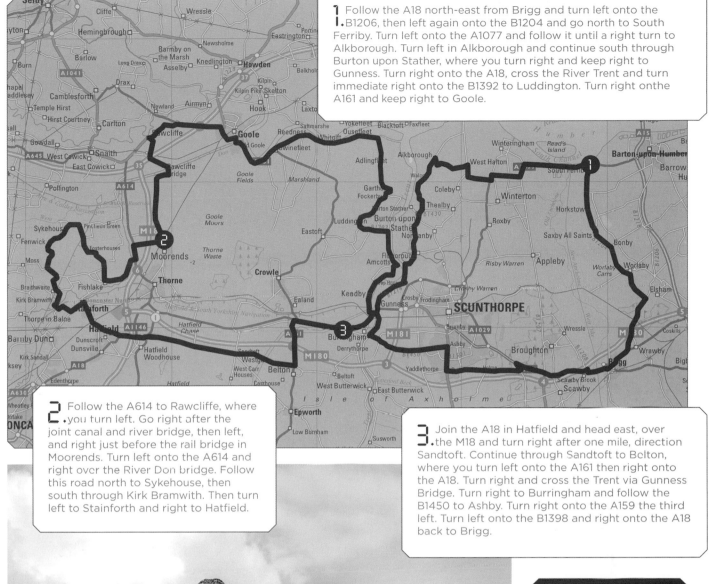

1. Follow the A18 north-east from Brigg and turn left onto the B1206, then left again onto the B1204 and go north to South Ferriby. Turn left onto the A1077 and follow it until a right turn to Alkborough. Turn left in Alkborough and continue south through Burton upon Stather, where you turn right and keep right to Gunness. Turn right onto the A18, cross the River Trent and turn immediate right onto the B1392 to Luddington. Turn right on the A161 and keep right to Goole.

2. Follow the A614 to Rawcliffe, where you turn left. Go right after the joint canal and river bridge, then left, and right just before the rail bridge in Moorends. Turn left onto the A614 and right over the River Don bridge. Follow this road north to Sykehouse, then south through Kirk Bramwith. Then turn left to Stainforth and right to Hatfield.

3. Join the A18 in Hatfield and head east, over the M18 and turn right after one mile, direction Sandtoft. Continue through Sandtoft to Belton, where you turn left onto the A161 then right onto the A18. Turn right and cross the Trent via Gunness Bridge. Turn right to Burringham and follow the B1450 to Ashby. Turn right onto the A159 the third left. Turn left onto the B1398 and right onto the A18 back to Brigg.

START + FINISH: Brigg

GETTING THERE: Brigg is on the A18, five miles east of Scunthorpe. There's a rail link from Gainsborough, where it's possible to connect with the national rail network.

BIKE SHOP: Sherwood Cycles on Bridge Street

CAFE: Brambles Cafe in the Market Place

LOCAL DELICACY: Haslet (pork meatloaf)

SOLWAY FIRTH

RIDE FACTS

Rating
Medium, hard if windy

Total climbing
1000 metres

Killer climb
Green How

'BECAUSE NOWHERE ON THIS RIDE IS A TOURIST DESTINATION, IT HAS A TRANQUILLITY TO MATCH ITS BEAUTY'

The Solway Firth separates a large part of England from Scotland with a wide expanse of water It's a haven of peace, and a sanctuary for wildlife The Scottish Solway coast attracts many more visitors than the English side because the mountains of Dumfries and Galloway are closer to it, and the English Lake District is just the hazy background for the first part for this ride, although you climb some of its foothills during the second half

Because nowhere on this ride is a tourist destination, it has a tranquillity to match its beauty. The first 35 miles or so run from busy Carlisle to the sea at Silloth, then down the coast to Maryport, passing marshes, mudflats and empty sandy beaches on the way. The wind can be your enemy here, because if it blows there's nowhere to hide, and it usually blows in off the sea.

In Victorian times, Maryport was a centre for boat building and a busy industrial port, where coal was exported from the local pits and iron ore imported for the steelworks at Workington. Trade began to dwindle when Workington built its own deep dock in 1927, and by 1933 nearly 60 per cent of the town were unemployed. Life has improved here, but it can still be hard.

The great advantage of living here lies inland from Maryport, where hillside buttresses lead up to the Cumbrian fells. Maryport is only eight miles from Cockermouth, gateway to one of Lakeland's finest valleys, Buttermere, but the route does a loop north before getting there.

I always thought Aspatria sounded Roman, but it's not; it's a Norse word meaning St Patrick's Ash Tree. Historians

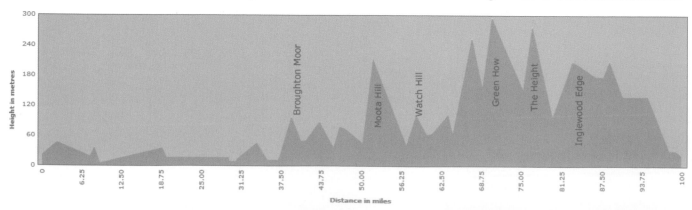

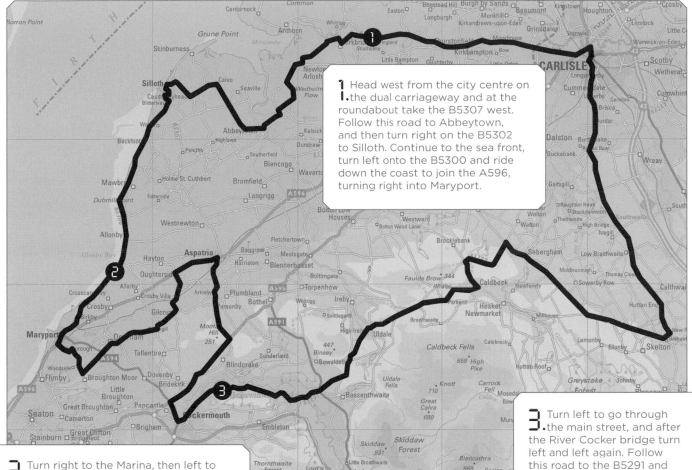

1. Head west from the city centre on the dual carriageway and at the roundabout take the B5307 west. Follow this road to Abbeytown, and then turn right on the B5302 to Silloth. Continue to the sea front, turn left onto the B5300 and ride down the coast to join the A596, turning right into Maryport.

2. Turn right to the Marina, then left to rejoin the A596. Turn left, then right to Ewanrigg. Turn right where the road levels, and continue uphill to Broughton Moor, where you turn left and cross the A954 to Dearham. Turn right, left and right at Greengill. Go left at Gilcrux and follow this road to the A596. Turn right to Aspatria, and there turn right onto the B5301. Climb Moota Hill, then turn right onto and left off the A595. Go through Blindcrake and turn left back onto the A595 then left onto the A594 to Cockermouth.

3. Turn left to go through the main street, and after the River Cocker bridge turn left and left again. Follow this road to the B5291 and turn left, cross the A591 and continue up the Green How climb. Descend to the B5299, turn right, and follow it through Caldbeck to the B5305 crossroads, where you turn right. Turn left in Unthank End and follow this road back to Carlisle.

believe the place was founded by some Vikings who had lived in Ireland. It has an even better view into the Lakes than Cockermouth, with the Ennerdale and Derwent fells, as well as Skiddaw, appearing close enough to touch.

Cockermouth was devastated by floods in 2009, with over 200 people having to be rescued by helicopter and boat. The route follows the River Derwent to the head of Bassenthwaite Lake — and a useful quiz fact. This is the only stretch of water in the Lake District that's called a lake. All the others have names ending in 'mere' or 'water'.

You already have a couple of hills behind you now, but the killer climb is to come, a double hill called Green How. It's located in part of the Lake District known as Back o' Skiddaw, which is an area of lower fells to the north of the 931-metre Skiddaw, the fourth-highest mountain in the Lake District.

This is another tourist-free zone. It has some of the charm of the Cumbrian fells, but it's wilder, bleaker and has a different geology. Although it attracts fewer visitors, it has committed residents. The climber Chris Bonington lives in Caldbeck, which was where the famous huntsman John Peel lived, and it's the base of the Northern Fells Group, a rejuvenation and preservation project.

The last section of the ride heads south-west towards Penrith before swinging north to shadow the M6 for a largely downhill run back to Carlisle. Try to visit the castle while you are there. Built from a rich red local stone, it's remarkably well preserved and still looks ready for a fight.

START + FINISH:
Carlisle

GETTING THERE: Carlisle is at Junctions 42 and 43 of the M6 and has a mainline rail station.

BIKE SHOP: Scotby Cycles on Church Street

CAFE: Circle Cafe Bar on Lowther Arcade

LOCAL DELICACY: Jennings Sneck Lifter beer

NORTH-WEST ENGLAND

NORTH LAKES

NORTH-WEST ENGLAND

RIDE FACTS

Rating
Very hard

Total climbing
1700 metres

Killer climb
Honister Pass

'CONQUERING THESE HILLS FEELS SPECIAL, AND CONQUERING THEM AS PART OF A 100-MILE RIDE IS VERY SPECIAL INDEED'

A word about the killer climb first: Honister gets the title, but it's pretty much a dead heat between the three big mountain passes. Kirkstone, Honister and Newlands are all hard and they require effort, commitment, patience and quite a bit of fitness. A compact chainset is your best friend here, but conquering these hills feels special, and conquering them as part of a 100-mile ride is very special indeed.

The ride is in one of the most famous beauty spots in Britain. I've picked out quieter, lesser-known roads where possible, but inevitably some of the roads are busy, so take extra care. It starts in Penrith, and the first leg in a day full of great places to ride is the one out and back along the south side of Ullswater.

The road stays near the lake until about halfway along. Ride over Hallin Fell, which is the only hill on this road, then turn around and come back. You then follow Ullswater's north side to the foot of Kirkstone Pass.

The climb starts at Hartsop, a name that's easy to misread because you'll feel like your heart is going to stop, or explode, in a few minutes. Kirkstone Pass is 2.6 miles long, and the first half is not too bad, but then it gets hard. The second half averages 10.5 per cent gradient in three distinct and much steeper steps, but your reward is a fantastic view and a long descent to Troutbeck and Windermere.

You ride around the largest lake in the north of England to enter Langdale and experience the magic of Elterwater. There's a short climb over to Grasmere, after which you play hide and seek with the main road going north over Dunmail Raise and around the unknown side of Thirlmere to Keswick. The Thirlmere road winds along the shore through a forest of dark conifers. It smells amazing and the view of Helvellyn

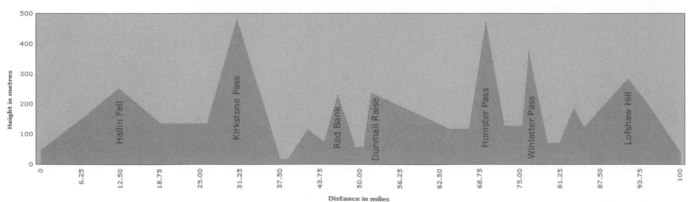

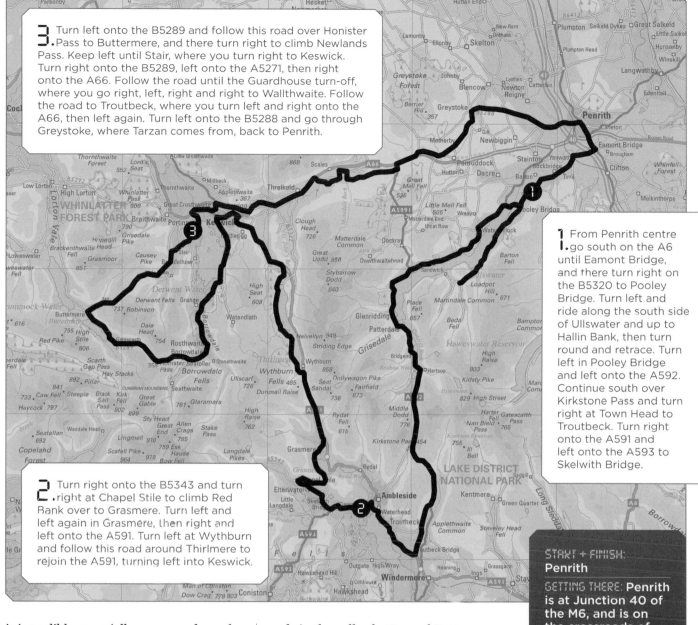

3. Turn left onto the B5289 and follow this road over Honister Pass to Buttermere, and there turn right to climb Newlands Pass. Keep left until Stair, where you turn right to Keswick. Turn right onto the B5289, left onto the A5271, then right onto the A66. Follow the road until the Guardhouse turn-off, where you go right, left, right and right to Wallthwaite. Follow the road to Troutbeck, where you turn left and right onto the A66, then left again. Turn left onto the B5288 and go through Greystoke, where Tarzan comes from, back to Penrith.

1. From Penrith centre go south on the A6 until Eamont Bridge, and there turn right on the B5320 to Pooley Bridge. Turn left and ride along the south side of Ullswater and up to Hallin Bank, then turn round and retrace. Turn left in Pooley Bridge and left onto the A592. Continue south over Kirkstone Pass and turn right at Town Head to Troutbeck. Turn right onto the A591 and left onto the A593 to Skelwith Bridge.

2. Turn right onto the B5343 and turn right at Chapel Stile to climb Red Bank over to Grasmere. Turn left and left again in Grasmere, then right and left onto the A591. Turn left at Wythburn and follow this road around Thirlmere to rejoin the A591, turning left into Keswick.

is incredible, especially on sunny days when its reflection crosses the water to meet you.

Keswick is the gateway to Borrowdale, where the mountains are volcanic in origin – and they look it. Most of the Lake District is made of igneous rock, created when an oceanic tectonic plate dipped beneath a continental plate. The descending rock melted, then bubbled upwards, creating an island arc, and later a landmass that geologists call Avalonia.

Honister Pass is at the head of Borrowdale, 1.5 miles of 10.5 per cent gradient with several bits of 25 per cent thrown in. It tops out on a knife-edge below a slate quarry, with probably the finest view in Lakeland in front of you. A breathtaking descent, with the towering scree slopes of Honister Crag above you,

ends in the valley bottom of Buttermere. Carry on riding for a bit, then look behind you, searching for a craggy top. That's Haystacks, a place beloved of Alfred Wainwright, the man who wrote the inspiring *Pictorial Guides to the Lakeland Fells*, and where his ashes are scattered.

Newlands Pass lifts you out of Buttermere, and then you weave through a network of lanes that are also the last leg of the formidable Bob Graham Round, a mountain challenge in which 42 Lakeland peaks have to be crossed on foot inside 24 hours. Try channelling the commitment of those who have achieved this extraordinary feat to power you back to Penrith, using a combination of lanes and short stretches of the A66.

START + FINISH:
Penrith

GETTING THERE: Penrith is at Junction 40 of the M6, and is on the crossroads of the A6 and the A66. It's also on the West Coast main line.

BIKE SHOP: Arragons on Brunswick Road

CAFE: Greystoke Cycle Cafe in Greystoke, which is five miles west of Penrith and on your route. Check www. greystokecyclecafe. co.uk for opening times.

LOCAL DELICACY: Cumberland sausages

ISLE OF MAN

RIDE FACTS

Rating
Hard

Total climbing
1400 metres

Killer climb
Snaefell

You get two rides in one with this 100-miler on the Isle of Man. Not only is it almost a circumnavigation of the island, it's nearly a lap of the famous TT circuit. But don't let almost and nearly put you off; this is a fantastic ride with superb sea views and great mountain climbs, and it pays tribute to two sports.

The Isle of Man is still part of motorcycle racing culture. The TT races are an annual event dating back to 1907, and are held on the TT circuit, a 37-mile lap, sometimes called the Mountain Circuit, that forms the last part of this ride. However, the island has also played a big part in cycling history, and not just because it's where Mark Cavendish comes from.

The Isle of Man Week was a festival of cycling with events held all over the island, culminating in the Isle of Man Grand Prix, which was over three laps of the TT circuit, so it was a gruelling race. Some of cycling's biggest names competed here, including three of the best pro racers ever: Fausto Coppi, Jacques Anquetil and Eddy Merckx. The bike races have gone now; 2003 was the last Cycling Week on the Isle of Man.

I've saved 'the lap' for later. There's something about riding around an island that's compelling. This ride sticks to the coast for as long as possible, but I was running out of distance towards the end, and had to take a short cut to the start of the TT circuit, or I'd have gone well over 100 miles.

There are plenty of interesting things to see, including the Laxey Wheel, the largest

working waterwheel in the world. It was built in 1854 to pump water from Laxey's mines, which produced lead, copper, silver and zinc. You have to go just off the route to find it, by going to the village centre then following the signs. Laxey is at the foot of Snaefell mountain, which you climb later

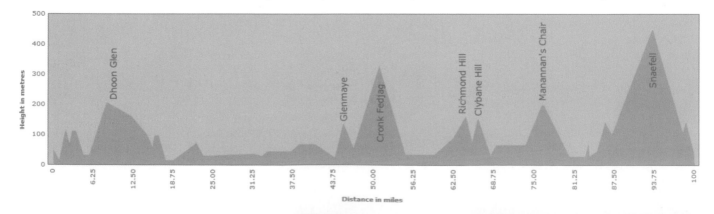

2. Follow the A4 south-west to Peel, where you turn right onto the A1 and left onto the A27. Go through Glenmaye, where the Cronk Fedjag climb begins. Near the summit turn right onto the A36 and descend to Ballagawne. Turn left onto the A27 to Ballabeg and right onto the A7 to Ballasalla.

1. Start at Onchan Head and follow the A11 coast road east then north to join the A2, where you turn right. Follow the A2 through Laxey and Ramsey, where you switch to the sea-front road and then join the A10 to ride round to the Cronk. Turn right and left in the Cronk, then right to Orrisdale. Turn right onto the A3 and then join the A4 in Kirk Michael.

3. Turn right at the first roundabout and follow the A5 to the A24 roundabout just outside Douglas. Turn left onto the A24, right onto the B32 to Union Mills, and there turn left onto the A1. You are now on the TT course. Turn right at Ballacraine onto the A3 and follow this road to the A14 junction on the Sulby straight. Turn right, climb over Snaefell and descend to Onchan Head.

and is part of the TT circuit, and a railway runs from the village to the summit.

After Laxey you continue north through Ramsey and its magnificent bay, and around the top of the island, which is significantly flatter than the rest of it. There are spectacular views of the Galloway coast in Scotland along this bit. Then you ride down the west coast to Peel. It's only the fourth-largest settlement on the island, but Peel is sometimes called a city, because the Isle of Man's only cathedral was built there. Like Peel's castle it's made of striking red sandstone, which leads to Peel's nickname of Rose City.

Peel is also where this ride starts to get hilly, and the climb of Cronk Fedjag from Glenmaye is tough. Another two

significant climbs come before you reach the TT course, which undulates all the way to the foot of Snaefell. It is hard cycling, and seeing and experiencing the terrain makes the fastest lap on a motorbike of 135 miles per hour even more incredible.

The road summit of Snaefell comes just after Bungalow station at 422 metres, and from there it's all downhill back to where you started in the Onchan suburb of Douglas. Snaefell's summit stands almost 200 metres higher than the road. It's possible to catch the electric tram from the station if you want to go up and have a look at what locals call the Six Kingdoms. They say that on a clear day you can see the Isle of Man, Wales, Scotland, England, Ireland and the Kingdom of Heaven.

START + FINISH:
Douglas

GETTING THERE:
Douglas is the Isle of Man's capital and main port. There are ferry services from Heysham, Liverpool, Belfast and Dublin. There are also lots of flights to Ronaldsway airport, which is ten miles south-west of Douglas.

BIKE SHOP: Eurocycles on Victoria Road

CAFE: Feegan's Continental Cafe

LOCAL DELICACY: Peel kippers

HOWGILL FELLS AND THE EDEN VALLEY

This ride is a like a good play; it holds your interest and there are plenty of scenery changes. The players are special too. The tall and muscular Howgill Fells are the hero; a delightful ride through the Eden Valley adds a soft feminine touch; and the wild and empty Shap Fells play the perfect villain, especially on a mucky, wet day.

The Howgills have a distinctive look. They are a high, steep-sided mass of rock with deep folds and a gently undulating top. Their surface looks smooth, like hand-finished clay tinted with every shade from light ochre to dark brown. And the

'THE WILD AND EMPTY SHAP FELLS PLAY THE PERFECT VILLAIN, ESPECIALLY ON A MUCKY, WET DAY'

shades change through each day as the sun shifts across the sky.

Sedbergh is the Howgill town, and your start point. It's in Cumbria now, but was once part of Yorkshire, and is still a sort of halfway house between the two. It's a book town, like Hay-on-Wye, with several independent retailers, and more importantly it's the start of today's first climb. Harter Fell is a long one, and it's the main road through the hills into the upper Lune valley.

From there you filter through to the Eden valley at Appleby-in-Westmorland. The town made do with Appleby as a name until 1974, when the government decided to do away with the county of Westmorland. It was incorporated with Cumberland and parts of Lancashire; Sedbergh was nicked from Yorkshire and the County Borough of Carlisle was dissolved; and the whole lot were rolled up together to form a new county called Cumbria.

Appleby is famous for its annual gypsy gathering called the Horse Fair, and it is a really beautiful place. Surrounded by high hills, and in one of the prettiest valleys in Britain, Appleby stands on the River Eden, which flows through an incredible slash of red sandstone that was deposited 270 million years ago in desert conditions.

After a brief loop out to the foot of Murton Fell, then back across the River Eden to leave it south of Penrith, you enter the third act of this ride, the wild and wonderful Shap Fells. This is where the direct Land's End to John o' Groats

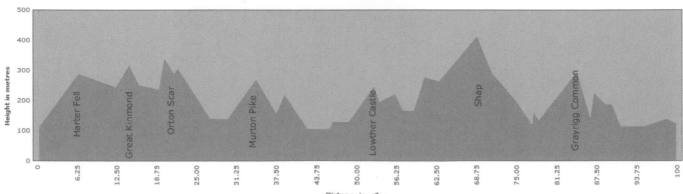

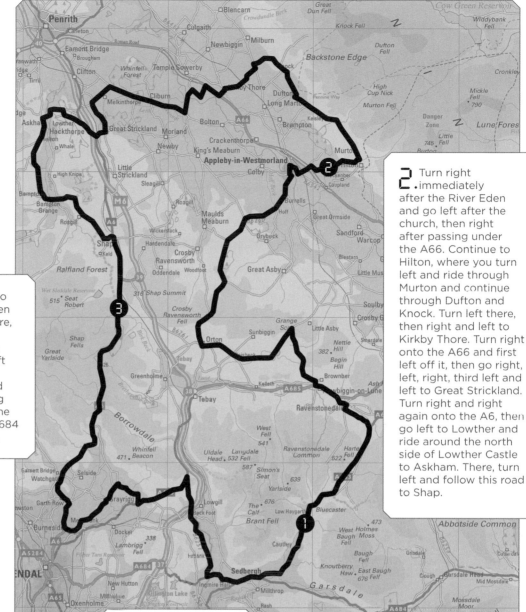

3. Turn right onto the A6 to climb Shap Fells and then descend to Garth Row. There, turn left, go up the steep hill and turn right to Patton Bridge. Turn left, second left and then right to Grayrigg. Turn left onto the A685 and climb to the top of Grayrigg Common. Turn right onto the B6257, then left onto the A684 and left again to Sedbergh.

2. Turn right immediately after the River Eden and go left after the church, then right after passing under the A66. Continue to Hilton, where you turn left and ride through Murton and continue through Dufton and Knock. Turn left there, then right and left to Kirkby Thore. Turn right onto the A66 and first left off it, then go right, left, right, third left and left to Great Strickland. Turn right and right again onto the A6, then go left to Lowther and ride around the north side of Lowther Castle to Askham. There, turn left and follow this road to Shap.

1. Head north-east out of Sedbergh on the A683 over Harter Fell, and turn left to Ravenstonedale. Turn left onto the A685 and right at Brownber. Go uphill, then turn left at the T-junction and descend to Raisbeck. Go through Raisbeck to Orton, and there turn right onto the B6260 to climb Orton Scar and continue to Appleby-in-Westmorland.

cycling route goes, and many a record attempt has foundered here. It's a long climb up the old A6, mostly straight, and with company in the early stages from the M6 and the West Coast main line. They all go through this pass, where Lakeland fells touch the Pennines.

You descend almost to Kendal, then veer off left for a lumpy ride that takes you through a string of tiny villages, across little-known rivers and eventually to the final climb, Grayrigg Common. The summit offers a spectacular view over the Lune valley, with the M6, the railway and the river running along it.

The Lune leads you back towards Sedbergh as you descend into its valley as far as the A684, turn left and pass Ingmire Hall. Half castle, half house, it was built in the 16th century from rock rubble and since then has been added to a lot, creating a bewildering mix of homeliness and battlements.

START + FINISH: Sedbergh

GETTING THERE: Sedbergh is on the A684, four miles east of Junction 37 of the M6. The nearest mainline rail station is Oxenholme, near Kendal, about ten miles west of Sedbergh.

BIKE SHOP: Justin Kirk Cycles

CAFE: The Sedbergh Cafe

LOCAL DELICACY: Sticky toffee pudding

FURNESS AND THE WESTERN FELLS

RIDE FACTS

Rating
Hard

Total climbing
1500 metres

Killer climb
Hardknott Pass

Some hills are rites of passage in cycling, and the Lake District has a good few of them, but none is as challenging as Hardknott Pass. It had to be included in this book, and I could have teamed it with its slightly less daunting brother the Wrynose Pass, but that's a tough ask on a 100-mile ride.

You start in Ulverston, birthplace of Stan Laurel and location of a lighthouse that's well over a mile from the sea. It's actually a replica of the third Eddystone Lighthouse and was built in 1850 as a memorial to another Ulverston man, Sir John Barrow, founder of the Royal Geographical Society.

The climbs on this ride come in two blocks, and the opening 30 miles or so are the first. You climb out of Ulverston and over Woodland Fell, then Broughton Moor, which are confusing names because there are very few trees on the fell and a big plantation of them on the moor. Then there's Brown Rigg, which is on the side of Ulpha Fell. This is wild now, but it must have been wilder. Ulpha comes from a Norse word meaning 'a hill where wolves live'.

There are lots of loops and crosses on this ride; there had to be to fit it all in. One of the places I wanted it to visit is Wasdale, the quietest of all the Lakeland valleys and I think the most spectacular. Wast Water is the deepest lake in England and it's surrounded by some of the highest mountains, including Scafell Pike, the highest of all, Scafell, Pillar, Great Gable, Yewbarrow — there are 16 of them around

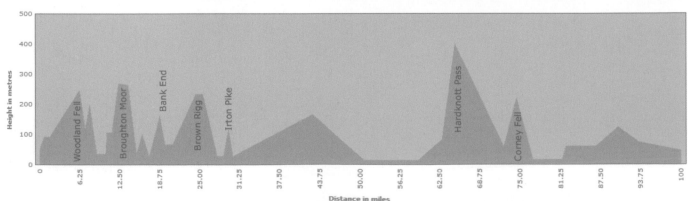

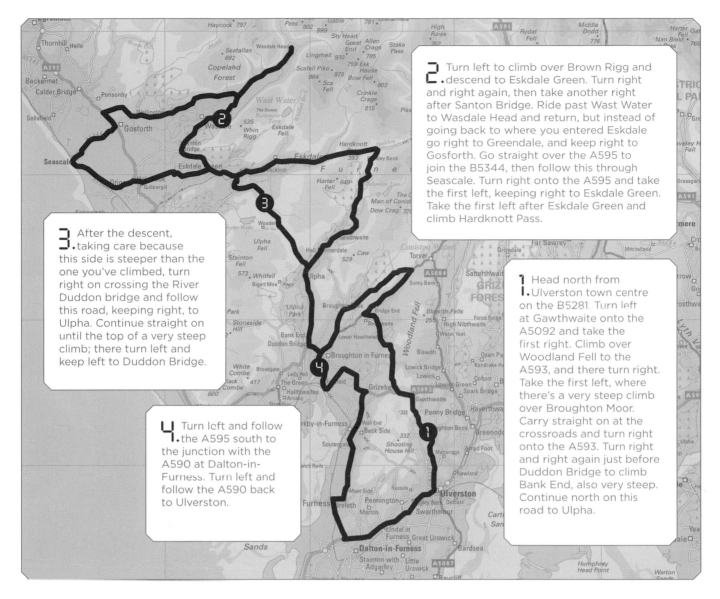

2. Turn left to climb over Brown Rigg and descend to Eskdale Green. Turn right and right again, then take another right after Santon Bridge. Ride past Wast Water to Wasdale Head and return, but instead of going back to where you entered Eskdale go right to Greendale, and keep right to Gosforth. Go straight over the A595 to join the B5344, then follow this through Seascale. Turn right onto the A595 and take the first left, keeping right to Eskdale Green. Take the first left after Eskdale Green and climb Hardknott Pass.

3. After the descent, taking care because this side is steeper than the one you've climbed, turn right on crossing the River Duddon bridge and follow this road, keeping right, to Ulpha. Continue straight on until the top of a very steep climb; there turn left and keep left to Duddon Bridge.

1. Head north from Ulverston town centre on the B5281. Turn left at Gawthwaite onto the A5092 and take the first right. Climb over Woodland Fell to the A593, and there turn right. Take the first left, where there's a very steep climb over Broughton Moor. Carry straight on at the crossroads and turn right onto the A593. Turn right and right again just before Duddon Bridge to climb Bank End, also very steep. Continue north on this road to Ulpha.

4. Turn left and follow the A595 south to the junction with the A590 at Dalton-in-Furness. Turn left and follow the A590 back to Ulverston.

Wasdale, all with ringing, evocative names. This is a splendid place, helped by the fact that it is west facing, which means a long car drive to get here from the rest of the Lake District. It's as near to being wild and unspoilt as almost anywhere in England.

The great fell runner Joss Naylor was a shepherd in this valley. I once saw him striding up a fell side doing his day job, a grey ghost of a man wearing a thick tweed coat fastened around his middle with bailer twine. I never saw anyone more at one with his place.

Wasdale Head is as far as the road goes, but if you are an ambitious mountain biker come back some time and press on to ride the bridleway over Sty Head Pass down into Borrowdale, or over Black Sail Pass and into Ennerdale. They are both amazing experiences and there's plenty to be amazed about here, but now you need to press on.

Next stop is Seascale, for a quick look at the Irish Sea, and then comes Eskdale, for the big-ticket item on this ride, Hardknott Pass. It's just over two kilometres long and gains 293 metres in that distance, so over 1000 feet. Its average gradient is 12.5 per cent, but there are much steeper pitches at the beginning and the end. The trick is to spread your effort and save some strength for the top part.

There's only one climb left now, up onto a shoulder of Corney Fell, then the rest of the route is in flat Furness, almost all the way down to Barrow. Once called Britain's Chicago because of the boom when some of the Royal Navy's greatest ships were built here, Barrow now only has a submarine yard. The town is right at the end of the Furness peninsula, and so remote that some locals say they live at the end of the longest cul-de-sac in Britain.

START + FINISH:
Ulverston

GETTING THERE:
Ulverston is on the A590, 23 miles west of Junction 36 of the M6. It also has a station on the Cumbrian Coast Line, which connects with the national rail network at Carnforth.

BIKE SHOP: Gill Cycles on The Gill

CAFE: The Hot Mango on King Street

LOCAL DELICACY: Morecambe Bay shrimps

SOUTH LAKES

RIDE FACTS

Rating
Hard

Total climbing
1050 metres

Killer climb
Warth Hill

In my mind the Lake District means mountains. For me the jaw-dropping beauty, the drama and intensity of the fells is even more wonderful than the lakes. There is another Lake District, though, and if you want to experience it on a bike it's best to do it here, to the south of those lofty peaks.

The ride starts at the mountain gateway of Kendal, the home of mint cake, and producer of pipe tobacco and snuff. Yes, they actually have a snuff works in Kendal; it's just east of the river, near one of the bridges. And Kendal has a whiff of antiquity about it. This is where in 1941 the Lakeland Bard, the irascible Alfred Wainwright, took a pay cut from his high-flying job in Blackburn's Town Hall to work in the borough treasurer's office. He'd fallen for the fells and yearned to be closer.

I like a bike ride with a ferry crossing. Unlike the Corran Ferry on the Moidart ride, this one is not necessary. The route could have gone around Windermere, but the ferry adds to the adventure, even if it does drop you off at the bottom of the short but steep Sawrey Hill.

That takes you up and over to Esthwaite Water and Hawkshead, where you enter the mountain-bike paradise of Grizedale Forest. It's a gorgeous place, full of footpaths, bike trails and surprises. These include an amazing sculpture trail, and it has a number of quiet villages hiding among the trees.

You ride south past the mountain-bike centre, where there's a cafe and a shop,

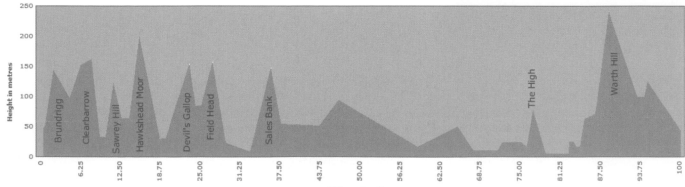

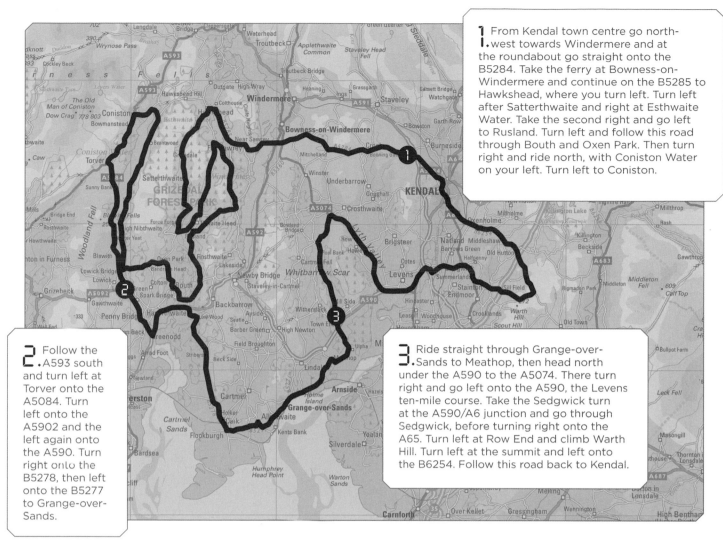

1. From Kendal town centre go north-west towards Windermere and at the roundabout go straight onto the B5284. Take the ferry at Bowness-on-Windermere and continue on the B5285 to Hawkshead, where you turn left. Turn left after Satterthwaite and right at Esthwaite Water. Take the second right and go left to Rusland. Turn left and follow this road through Bouth and Oxen Park. Then turn right and ride north, with Coniston Water on your left. Turn left to Coniston.

2. Follow the A593 south and turn left at Torver onto the A5084. Turn left onto the A5902 and the left again onto the A590. Turn right onto the B5278, then left onto the B5277 to Grange-over-Sands.

3. Ride straight through Grange-over-Sands to Meathop, then head north under the A590 to the A5074. There turn right and go left onto the A590, the Levens ten-mile course. Take the Sedgwick turn at the A590/A6 junction and go through Sedgwick, before turning right onto the A65. Turn left at Row End and climb Warth Hill. Turn left at the summit and left onto the B6254. Follow this road back to Kendal.

'THE ROUTE COULD HAVE GONE AROUND WINDERMERE, BUT THE FERRY ADDS TO THE ADVENTURE'

then loop back north, south and west before you end up riding north again, next to Coniston Water. Look out for John Ruskin's house, Brantwood, on your right, as you get close to the northern end of the lake, and think of Donald Campbell, who perished in the waters here.

In 1967 Campbell was already the only man ever to have held the world land and water speed records, and he still is. He was making his second run along the lake in his boat *Bluebird K7* when he lost control at 320 mph. The boat took off, cart-wheeled and then crashed down into the water; it's

thought that Campbell died instantly. He's buried in Coniston Cemetery.

The route goes south from Coniston to the Leven estuary and to Morecambe Bay, then east to Grange-over-Sands. Historically, this and much of the southern part of the ride was Lancashire, and it's still part of the Duchy of Lancaster.

This is a ride of loops, and the next goes around a limestone outcrop called Whitbarrow before joining the A590 for a short stretch along one of the fastest ten-mile time-trial courses in Britain. Time trialling grew as a sport almost separate from the rest of cycling in this country. Race courses have tended to be chosen for their speed potential rather than for their challenge, and personal bests for standard distances, such as 10, 25 or 50 miles, are racing currency. Many keen time triallists would rather finish 20th with a fast time than win a race with a slow time. However, speed will be the last thing on your mind during the final 15 miles of this ride, which is quite undulating and contains today's killer climb, Warth Hill.

START + FINISH: Kendal

GETTING THERE: Kendal is on the A684, six miles west of Junction 37 of the M6. Oxenholme rail station, about a mile out of town, is on the West Coast Main Line, and has a rail link with Kendal and other stations in the Lake District.

BIKE SHOP: Askew Cycles in the Old Brewery is an independent shop in Kendal, where there is also a branch of the Evans chain.

CAFE: The Joshua Tree on Stramongate

LOCAL DELICACY: Mint cake. Take some on the ride – you'll be hooked.

FOREST OF BOWLAND

RIDE FACTS

Rating
Hard

Total climbing
1350 metres

Killer climb
Trough of Bowland

> 'IT MIGHT BE WORTH STOPPING FOR A CUPPA AND A STICKY BUN TO BUILD STRENGTH FOR THE KILLER CLIMB'

The Forest of Bowland is the pride of Lancashire. It's where many Lancashire cyclists do their long rides. I say 'long' because there aren't many roads through this area, so if you want to sample what it has to offer you need a fair bit of commitment.

I've started the ride in Settle, even though it's in Yorkshire, because doing so takes advantage of prevailing westerly winds on the final leg. Anyway, you leave the white rose county for its red rose neighbour fairly quickly. The border crossing is at Tosside, and it's followed by this ride's first serious climb, Stephen Moor.

The descent ends in Slaidburn, a pretty stone village that has given its name to one of the most popular pieces of brass-band music, and you can't get more northern than that. It's also the start of the day's second climb, over the Newton Fells and down to Clitheroe.

Some of the Lancashire villages you've ridden through were Yorkshire villages before 1974, and you can still see county signs where the red rose is painted over in white, but Clitheroe is Lancashire, always has been, and proud of it. The jet engine was developed in Clitheroe during the Second World War. The houses on Whittle Close were built on the site of the jet test beds and were named after Sir Frank Whittle, the jet's inventor.

The route now joins up again with the River Ribble, which starts in Yorkshire and which you followed out of Settle. You turn north around cigar-shaped Longridge Fell and head for Chipping. There's a cafe here called Cobbled Corner, a regular cyclist's stop. It's on Club Lane, which is left where the route turns right. It might be worth stopping for a cuppa and a sticky bun to build strength for the killer climb.

The Trough of Bowland follows the valley made by a tributary of the River Hodder, and is the main pass between Lancaster and Clitheroe through Bowland, which the trough splits into two distinct blocks. The descent has a really steep bit near the end as you enter Wyresdale. This section is gorgeous. The route follows the River Wyre upstream, through little woods and tiny villages, until just after Abbeystead. It's a place to come back to and explore fully one day.

You've now got another climb to do, out of Wyresdale up the side of Abbeystead Fell and past the Jubilee Tower. This is a piece of exuberance built by a resident of nearby Hare Appletree, James Harrison. He was a Liverpool shipbuilder and he built the tower to celebrate Queen Victoria's Golden Jubilee in 1887. Look west and you can see Lancaster, Morecambe Bay and the Lakeland fells beyond.

A short, quite complicated section leads to the Lune valley at Caton, where you begin the final leg. Note the aerial ropeway up the fellside between Claughton brickworks and a clay pit up on Claughton Moor. You enter Yorkshire again at Low Bentham, and then there are a couple of short, sharp climbs to do before Settle.

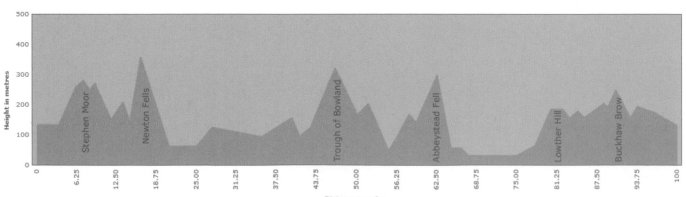

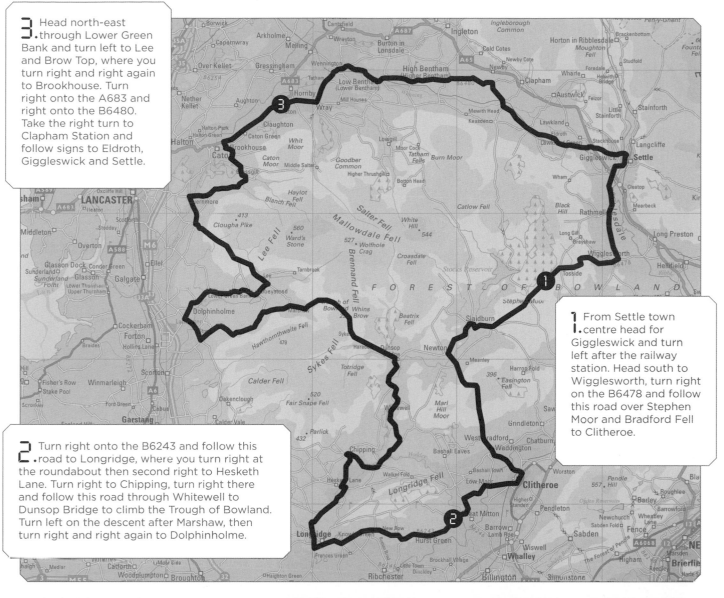

3. Head north-east through Lower Green Bank and turn left to Lee and Brow Top, where you turn right and right again to Brookhouse. Turn right onto the A683 and right onto the B6480. Take the right turn to Clapham Station and follow signs to Eldroth, Giggleswick and Settle.

1. From Settle town centre head for Giggleswick and turn left after the railway station. Head south to Wigglesworth, turn right on the B6478 and follow this road over Stephen Moor and Bradford Fell to Clitheroe.

2. Turn right onto the B6243 and follow this road to Longridge, where you turn right at the roundabout then second right to Hesketh Lane. Turn right to Chipping, turn right there and follow this road through Whitewell to Dunsop Bridge to climb the Trough of Bowland. Turn left on the descent after Marshaw, then turn right and right again to Dolphinholme.

START + FINISH: Settle

GETTING THERE: Settle is just east of the A65, 13 miles north-west of Skipton. It has rail links with Bradford and Leeds as well as the West Coast Main Line through Carnforth.

BIKE SHOP: 3 Peaks Cycles in the Market Place

CAFE: Ye Olde Naked Man in the Market Place. An eye-catching name in a place where every other building is a cafe; it's a nice place, too.

LOCAL DELICACY: Lancashire cheese

LANCASHIRE PENNINES

This is a hard old slog with very little flat road and some pretty challenging hills. Two of them have been used by cyclists as venues for national hill climb titles. It's a rugged part of the country, full of gaunt valleys, witchy heights, squat little villages and big industrial towns.

The start is in Bury, birthplace of the first British racing cyclist to become a household name here and abroad. Reginald Hargreaves Harris was the Sir Chris Hoy of his day. He won Olympic medals, but the Olympics were restricted to amateurs back then; the real glory boys of the velodrome were the professional sprinters. Harris won four world professional sprint titles between 1949 and 1954, and he was dubbed 'Milord' by European track-racing fans for his fine manners and his love of fast cars and good living.

Bury is on the outskirts of Manchester and at the foot of the Pennines, which you enter at Ramsbottom — and with a bang. You don't have to climb the Rake — you can avoid it by carrying straight on where the route turns right as you enter town — but getting to the top of its 25 per cent slope feels good. Anyway, it's only 950 metres long and the only really steep bit is at the start, and near the top, and ... well, the bit in the middle is steep, too.

A string of mill towns comes next as you follow the Rossendale valley over into Yorkshire and Todmorden, where the route switches into the upper Calder valley to climb onto Todmorden Moor. There's a huge wind farm here along a high road called the Long Causeway, which eventually rewards you with amazing views over Burnley, Nelson and Colne, with the great bulk of Pendle Hill looming in the distance.

Pendle Hill is an outlier of the Yorkshire Dales hills, and you brush the Dales in Barnoldswick. The route swings west from here to Clitheroe, where you enter witch country.

The road over Pendle Hill crosses a lower peak called the Nick of Pendle, which is another regular hill-climb venue. It's also the scene of a harrowing tale from the 17th century, when a number

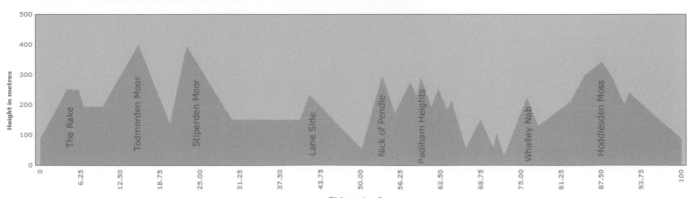

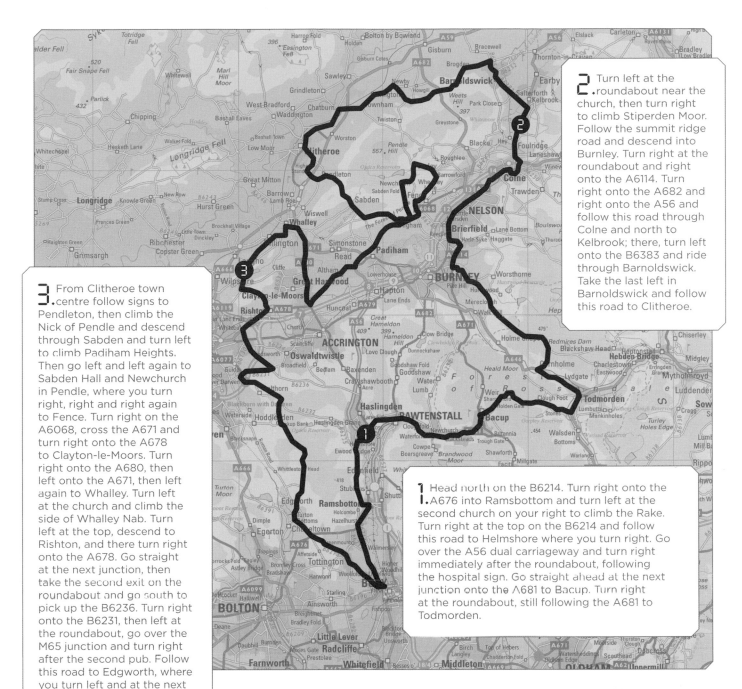

2. Turn left at the roundabout near the church, then turn right to climb Stiperden Moor. Follow the summit ridge road and descend into Burnley. Turn right at the roundabout and right onto the A6114. Turn right onto the A682 and right onto the A56 and follow this road through Colne and north to Kelbrook; there, turn left onto the B6383 and ride through Barnoldswick. Take the last left in Barnoldswick and follow this road to Clitheroe.

3. From Clitheroe town centre follow signs to Pendleton, then climb the Nick of Pendle and descend through Sabden and turn left to climb Padiham Heights. Then go left and left again to Sabden Hall and Newchurch in Pendle, where you turn right, right and right again to Fence. Turn right on the A6068, cross the A671 and turn right onto the A678 to Clayton-le-Moors. Turn right onto the A680, then left onto the A671, then left again to Whalley. Turn left at the church and climb the side of Whalley Nab. Turn left at the top, descend to Rishton, and there turn right onto the A678. Go straight at the next junction, then take the second exit on the roundabout and go south to pick up the B6236. Turn right onto the B6231, then left at the roundabout, go over the M65 junction and turn right after the second pub. Follow this road to Edgworth, where you turn left and at the next junction take the B6213 back to Bury.

1. Head north on the B6214. Turn right onto the A676 into Ramsbottom and turn left at the second church on your right to climb the Rake. Turn right at the top on the B6214 and follow this road to Helmshore where you turn right. Go over the A56 dual carriageway and turn right immediately after the roundabout, following the hospital sign. Go straight ahead at the next junction onto the A681 to Bacup. Turn right at the roundabout, still following the A681 to Todmorden.

of Pendle women were blamed for some deaths in the area, convicted of witchcraft and hanged. The story gives the hill a spooky air and it's said to be one of the most haunted places in the country.

From Pendle the route dips into the Hyndburn district, skirts Accrington and then goes through the pretty village of Whalley. As you climb up the side of Whalley Nab, check out Whalley Arches on your right; it's a 48-span viaduct across the Calder valley. Whalley was where the first

Roses cricket match between Lancashire and Yorkshire was played back in 1867.

It's not easy to find a countryside way through the ribbon of towns above Bury, but there's one between Blackburn and Oswaldtwistle, which leads out onto the Hoddlesden moors and over to Edgworth for a moorland run back to the black-pudding capital of Britain.

It's said that so much of this sausage made from pig's blood is consumed in Bury that the standard test for possible bowel cancer, blood in faeces, doesn't work here. There, I bet you are glad you know that. On a lighter and more wholesome note, the Bury Black Pudding Company supply Harrods with the delicacy.

START + FINISH: Bury

GETTING THERE: Bury is five miles north of Manchester. It has tram and train links with the city.

BIKE SHOP: Pilkington Cycles on Bolton Road

CAFE: There are loads in and around Bury Market

LOCAL DELICACY: Black pudding

WEST LANCASHIRE

'THERE'S A GOOD CHANCE YOU'LL SEE SOME KIND OF CHAMPION AS YOU RIDE AROUND WEST LANCASHIRE'

A lot of Britain's best racing cyclists live and train in this part of the country, including Tour de France winner Bradley Wiggins, so there's a good chance you'll see some kind of champion, or an aspiring one, as you ride around West Lancashire.

Bolton is the start and finish. It's home to Olympic sprint champion Jason Kenny and the comedian Peter Kay. The late Fred Dibnah was also a Bolton man. He was a steeplejack and steam-engine enthusiast who became a household name through the raw enthusiasm of his TV documentaries.

There's a hill to climb from the start. Then after Horwich the route undulates through some very pleasant countryside, while threading its way around densely populated places like Wigan and Skelmersdale, once a centre for wool processing and coal.

You cross from Lancashire into Merseyside at Lydiate, to head for Liverpool Bay and the beach at Crosby, the site of Antony Gormley's installation *Another Place*. Cast-iron men, each one weighing 650 kilograms and one metre 89 centimetres tall, stand on the beach, looking out to sea.

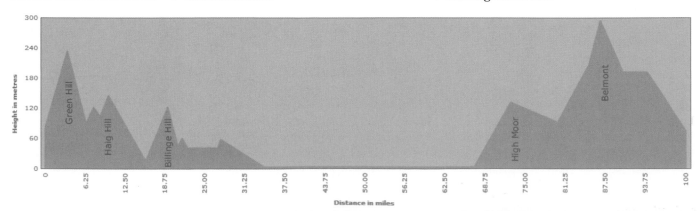

NORTH-WEST ENGLAND

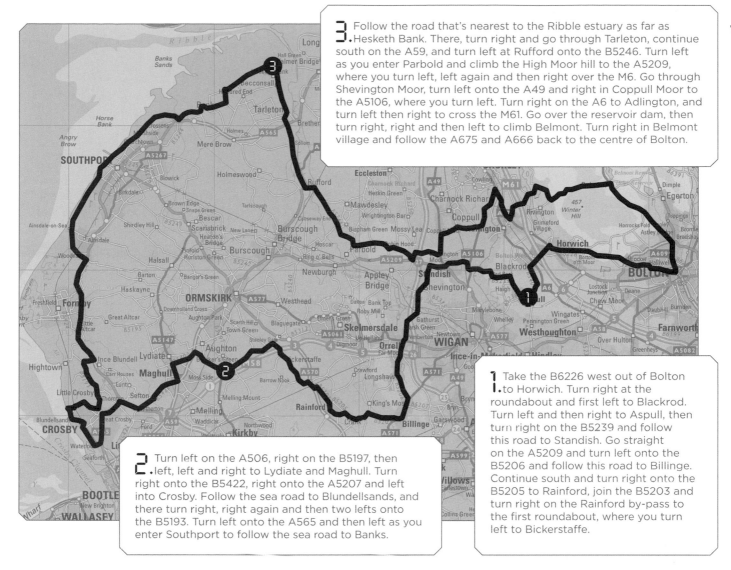

3. Follow the road that's nearest to the Ribble estuary as far as Hesketh Bank. There, turn right and go through Tarleton, continue south on the A59, and turn left at Rufford onto the B5246. Turn left as you enter Parbold and climb the High Moor hill to the A5209, where you turn left, left again and then right over the M6. Go through Shevington Moor, turn left onto the A49 and right in Coppull Moor to the A5106, where you turn left. Turn right on the A6 to Adlington, and turn left then right to cross the M61. Go over the reservoir dam, then turn right, right and then left to climb Belmont. Turn right in Belmont village and follow the A675 and A666 back to the centre of Bolton.

1. Take the B6226 west out of Bolton to Horwich. Turn right at the roundabout and first left to Blackrod. Turn left and then right to Aspull, then turn right on the B5239 and follow this road to Standish. Go straight on the A5209 and turn left onto the B5206 and follow this road to Billinge. Continue south and turn right onto the B5205 to Rainford, join the B5203 and turn right on the Rainford by-pass to the first roundabout, where you turn left to Bickerstaffe.

2. Turn left on the A506, right on the B5197, then left, left and right to Lydiate and Maghull. Turn right onto the B5422, right onto the A5207 and left into Crosby. Follow the sea road to Blundellsands, and there turn right, right again and then two lefts onto the B5193. Turn left onto the A565 and then left as you enter Southport to follow the sea road to Banks.

There's something about them. They are identical, and they are covered by each tide. Sometimes they stand clear of the sand, sometimes it builds up around them. I don't know enough to say what they symbolise, but to me they are about endurance, about standing firm no matter what. Being resolute is a good cycling quality, too.

You keep the coast company for a while now. You pass Formby, where the dunes are one of the last habitats of the rare natterjack toad, then follow part of the Trans Pennine Trail cycling route across the sands of Southport.

Eventually you reach the south side of the Ribble estuary, a hugely fertile area famous for vegetables grown both out in the open and under glass. The flat part of the ride, which has lasted over 40 miles, ends after following the Leeds and Liverpool Canal south as far as Rufford. This is where the long but not too steep climb up to High Moor begins.

You really are in Bradley Wiggins country now. He lives close to here, and by strange coincidence, even though he was born in Belgium, his father was Australian and he grew up in London, his name is a word in the local dialect. There's a Wiggins Lane on this ride, and a pub on Parbold Hill, which runs parallel to the High Moor climb, used to be called the Wiggin Tree. A Wiggin tree is a rowan or mountain ash around here, or at least it was. Now, you don't get better or more trivial sporting trivia than that.

The next destinations are Rivington and Anglezarke reservoirs. The 2002 Commonwealth Games triathlon and the cycling road race were based here, while the mountain-bike event was up Rivington Moor. This route goes between the two reservoirs and then between Anglezarke and Rivington moors to climb today's killer. Known locally as Belmont, it's named after the village on the other side, and it's a tough end to 100 miles, but from the summit it will be downhill all the way to Bolton.

START + FINISH: Bolton

GETTING THERE: Bolton is at Junction 3 of the M61, about 10 miles north-west of Manchester. It has a rail link with both of Manchester's big stations.

BIKE SHOP: MK Cycles on Tonge Moor Road

CAFE: There are a lot of cafes in Bolton, but The Barn in Rivington Country Park is a local cyclist's favourite.

LOCAL DELICACY: Tripe and onions

THE WIRRAL

RIDE FACTS

Rating
Easy

Total climbing
550 metres

Killer climb
Kelsall Hill

'THE EUREKA CAFE IN TWO MILLS IS A CYCLING HERITAGE SITE, A TRULY TRADITIONAL CYCLISTS' CAFE'

The Wirral peninsula lies between the Dee and Mersey estuaries and has something of an island feel because of it. It's a busy place; the whole north-east side of the Wirral is built up and is really part of the Greater Merseyside conurbation, although the only links to Liverpool are via tunnels and on the famous ferry.

The Wirral is also a hive of cycling activity, with many small lanes on the peninsula itself and the whole of North Wales lying just across the Dee. There are lots of cyclists here. The Olympic gold medallist, Tour de France stage winner and world record holder Chris Boardman is from the Wirral and still rides in the lanes. A number of other internationals and national champions also come from here.

The Wirral is only 15 miles long and seven miles wide, so inevitably a 100-mile ride is going to spill over. This one starts in Chester, and 13 of the first 14 miles are in North Wales. No mountains, though, just the climb of Northop Hill above Connah's Quay, although you do get a nice view of the Clwydian Range over in the west.

Chester used to be a thriving sea port, much bigger than Liverpool, but the Dee silted up, leaving a magnificent ecosystem for birds but favouring Liverpool, on the Mersey, as the major port of the industrial north-west. The ride threads around the Dee estuary, with a small detour inland through Two Mills. The Eureka Cafe in Two Mills is a cycling heritage site, a truly traditional cyclists' cafe, and it's stuffed with bike-racing memorabilia.

The next 45 miles follow the outline of the peninsula. You go along the north bank of the Dee to Hoylake, then along the Liverpool Bay coast to the sea front at New Brighton. This was once a popular holiday resort; created to rival Blackpool, it had its own tower with a glittery ballroom underneath.

The next section is through Birkenhead, another place in northern England where fortunes changed, but here they did so with breathtaking speed. The shipbuilders Cammell Laird built some great vessels in Birkenhead, but it wasn't long before they were hit by the slump in shipbuilding in the UK. In the short boom Birkenhead built a fabulous town centre, but that was it – the money ran out, and the magnificent buildings sit in the middle of town like an abandoned film set.

The route avoids the busiest parts by sticking to a B-road that runs south-west to the pretty village of Willaston, then through Ellesmere Port, close to the Vauxhall car factory and the massive Stanlow oil refinery, and out of the Wirral. This section of ride is unashamedly industrial. As you climb Helsby Hill and even more so through Frodsham you get amazing views of Stanlow, the Mersey beyond it, and Runcorn and Widnes straddling the river. You can also see the Manchester Ship Canal, just south of the Mersey, built to enable ships to come straight from the sea and sail directly to Manchester for off-loading there.

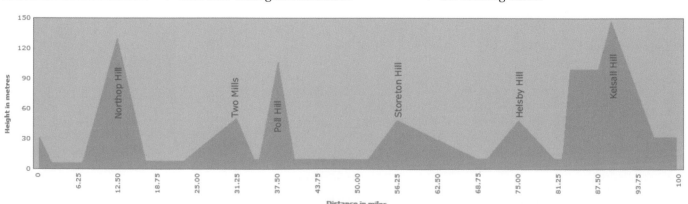

Height in metres — Distance in miles

Northop Hill · Two Mills · Poll Hill · Storeton Hill · Helsby Hill · Kelsall Hill

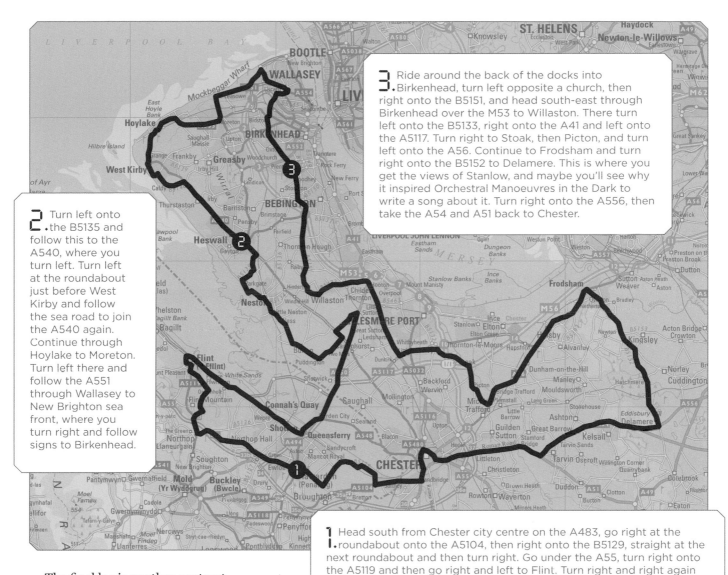

3. Ride around the back of the docks into Birkenhead, turn left opposite a church, then right onto the B5151, and head south-east through Birkenhead over the M53 to Willaston. There turn left onto the B5133, right onto the A41 and left onto the A5117. Turn right to Stoak, then Picton, and turn left onto the A56. Continue to Frodsham and turn right onto the B5152 to Delamere. This is where you get the views of Stanlow, and maybe you'll see why it inspired Orchestral Manoeuvres in the Dark to write a song about it. Turn right onto the A556, then take the A54 and A51 back to Chester.

2. Turn left onto the B5135 and follow this to the A540, where you turn left. Turn left at the roundabout just before West Kirby and follow the sea road to join the A540 again. Continue through Hoylake to Moreton. Turn left there and follow the A551 through Wallasey to New Brighton sea front, where you turn right and follow signs to Birkenhead.

The final leg is another contrast because it runs through Delamere Forest, a tiny remnant of the old forests of Mara and Mondrem, two huge areas of woodland that covered all of north-west Cheshire. It still makes a very pleasant ride back to Chester.

1. Head south from Chester city centre on the A483, go right at the roundabout onto the A5104, then right onto the B5129, straight at the next roundabout and then turn right. Go under the A55, turn right onto the A5119 and then go right and left to Flint. Turn right and right again to Queensferry, where you turn left. Join the A494, then the A550 going through Two Mills, and then take the second left. Go right onto the A540 and first left to Burton and Neston.

START + FINISH: Chester

GETTING THERE: Chester is at the western end of the M56, about 40 miles south-west of Manchester. It's served by two rail stations and well connected to the national network.

BIKE SHOP: The Bike Factory in Boughton, which is right next to Chester city centre

CAFE: There are a number of cafes in Chester, but it's also worth visiting the Eureka in Two Mills. It's one of those things every cyclist should do at least once, just to say you've been.

LOCAL DELICACY: Wirral watercress

CHESHIRE

RIDE FACTS

Rating
Medium/hard

Total climbing
1000 metres

Killer climb
Mow Cop

A bike ride isn't a bike ride without hills. Well, that's my excuse for sticking some killer hills in at the end of this one. Most of them aren't even in Cheshire, but in neighbouring Staffordshire. However, they provide a fantastic view over the Cheshire Plain, one where on a clear day you can trace the route you've just ridden by the landmarks you've passed.

Cheshire is a place of contrasts, swinging from working-class towns like Crewe and Macclesfield to the WAGs' world of Wilmslow and Knutsford. Congleton is somewhere in between. Respectable now, and edging more into footballer territory as time goes on, it wasn't at all respectable in the early 17th century. That's when the locals raided a fund set aside to buy a new Bible and used

it to buy a bear – because the one the town had for bear baiting was getting too old. That's why there's a bear on the town signs today.

The route starts with a gentle climb towards the outskirts of Macclesfield and Alderley Edge. This is where WAG world starts, but it's also the place where Congleton-born Alan Garner grew up and based some of his children's fantasy novels. He was inspired by the countryside around the Edge, which is an escarpment with mysterious caves underneath it.

David Beckham and Christiano Ronaldo lived in Alderley Edge, as well as numerous TV personalities, and you'll notice the Ferraris and Aston Martins coming thick and fast for the next few miles. Knutsford has a McLaren showroom, and Wilmslow is so affluent that I counted ten sunglasses shops but not one butcher's in the town centre. The route skirts the edges of this madness before doing a loop around Tatton Park and heading off to Cheshire's salt towns.

There are huge reserves of salt under Cheshire, with mines so big that lorries drive around in them. Northwich, Middlewich, Nantwich and Winsford all had salt mines, but Middlewich, where food salt is produced, and Winsford, where they mine rock salt for treating icy roads, are the only ones with working salt mines today.

The River Weaver, which you follow towards Crewe, was crucial to the salt

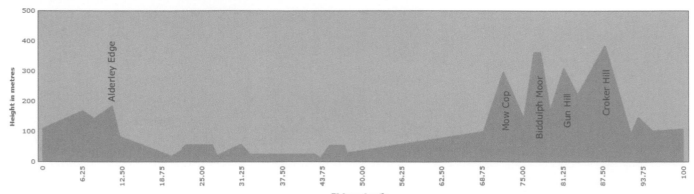

2. Turn right onto the A54 and follow this road to Winsford town centre. Turn left onto the B5074 at the roundabout and follow this road to Nantwich. Turn left at the first roundabout onto the A500, and left at the next roundabout onto the A530, and follow this to the hospital on the north-west edge of Crewe. Turn right just before the hospital and right onto the B5076, then go straight at the next roundabout and follow this road to Haslington. Go south straight through Haslington, then turn left onto the B5077 to Alsager.

1. Take the A536 going north-east out of Congleton, turn left at Warren, then first right and continue straight to the B5087, where you turn left to Alderley Edge. Turn right onto the A34 and second left off it onto the B5085 to Mobberley. Turn right after Mobberley, then left and left again to ride around the edge of Tatton Park. Turn right as you enter Knutsford. Cross the A50, and after the M6 bridge go straight over the A556 onto the B5391. Take the second right, then go right then left to the A559 where you turn left. Turn left onto the A530 and continue south-east to Middlewich.

3. Turn left in Alsager following signs to the Leisure Centre, then turn right after crossing a disused railway. Turn right to Rode Heath and right after crossing the canal, then first right and right again to the A34. Turn left, then second right to climb Mow Cop. Turn left at the top, then right to Biddulph. Continue through Biddulph and Biddulph Moor. Turn left to Rushtonhall, and there turn right to Ryecroft Gate. Cross the A523 and ride straight up Gun Hill. Turn left at the top and go north to Danebridge and Wincle, where you turn right. Then go left onto the A54 over Croker Hill and continue on this road back to Congleton.

trade, as it flows into the Mersey near Runcorn. Some say Crewe is the start of the north, and it certainly feels northern. Rolls-Royce cars were made here, and Bentleys still are. It has one of the largest rail junctions in the country, and British Rail's Crewe works once employed 20,000 people. Crewe's neighbour Alsager is the start of the hilly last part of this ride. Mow Cop is an experience; you climb straight off the Cheshire Plain in just under a mile of over 11 per cent gradient, and the top bit is well over that. The summit is in Staffordshire, and the view over Cheshire as you ride along what's called the Staffordshire Gritstone Edge is incredible. There's Jodrell Bank straight ahead, with busy Manchester Airport behind and the sprawl of Manchester in the distance. That's Liverpool and the sea to the north-west, the Wirral is just south of it, and then there's Snowdonia.

The next two climbs are part of the Staffordshire Moorlands. Biddulph Moor and Gun Hill, a climb made famous by local professional cyclist Les West, who was unbeaten up this hill in the 1960s and 1970s. The final hill, Croker Hill, is in Cheshire. Look for a conical hill called the Cloud over to your left, another natural feature that fired Alan Garner's imagination.

START + FINISH:
Congleton

GETTING THERE:
Congleton is on the A34, 12 miles north of Stoke and 20 miles south of Manchester city centre. It has rail links to both.

BIKE SHOP: The Cycle Store on West Road

CAFE: Coffee Beans Cafe on Bridge Street

LOCAL DELICACY: Cheshire cheese

DERBYSHIRE DALES

RIDE FACTS

Rating
Hard

Total climbing
2300 metres

Killer climb
Taddington Moor

'MOST OF
THE RIDING
SO FAR HAS
BEEN EITHER
ALONG OR IN
AND OUT OF
THE STEEP
VALLEYS'

The Derbyshire Dales are the southern half of the Peak District. They are also known as The White Peak, because they are made of light-grey limestone, which contrasts sharply with the millstone grit of the Dark Peak further north. The natural colour of millstone grit is a rich dark yellow, but when exposed it's weathered almost black by atmospheric pollution.

The ride starts in Ashbourne, the southern gateway to the Dales, and in keeping with the rest of the route, it begins with a climb. You scale Hognaston Winn to Carsington Reservoir, a place well known to triathletes for the heartbreaking hills they encounter in several famous events held there each year.

There's a left turn at the top and you descend through Brassington, ride over a low ridge then reach the A5012, known locally as the Via Gellia. It's not a Roman Road but was named after Philip Eyre Gell, who built it in the late 1700s. Gell affected Roman descent, so its name is a bit of local mickey-taking.

The road leads to Cromford, home of Arkwright's spinning mill. Built right at the beginning of the Industrial Revolution, it's the template for the whole factory concept. This part of Derbyshire was a great textiles area. The wool/cotton mix fabric Vyella was named after the Via Gellia, and was developed and produced at the nearby Hollins Mill.

The next climb takes you out of the Derwent valley to Crich, where there's a tram museum, then over to Matlock. Next is Derbyshire's Wensley Dale (two words, notice), which leads to Elton.

The historic names come thick and fast on this ride. Back in the Derwent valley you pass the 'Palace of the Peaks', Chatsworth House, then make a long climb to Eyam, the village that shut itself off when a resident fell victim to bubonic plague during the 1660s. Doing so condemned many villagers to death but probably prevented a national epidemic.

You hit some cycling history next. A descent to the River Wye takes you to Monsal Dale and a short but steep climb where the river switches course from south to west. This is Monsal Head, a famous hill-climb race venue.

You go straight on, but the Wye curves west then east and you meet it again in chocolate-box pretty Ashford in the Water. There's a stretch of main road now, before a taste of the Dale tops. Most of the riding so far has been either along or in and out of the steep valleys, but originally the Dales were mostly a huge limestone plateau, with today's rivers forming subterranean caverns in a lot of places. The caverns became valleys when their roofs collapsed.

Flagg Moor is a great example of what the plateau looked like. It's only a quick look, though, because you soon drop into Dovedale and begin the undulating final run back to Ashbourne. This passes through Tissington, which gives its name to a Jacobean mansion and a modern 13-mile off-road cycling trail.

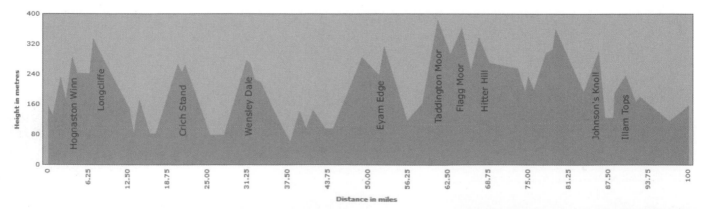

2. Turn right onto the A6, then left in Darley Dale onto the B5057 to Winster. Go straight on at the crossroads to Elton, then follow the road to Middleton, Youlgreave, Alport and the A6, where you turn right. Turn left onto the B6012 at Rowsley and ride past Chatsworth. Turn right onto the A619 and left onto the A623 at Baslow. Turn right onto the A625 and immediately left onto the B6001 and left again onto the B6521 to Eyam. Continue to Foolow, where you go left then right onto the A623 and left onto the B6465. At the top of the hill turn right and descend into Monsal Dale. Turn left and climb Monsal Head, and then turn right onto the B6465 to Ashford in the Water.

3. Turn right onto the A6 and left at Taddington. Keep left and continue to Flagg. After the village go left onto the A515, turn first right to Crowdecote, then right to Earl Sterndale. Turn left onto the B5053 up Hitter Hill. Follow this road to the B5054 junction and turn left through Hartington, then go right, uphill to the A515, where you turn right. Turn right to Alstonefield and left to Ilam, then left to Tissington, crossing the A515. Turn right on the B5058, then left on the A515 back to Ashbourne.

1. Find the B5035 and head north-east on it. Turn left just as you reach Carsington Water to Brassington. Turn right at Longcliffe, then right again onto the A5012 to Cromford, and there turn right onto the A6. Turn left onto the B5035, go through Crich and turn left at the sharp right bend after the village. Follow this road, keeping right except for one left at Plaistow, to the A615, where you turn left to Matlock.

START AND FINISH:
Ashbourne

GETTING THERE:
Ashbourne is 11 miles north-west of Derby on the A52. Derby is also the nearest rail link.

BIKE SHOP: Pedal Power Bikes

CAFE: The Flower Cafe in the Market Place

LOCAL DELICACY:
Bakewell tart

NOTTINGHAMSHIRE

RIDE FACTS

Rating
Easy/medium

Total climbing
520 metres

Killer climb
Long Dale

This ride explores two contrasting halves of the county, the Trent Valley and Sherwood Forest. All but one of the ride's hills come in the second half, the Sherwood side, and it keeps to the county's back roads, avoiding the busy main ones. Nottinghamshire often gets overlooked; it's a place people tend to drive through on their way somewhere else, but they shouldn't. This ride shows it has a lot to offer.

You start in Retford, a red-brick market town in the north of the county, and you start with a climb. It's not too hard, and there's a long descent to the giant Trent power station at Cottam. Watch for the working windmill on your left as you pass through North Leverton.

A string of villages follows. You go through Treswell and Rampton, which has seen a number of high-profile murderers treated in its maximum-security hospital, then on south to Laneham, past another power station at High Marnham, to Sutton on Trent and the Old Great North Road.

This was the stagecoach route between London and York, and later to Edinburgh. When our roads were numbered this was the first, the A1, which of course still exists but is all dual carriageway and motorway now. The new A1 follows much of the old route, but there are places along its route, like this bit between Sutton and Tuxford, that have been bypassed. These are good roads to ride; wide and well surfaced, but with little traffic.

'THESE ARE GOOD ROADS TO RIDE; WIDE AND WELL SURFACED, BUT WITH LITTLE TRAFFIC'

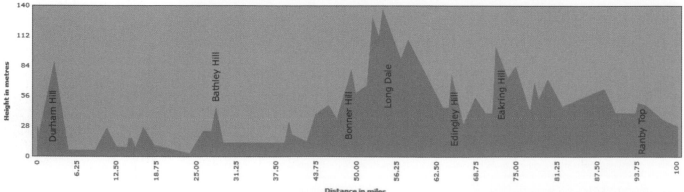

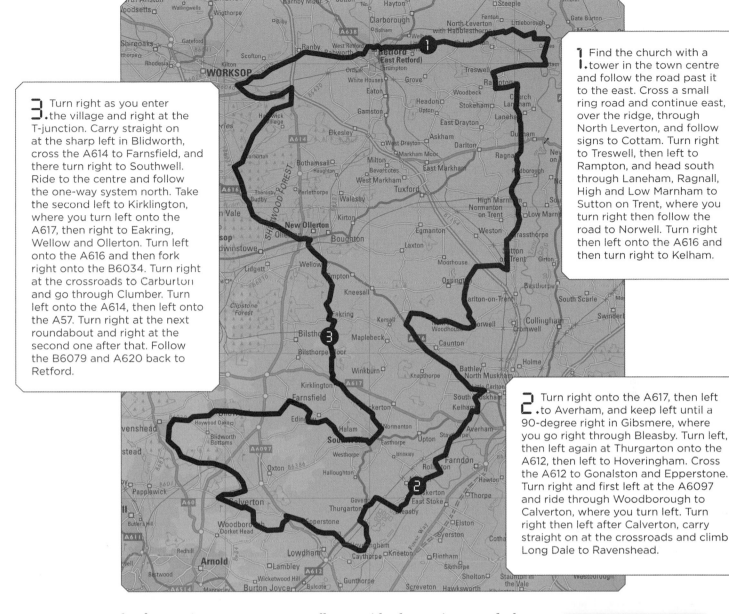

3. Turn right as you enter the village and right at the T-junction. Carry straight on at the sharp left in Blidworth, cross the A614 to Farnsfield, and there turn right to Southwell. Ride to the centre and follow the one-way system north. Take the second left to Kirklington, where you turn left onto the A617, then right to Eakring, Wellow and Ollerton. Turn left onto the A616 and then fork right onto the B6034. Turn right at the crossroads to Carburton and go through Clumber. Turn left onto the A614, then left onto the A57. Turn right at the next roundabout and right at the second one after that. Follow the B6079 and A620 back to Retford.

1. Find the church with a tower in the town centre and follow the road past it to the east. Cross a small ring road and continue east, over the ridge, through North Leverton, and follow signs to Cottam. Turn right to Treswell, then left to Rampton, and head south through Laneham, Ragnall, High and Low Marnham to Sutton on Trent, where you turn right then follow the road to Norwell. Turn right then left onto the A616 and then turn right to Kelham.

2. Turn right onto the A617, then left to Averham, and keep left until a 90-degree right in Gibsmere, where you go right through Bleasby. Turn left, then left again at Thurgarton onto the A612, then left to Hoveringham. Cross the A612 to Gonalston and Epperstone. Turn right and first left at the A6097 and ride through Woodborough to Calverton, where you turn left. Turn right then left after Calverton, carry straight on at the crossroads and climb Long Dale to Ravenshead.

You pass under the new A1 at Cromwell, then ride through ancient Norwell before picking up the Trent again at Kelham, just west of Newark, where the river changes its direction from east to north. The river didn't always do that; before the Ice Age the Trent continued east through a space in the Lincolnshire ridge called the Ancaster Gap to reach the sea. The change of direction came when the Gap was blocked by ice, and the river stayed that way after the thaw.

You finally leave the big river at Hoveringham and head north-west through some of Nottingham's prosperous satellite villages. The ride gets hillier now, with the high point reached after a long but gentle climb up Long Dale from Calverton to Ravenshead.

Southwell is the next place of interest, a small town with a huge minster and a lot of history. Charles I spent his last night of freedom in the half-timbered King's Head Inn, and Southwell is the birthplace of the Bramley apple.

You had a brief taste of Sherwood Forest around Ravenshead, but at Ollerton you enter its heart. In nearby Edwinstowe is Robin Hood's supposed hideout, the Major Oak – 800 years old, supported by props, but still producing acorns. The route goes through Lime Tree Avenue in Clumber Park, the longest in Europe. Clumber was the home of the Dukes of Newcastle, and this part of Nottinghamshire contains many similar homes, so many that it's called the Dukeries. It's pleasant and pastoral, all green rolling acres. Those Dukes knew about 'location, location' centuries ago.

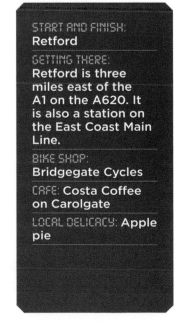

START AND FINISH:
Retford

GETTING THERE:
Retford is three miles east of the A1 on the A620. It is also a station on the East Coast Main Line.

BIKE SHOP:
Bridgegate Cycles

CAFE: Costa Coffee on Carolgate

LOCAL DELICACY: Apple pie

LINCOLNSHIRE WOLDS

RIDE FACTS

Rating
Medium

Total climbing
1150 metres

Killer climb
Limber Hill

The Lincolnshire Wolds feel higher than they are. They don't reach much above 150 metres, but fresh air sweeps in from the North Sea to cleanse them, and a ride here really blows away the cobwebs. But just to make this ride even more bracing, it starts with a quick sprint along the Lincolnshire coast.

'Skegness Is So Bracing' was the slogan of the county's most famous resort. Its delights lie to the south of this ride, but you'll understand what they meant when you meet the North Sea. Your start town is Louth, the eastern gateway to the Wolds, but a flat bit of coasting makes a perfect warm-up.

You hit the hills at Ludborough and this ride's killer climb, Limber Hill. It isn't too bad – there are some steep hills in the Wolds, but I've avoided them. That makes this a perfect 100 miles for anyone graduating from flatter 100s and on their way to tougher stuff.

You descend to Binbrook and pass the old airfield there. Because it's largely flat and close to the North Sea, Lincolnshire has a long association with the RAF. It reached its peak during the Second World War, when the county was home to Bomber Command and almost every other Lincolnshire village had an RAF base. Even the plateau parts of the Wolds were pressed into use, and memories of the many who didn't come back still haunt the county.

The ride undulates north then south in a loop of nearly 19 miles that ends at the top of Bully Hill, where it joins High Street. Today this is the B1225, but it was built by the Romans between two towns they founded, Caistor and Horncastle. The Romans had a great eye for the best line, and although the road crosses hilly country it does so without encountering steep hills.

Horncastle leads to the final section of the ride, and roads that are the heart of the Wolds. These were built after the Romans, using the footpaths and bridleways between towns and villages, and even between fields. They also used more direct routes, because they were designed for legs and not wheels. The contrast between these and Roman High Street is repeated throughout the country, as successive generations built a dense, interconnecting network of arteries on the skeleton of great roads left by the Romans.

You pass another place with RAF associations, the Aviation Museum at East Kirkby, then face a wicked climb from Old Bolingbroke to Mavis Enderby. In fact it's all hills on the final leg, as you

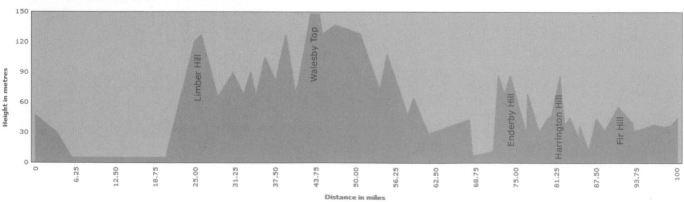

2. Follow the main road through Rothwell, which eventually swings south. Turn right at the next crossroads and left onto the B1225. Follow this road until it joins the A158 just north-west of Horncastle.

1. Go south then east on the B1200. Turn left onto the A1031 at Saltfleetby St Clements. Take the first left in Wragholme and head west to join the A18. Turn first left off the A18 (which is really straight on) to climb Limber Hill. Turn right at the top. Turn right in Binbrook onto the B1203, and then take the second left to Rothwell.

3. Turn right onto the A153, then left onto the B1183 and left again onto the A155. Turn left at the Old Bolingbroke sign and go through the village to Mavis Enderby. There, turn right onto the B1195 and then left to Hagworthingham, where you turn right to Brinkhill and South Ormsby. Turn right, then left to cross the A16, then turn left and left in South Thoresby. Join the A157 after Little Cawthorpe and continue straight on the B1200 to Louth.

pass through Hagworthingham and South Thoresby, names left us by the Vikings, before the run back to Louth.

Louth is a nice place, full of old buildings and antique shops, and the skyline is dominated by the spire of St James's Church, at 295 feet the tallest of any parish church in Britain. The Greenwich Meridian runs through Louth on Eastgate; there's a plaque indicating exactly where on the north side of the street.

'A RIDE HERE REALLY BLOWS AWAY THE COBWEBS'

START AND FINISH: Louth

GETTING THERE: Louth is on the intersection of the A16 and A157, 17 miles south of Grimsby and 24 miles north-east of Lincoln. The nearest rail lines are in those two places.

BIKE SHOP: Louth Cycle Centre

CAFE: Chuzzlewits Tea Rooms on Upgate

LOCAL DELICACY: Grimsby fishcakes

SOUTH LINCOLNSHIRE

RIDE FACTS

Rating
Easy

Total climbing
150 metres

Killer climb
None, really

You could ride 100 miles, never be more than ten miles from Boston, and never cover more than 400 metres of the same road twice. The same goes for the other Wash towns, as you will see in the Fenland ride. The whole area has a fine network of medium, small and tiny roads; so many that on the map they look like lacework.

Boston is your start and finish, and if visibility is good it's your navigation point throughout the ride. Boston Stump is the name given to the tower of St Botolph's Church in the heart of town. It's 83 metres high and can be seen for miles because the surrounding countryside is pan flat. This is a great ride if you don't like hills. There's only one, almost exactly halfway round, at Toynton All Saints, and it's only 45 metres high.

The first section hugs the north-eastern side of the Wash, the bay that looks like a big square bite out of of eastern England, and which is fed by the rivers Witham, Welland, Nene and Great Ouse. The story goes that King John's crown jewels were lost in the Wash. He sent them ahead when he was travelling through the area, and the wagon carrying them was caught by the high tide while crossing the River Welland. However, some historians think this story is a cover and that the king put them up as security on a loan and, having obtained it, conveniently 'lost' them.

If you are expecting the coastal run to be full of wide sea views and crashing waves, prepare to be disappointed. The Wash is shallow and separated from the road by half a mile of salt marsh. It's a haven for wildlife, though, and this section of the ride includes a trip out to Gibraltar Point, a nature reserve that stands where the Wash joins the North Sea.

You continue north for a few more miles, then head inland and cross the first contour of the ride at Gunby, after nearly 40 miles. Spilsby and Toynton All Saints stand on a small outlier of the Lincolnshire Wolds. The oldest towns and villages were built on little areas of higher ground like this, often with a windmill to catch the winds blowing off the flatlands, like the one on top of the hill at Toynton.

The flatlands here are called fens. Often man-made, or at least man-helped, they are extremely fertile. This was a natural phenomenon, created by regular flooding bringing dissolved nutrients, and the fact that much of the area was formerly peat bog. Now this part of Lincolnshire is farmed intensely on an industrial scale, using a lot of fertilisers.

After riding north, west and then south on generally quiet roads, even the main ones, you have to take a section of the busy A52 when you swing east and

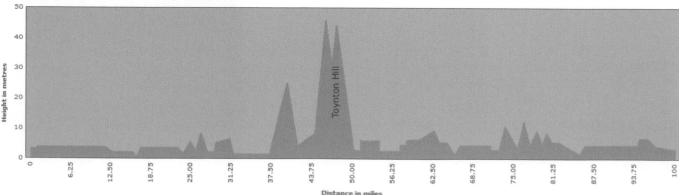

2. Turn left at the Marine Zoo then right onto the A52 to Ingoldmells. Turn left to Addlethorpe and Gunby. Take the third exit onto the A158 then turn right on the B1195 to Spilsby, where you turn left onto the A16. Turn left to Toynton All Saints, and after the village turn right to rejoin the A16 and go left to Stickney. Turn right and follow signs to Coningsby; the castle at adjoining Tattershall will be an aid to navigation here.

1. Go north-east on the A52 and turn right at Benington, then continue on this minor road that runs parallel with the A52 to Wrangle. Turn left into Wrangle, then right onto the A52 to a very sharp right bend where you go straight on. Continue north-east through Friskney and Wainfleet All Saints, then turn right and keep right to go left onto the A52 to Skegness. Turn right, head for the sea front and follow signs to Gibraltar Point; then retrace to Skegness.

3. Turn left onto the A153. Carry straight on after North Kyme where the A-road goes sharp right, fork right and then keep left to Heckington. There you join the B1394 and continue south on it to the A52, where you turn left. Turn right onto the A152 in Donington. Turn left onto the B1397 in Gosberton and follow this road back to the edge of Boston, where you join the A16 and turn left near the Black Sluice.

'THIS IS A GREAT RIDE IF YOU DON'T LIKE HILLS'

head back to Boston. It's the only way over the South Forty-Foot Drain, one of the major man-made ditches into which smaller ditches empty in order to keep the Fens dry. The last section to Boston goes through the area of lacework lanes mentioned at the beginning.

START AND FINISH: Boston

GETTING THERE: Boston is on the A52, 35 miles south-east of Lincoln. It has a rail connection with Sleaford, through which the rest of the rail network can be accessed.

BIKE SHOP: Noel Craft Cyclelife

CAFE: Boston Lock Cafe at the Black Sluice Centre, which you pass very close to the end of the ride

LOCAL DELICACY: Lincolnshire sausages

NORTH SHROPSHIRE

RIDE FACTS

Rating
Hard

Total climbing
1120 metres

Killer climb
Walton Hill

'IT'S QUITE A HARD RIDE, WITH LOTS OF LUMPS AND BUMPS BETWEEN THE SET-PIECE CLIMBS'

I think Shropshire is an underrated cycling destination. It's close to Wales, and that's where people tend to go to do epic rides. This one dips into the Principality a couple of times, but of the two big climbs, one is entirely on the Shropshire side, and the other one mostly. It's quite a hard ride, with lots of lumps and bumps between the set-piece climbs.

The county town, Shrewsbury, is the base of operations and the route heads straight to Wales and the Long Mountain. This is exactly what it says it is: a long, slender mountain with very steep sides.

To reach the top you are going to climb Walton Hill, a little over two miles long with an average gradient of 8 per cent and a wicked bit of 25 per cent about a third of the way up. The top is a wonderful place, from which you can look west over Welshpool and towards the Cambrian Mountains, and due east you can see the Wrekin, near Telford, the other big climb on this ride, and the West Midlands conurbation beyond that.

Off the mountain the route plays with the Welsh border as it works its way north to Oswestry, which is English now but has been Welsh, several times. You climb up a hill towards Old Oswestry, an Iron Age fort, then head south for a short run along the A5 London to Holyhead road. Built by Thomas Telford, the road once hosted a famous cycling road race that ran the whole length of it, 260 miles in a single day.

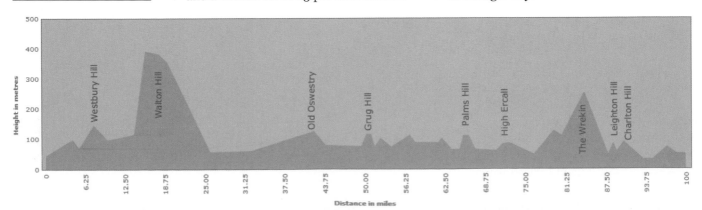

Height in metres

500
400
300
200
100
0

Westbury Hill · Walton Hill · Old Oswestry · Grug Hill · Palms Hill · High Ercall · The Wrekin · Leighton Hill · Charlton Hill

0 · 6.25 · 12.50 · 18.75 · 25.00 · 31.25 · 37.50 · 43.75 · 50.00 · 56.25 · 62.50 · 68.75 · 75.00 · 81.25 · 87.50 · 93.75 · 100

Distance in miles

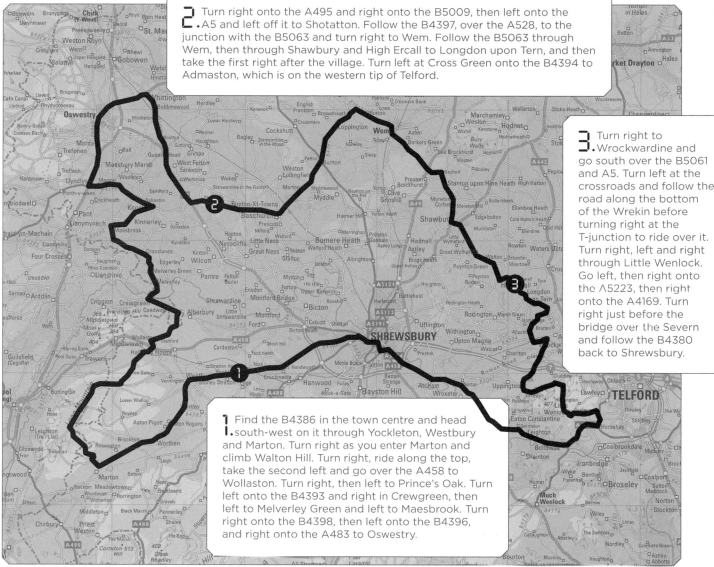

2. Turn right onto the A495 and right onto the B5009, then left onto the A5 and left off it to Shotatton. Follow the B4397, over the A528, to the junction with the B5063 and turn right to Wem. Follow the B5063 through Wem, then through Shawbury and High Ercall to Longdon upon Tern, and then take the first right after the village. Turn left at Cross Green onto the B4394 to Admaston, which is on the western tip of Telford.

3. Turn right to Wrockwardine and go south over the B5061 and A5. Turn left at the crossroads and follow the road along the bottom of the Wrekin before turning right at the T-junction to ride over it. Turn right, left and right through Little Wenlock. Go left, then right onto the A5223, then right onto the A4169. Turn right just before the bridge over the Severn and follow the B4380 back to Shrewsbury.

1. Find the B4386 in the town centre and head south-west on it through Yockleton, Westbury and Marton. Turn right as you enter Marton and climb Walton Hill. Turn right, ride along the top, take the second left and go over the A458 to Wollaston. Turn right, then left to Prince's Oak. Turn left onto the B4393 and right in Crewgreen, then left to Melverley Green and left to Maesbrook. Turn right onto the B4398, then left onto the B4396, and right onto the A483 to Oswestry.

You leave the A5 after the West Felton cutting and head for Wem. It's a good name, but it was even better during Saxon times when Wem was Wamm. It sounds brilliant, but Wamm was Saxon for marsh, so it was probably a bit of a muddy place as the town is low lying and on the confluence of the River Roden and Sleap Brook. The sweet pea was invented in Wem, cultivated by Henry Eckford and introduced commercially in 1882.

The route follows the River Roden south towards Telford, but you keep to the west of the town heading for the Wrekin, which dominates the horizon for miles around. The top stands 407 metres above the maturing valleys of the Roden, Tern and Severn. The Wrekin's geology is complicated but basically it's part of the Shropshire Hills, which are a good few miles south-west. The Wrekin is isolated from them by a number of fault lines.

The road doesn't go all the way to the top, just over a flat-topped subsidiary peak on the Wrekin's east side. As you climb, think about Hugh Porter. He's the BBC cycling commentator now, but he was the world track pursuit champion four times back in the 1970s. He trained on this road, sometimes riding up it without holding the handlebars in order to build core strength – long before the fitness experts even coined the term.

You descend into the Severn valley and follow its course upstream back to Shrewsbury. Look out for Wroxeter: now a tiny village, it was once the fourth-largest city in Roman Britain and called Viroconium Corniovium. You can still see ruins of the public baths, and the poet A. E. Housman celebrated 'the Uricon city', as he called it, in a poem with the line 'Today the Roman and his trouble are ashes under Uricon'.

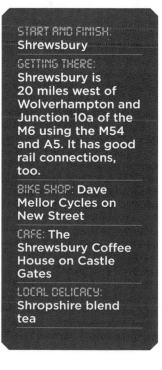

START AND FINISH:
Shrewsbury

GETTING THERE:
Shrewsbury is 20 miles west of Wolverhampton and Junction 10a of the M6 using the M54 and A5. It has good rail connections, too.

BIKE SHOP: Dave Mellor Cycles on New Street

CAFE: The Shrewsbury Coffee House on Castle Gates

LOCAL DELICACY: Shropshire blend tea

MIDLANDS

NORTH STAFFORDSHIRE

RIDE FACTS

Rating
Medium

Total climbing
920 metres

Killer climb
Ipstones Edge

This is a mixed ride of mature river valleys, woods, rural lanes and just a touch of the Staffordshire Moorlands; and it's also full of industrial heritage. It starts in Barton-under-Needwood with a lovely road that runs north towards the great brewing town of Burton upon Trent and into Needwood Forest.

As with many of our ancient forests, Needwood's true glory has gone, a victim of the 1803 Enclosure Act and the need for farmland, but it was written about in poetry by Erasmus Darwin and painted by the landscape artist Joseph Wright. What remains is a ring of smaller forests and woods on the edge of the plateau it covered. You pass one, Bagot Forest, as you leave Abbots Bromley.

This is middle England, old England in many ways. Traditions endure here, like the Abbots Bromley Horn Dance. It's a complicated affair, half pagan ritual, half Morris dance, and widely held to date back to when this was the kingdom of Mercia, although some historians think the whole thing might have been made up later as an excuse to party.

The route continues south of Uttoxeter and crosses the River Dove at Aston Bridge to go north towards Ashbourne and the Peak District, getting hillier all the time. Take care on the short stretch of main road past Darley Moor, a motor-racing circuit that hosts of lot of cycling events, after which you head east over the Dove again and enter the hilliest part of the ride.

At Alton you descend into the Churnet valley and past Alton Towers, then do an up and back to Ipstones Edge purely for the view. At 380 metres, this is the high point of the ride. You are in the Staffordshire Moorlands district now, the southern extremity of the Peak District, and the view north is full of famous hilltops.

This is also the northern tip of the ride. You descend south through Ipstones to Froghall, where there's a wharf on the Caldon Canal. You also meet the Churnet Valley Railway here. Kingsley & Froghall is one of the principal stations on this revived steam and diesel route. The Thomas Bolton Copperworks stands by the rail line, which itself makes a splendid journey, especially by steam, as it winds through the deep, wooded valley. This is

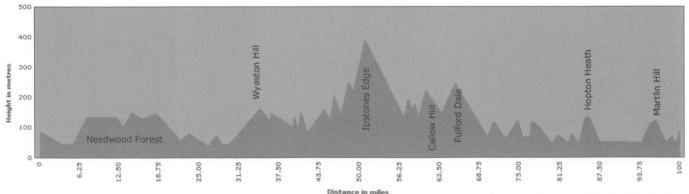

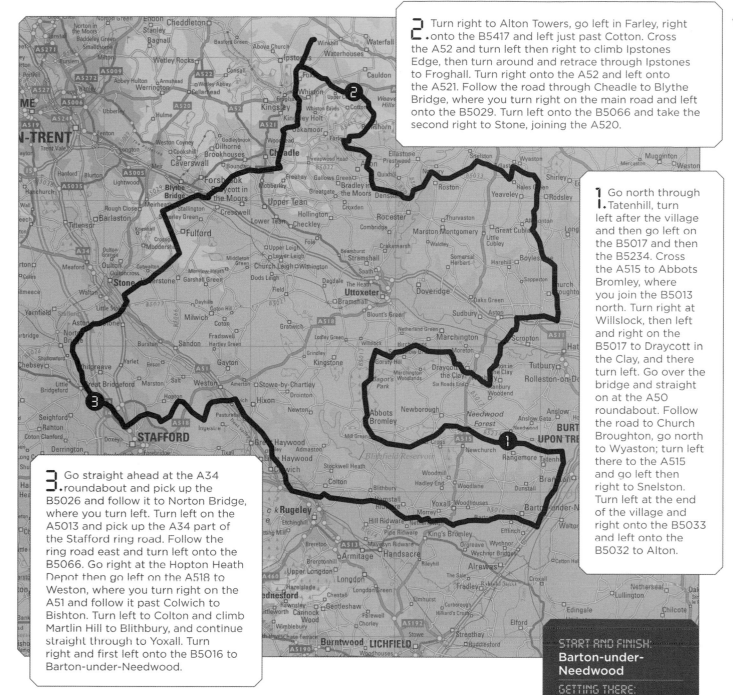

2. Turn right to Alton Towers, go left in Farley, right onto the B5417 and left just past Cotton. Cross the A52 and turn left then right to climb Ipstones Edge, then turn around and retrace through Ipstones to Froghall. Turn right onto the A52 and left onto the A521. Follow the road through Cheadle to Blythe Bridge, where you turn right on the main road and left onto the B5029. Turn left onto the B5066 and take the second right to Stone, joining the A520.

1. Go north through Tatenhill, turn left after the village and then go left on the B5017 and then the B5234. Cross the A515 to Abbots Bromley, where you join the B5013 north. Turn right at Willslock, then left and right on the B5017 to Draycott in the Clay, and there turn left. Go over the bridge and straight on at the A50 roundabout. Follow the road to Church Broughton, go north to Wyaston; turn left there to the A515 and go left then right to Snelston. Turn left at the end of the village and right onto the B5033 and left onto the B5032 to Alton.

3. Go straight ahead at the A34 roundabout and pick up the B5026 and follow it to Norton Bridge, where you turn left. Turn left on the A5013 and pick up the A34 part of the Stafford ring road. Follow the ring road east and turn left onto the B5066. Go right at the Hopton Heath Depot then go left on the A518 to Weston, where you turn right on the A51 and follow it past Colwich to Bishton. Turn left to Colton and climb Martlin Hill to Blithbury, and continue straight through to Yoxall. Turn right and first left onto the B5016 to Barton-under-Needwood.

'THIS IS ALL MAGIC STUFF IF YOU ARE INTO INDUSTRIAL HERITAGE'

all magic stuff if you are into industrial heritage.

The industrial theme continues in Cheadle, home of one of the Wedgwoods. An army major, Cecil Wedgwood was awarded the DSO during the Boer War and was killed during the Battle of the Somme in 1916. The Wedgwoods were pottery manufacturers, and after Cheadle you are in the Potteries, the name given

to the city of Stoke-on-Trent and the five towns that surround it.

Next on the heritage trail is Stone, home of the canal builder James Brindley. Through it passes one of his best works, the Trent and Mersey Canal, which links the two great rivers and thus the country's east and west coasts. You follow quite a bit of its route south-east on the final leg back to Barton-under-Needwood.

START AND FINISH:
Barton-under-Needwood

GETTING THERE:
Barton-under-Norwood is just off the A38, five miles south-west of Burton upon Trent.

BIKE SHOP: Cadence Sport in Barton-under-Needwood is owned by former Tour de France racer Adrian Timmis.

CAFE: The Skinny Kitten

LOCAL DELICACY: Staffordshire oatcakes

VALE OF BELVOIR

RIDE FACTS

Rating
Easy

Total climbing
530 metres

Killer climb
Belvoir Castle

'THE LANES
ARE QUIET,
THEY
UNDULATE
GENTLY AND
YOU CAN SEE
FOR MILES'

In many ways the Vale of Belvoir is Thatcher's Britain. Former Prime Minister Margaret Thatcher was born in Grantham; you pass what was her father's corner shop on North Parade near the centre of town. The Vale is foxhunting country, conservative to its core, a place where entrepreneurism brings rewards and life is good. Perhaps Thatcher thought everywhere could be like this, when it probably can't.

It's great cycling country, too, and has been a favourite destination for cycling clubs from the Nottingham and Leicester areas for many years. The ride starts in Melton Mowbray, famous for pork pies and Stilton cheese. The Melton Mowbray pie was given protected geographical status by the European Union in 2008,

and even though Stilton is named after a Cambridgeshire village on the A1 it's never been made there, only in Melton or in villages near it.

The term 'painting the town red' was also born in Melton when the Marquess of Waterford and some mates, celebrating a successful hunt, got a bit the worse for drink, found some red paint and defaced several buildings with it. The first section of the ride undulates north-east to Woolsthorpe by Colsterworth, where the manor house is the birthplace of Isaac Newton. You pass it heading north, as the route begins to shadow the A1 to Grantham. Newton went to school in Grantham, and as well as producing Britain's first woman prime minister, Grantham was the first place to recruit

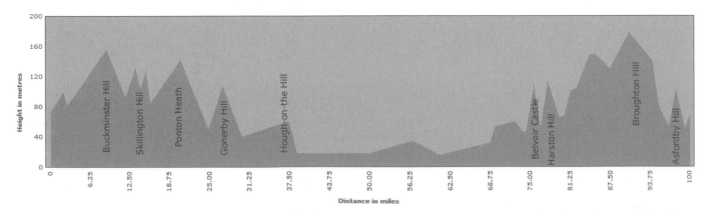

2. Continue north on the B1174 over Gonerby Hill. Turn right in Great Gonerby, then left onto the A607. Turn left in Caythorpe and right in Hough-on-the-Hill, then right and left in Brandon. Turn right after Claypole and again just before the A1. Go over the A1 bridge at Balderton and turn left. Continue south until the right turn to Flawborough. There are so many lefts and rights now it's simpler to follow the signposts to Flintham, then Car Colston, then Scarrington, then Langar and Harby.

3. Turn left in Harby, then right where you see a Redmile sign pointing left. Climb past Belvoir Castle to Woolsthorpe by Belvoir, turn right to Harston and then do the signpost routine again to Knipton, Branston and Eaton. Turn left after Eaton and follow this road through Eastwell across the A606 to the junction with the A6006, where you turn left and head back to Melton Mowbray.

women police officers.

You climb over Gonerby Hill, where Oliver Cromwell had his first victory of the Civil War, then up onto the shoulder of the Lincoln Ridge. This is an elongated upland area that runs the length of Lincolnshire, and it carried one of the most important Roman roads, Ermine Street.

The true Vale of Belvoir is the flat land to the west of the first section of this ride, and you enter it at Hough-on-the-Hill. The route turns south at Balderton, then flits through several beautiful red-brick villages, heading generally south to Colston Bassett. This section, and the one that travels up the other side of the Vale to Belvoir Castle, is idyllic. The lanes are quiet, they undulate gently and you can see for miles. Bikes were made for rides like this.

Belvoir Castle is built on a shelf of land near the top of Blackberry Hill and has the most commanding view, not just of the Vale but a 180-degree slice of the Midlands from Nottingham in the west, through Newark and Lincoln in the north, to Grantham and beyond in the east. The castle dates from Norman times, but the present building comes from the early

1. Head east on the B676 and turn left just before Colsterworth to Woolsthorpe, where Newton's birthplace is on your right. Turn left then right, then go straight at the crossroads to Skillington. Turn right and keep left to Hungerton. Turn right and right again, and after crossing the A1 bridge go left onto the B1174 to Grantham. Margaret Thatcher's birthplace is on your right as you go through town. It was a shop called Roberts when she lived there, but not any more.

19th century. It's still the home of the Manners family, who live in a small part of the castle, but much of the rest is given over to earning money. It has been used as a set for several major film and TV productions, including *The Da Vinci Code*.

The climb to Belvoir Castle is quite steep, as is Harston Hill just after it. Then you start the long climb of Broughton Hill, which is a steep-sided ridge, but you climb its gentler long axis. The last leg goes east back to Melton, and the descent of Asfordby Hill provides a high-speed entrance to the town. So, with 100 miles of calories burned, you've earned a pork pie. Go on, you know you want one.

START AND FINISH: Melton Mowbray

GETTING THERE: Melton Mowbray is on the A607, 16 miles east of Junction 23 of the M1.

BIKE SHOP: Halfords

CAFE: Cafe Italia on Church Street

LOCAL DELICACY: Melton Mowbray pork pies

CHARNWOOD FOREST

RIDE FACTS

Rating
Medium

Total climbing
950 metres

Killer climb
Beacon Hill

'YOU'LL HAVE TO LOOK SHARP FOR THIS RIDE, BECAUSE IT STARTS IN THE FITNESS CAPITAL OF ENGLAND'

By the time you've waded through this book you'll realise that I really like forests. There's something about them – the mystery maybe. You can't see the horizon in a forest and anything could hide among the trees. Maybe I read too much Tolkien when I was younger, but they are beautiful; forests do something to the light, to the air, and they smell deep and rich, but fresh, too. This ride finishes by exploring an old one, but as with most of our natural forests there's only a remnant of Charnwood left.

You'll have to look sharp for this ride, because it starts in the fitness capital of England. Sports science is Loughborough University's speciality, and fit young people roll up here every year to study and to train. British Triathlon is based here, so there could be some pretty nippy cyclists zipping about on the roads, although they're probably not doing 100 miles.

The route heads west first to Ashby de la Zouch, which is an old place in a new forest. The National Forest was planted during the second half of the 1990s across 200 square miles of the Midlands. There are eight million trees in it, 85 per cent broadleafed, and after looking a bit like a bad hair replacement when it was first planted, the forest is taking shape. It will be glorious one day.

There's a short loop north through Melbourne, then you head south through the western edge of Coalville to a change of landscape. Coalville stands on coal that was mined here as early as the Middle Ages. It was later worked on an industrial

scale, and the town and surrounding villages also had quarries and produced textiles and rail wagons.

You head west again at Ibstock, then south to Twycross, home of a famous zoo, and east towards Market Bosworth. On the way, just after Congerstone, you'll see the Battlefield Line. It's a heritage railway that runs for 4.5 miles from Shackerstone to Shenton, which is close to Bosworth Field. This is where the final battle of the Wars of the Roses was fought, so it's where, in Shakespeare's play, Richard III uttered the classic line, 'A horse, a horse, my kingdom for a horse!' You pass the battlefield just south of Market Bosworth. It lies on your right where you turn sharp left. If you carry straight on there's a great farm shop and cafe about 200 metres further down the road.

Soon afterwards you ride through Kirkby Mallory and through a bit of cycling history. Cyclists still race on the Mallory Park motor racing circuit, but in 1970 it and the roads around it hosted the world road race championships. It was the first time for the UK, and all the best riders of the day were here, including the greatest pro road racer ever, Eddy Merckx.

The last section of this ride switches back and forth through Charnwood Forest and culminates with a long climb up Beacon Hill. Many of the trees have gone, but the underlying geology is much less transient. Some rock outcrops in Charnwood are Precambrian, so

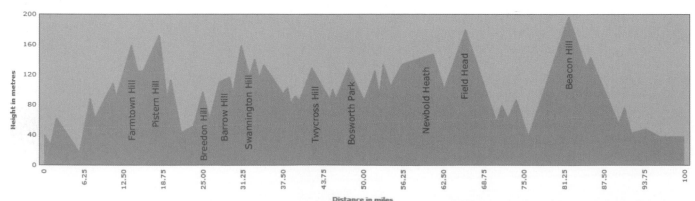

1. Go due north to Stanford on Soar, turn left to Normanton on Soar and go left onto the A6006. Join the B5324 at the A6 junction and continue past Coleorton Hall, then go right and left onto and off the A512, turn right, then go right and left onto and off the A511. Turn right to Ashby de la Zouch and go north through the middle of town, joining the B5006. Turn right past Calke Park then left onto the B587 to Melbourne. On entering town turn right to Wilson, then left to Breedon on the Hill. Go right one mile after the A42 flyover and follow the road south, joining the A447 at the A511 junction, to Ibstock.

2. Turn right towards Measham and go left just before there onto the B4116. Turn left just before Twycross and ride through Bilstone and Congerstone to Market Bosworth. Turn right and right again in the town centre and follow the battlefield signs south. Go under a railway bridge and turn left to go under another. Turn left in Sutton Cheney then right onto and left off the A447 to Kirkby Mallory. Turn left after Peckleton and ride to Desford, and there go left onto the B582 to Newbold Heath. Turn right to Botcheston, then left to Markfield.

they date back over 600 million years. The first fossil ever discovered of the first complex animal was found in Charnwood Forest.

3. Head east under the A50 to Newton Linford, and there turn left to Anstey. Follow the road to Cropston, where you go right then second left to Quorn. Turn left to Woodhouse, then keep left to The Brand and go right just after Roecliffe Manor. Then do a left and a right twice to climb up to the small pass between Beacon Hill and Bawdon Castle Farm. Go under the M1 and follow this road around the western edges of Shepshed to Hathern. Turn right to Loughborough.

START AND FINISH:
Loughborough

GETTING THERE:
Loughborough is on the A512, one mile east of Junction 23 of the M1. It has a mainline rail station.

BIKE SHOP: **Pedal Power on Ashby Road**

CAFE: **Costa in the Market Place**

LOCAL DELICACY: **Livesey Brothers mushrooms**

RUTLAND

RIDE FACTS

Rating
Medium

Total climbing
1130 metres

Killer climb
Tilton on the Hill

This is a convoluted ride, because at only 18 miles by 17 miles at its widest place, Rutland is our smallest county. It would have been even more convoluted had I not allowed it to cross a border once or twice on the way.

The ride starts and finishes at Oakham, the county town and a gorgeous old place on the western edge of Rutland Water. This massive reservoir fills much of what was the Vale of Catmose and is one of the largest man-made lakes in Europe. It's a great place for bird watching, water sports and family cycling on the 25-mile route around it.

The first section leaves Oakham and heads north-east past Cottesmore RAF base and under the A1 to enter Lincolnshire and approach from the north the beautiful old town of Stamford. The main street is so well preserved that it's been used in a number of period films and TV programmes, including the classics *Pride and Prejudice* and *Middlemarch*.

You head west out of Stamford and back into Rutland, then follow the southern shore of Rutland Water before switching south at Manton and west to Uppingham. This is Rutland's other town, and home of one of Britain's oldest public schools. You leave the town by climbing King's Hill past Eyebrook Reservoir, where Lancaster bomber crews of the 'Dambuster' squadron trained during the Second World War.

This is a hilly ride, and the hills get harder and more frequent from now on. There's a brief dip into Northamptonshire

at Weston, then the route swings north to Tilton on the Hill and Somerby.

This is the heart of Rutland Classic country. The Rutland Classic is Britain's

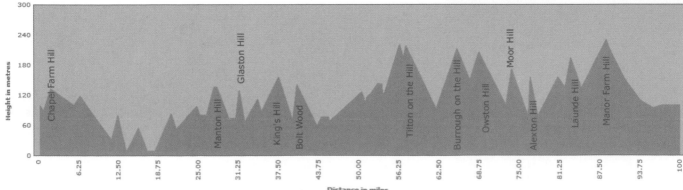

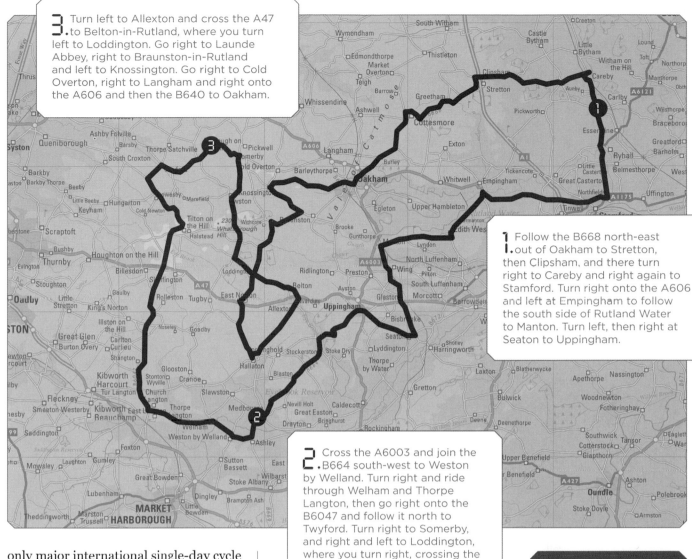

3. Turn left to Allexton and cross the A47 to Belton-in-Rutland, where you turn left to Loddington. Go right to Launde Abbey, right to Braunston-in-Rutland and left to Knossington. Go right to Cold Overton, right to Langham and right onto the A606 and then the B640 to Oakham.

1. Follow the B668 north-east out of Oakham to Stretton, then Clipsham, and there turn right to Careby and right again to Stamford. Turn right onto the A606 and left at Empingham to follow the south side of Rutland Water to Manton. Turn left, then right at Seaton to Uppingham.

2. Cross the A6003 and join the B664 south-west to Weston by Welland. Turn right and ride through Welham and Thorpe Langton, then go right onto the B6047 and follow it north to Twyford. Turn right to Somerby, and right and left to Loddington, where you turn right, crossing the A47, to Hallaton.

only major international single-day cycle race. It's inspired by the Classic races held each year in Europe, particularly one in Belgium called the Tour of Flanders, and another in France known as Paris–Roubaix. Rutland's roads are similar to the ones where the Tour of Flanders is decided, and the race organisers have linked them with off-road sections, mimicking the cobbled tracks that are at the heart of Paris–Roubaix.

The Rutland Classic uses lots of roads around Burrough on the Hill, Somerby and Owston, visiting each village a number of times, but you just go through them once to head south again to Hallaton.

If you time this ride for Easter Monday you'll see the annual bottle-kicking contest in Hallaton. The bottles are barrels, there are three of them, and the contest is between teams from Hallaton and Medbourne, who meet in a field between two streams one mile apart. The contest is the best of three and the idea is for each village to get the barrel over 'their' stream.

'RUTLAND'S ROADS ARE SIMILAR TO THE ONES WHERE THE TOUR OF FLANDERS IS DECIDED'

The only rules are: 'No eye gouging, no strangling and no use of weapons.' The final section goes north and east back to Oakham, past Launde Abbey, where Launde Hill is short but the steepest on the ride. The abbey is so beautiful that the man responsible for the Dissolution of the Monasteries, Thomas Cromwell, kept it for himself. He was executed for treason before he could live there, but his son Gregory did, in the present house, which he built.

START AND FINISH:
Oakham

GETTING THERE:
Oakham is on the A606, 11 miles west of Stamford and the A1, and nine miles south-east of Melton Mowbray.

BIKE SHOP: Rutland Cycling is a massive bike shop on the south shore of Rutland Water.

CAFE: Castle Cottage Cafe near All Saints Church

LOCAL DELICACY: Rutland duck charcuterie

WENLOCK AND THE WELSH BORDERS

RIDE FACTS

Rating
Very hard

Total climbing
1250 metres

Killer climb
Long Mynd

'THE DESCENT INTO CHURCH STRETTON IS SPECTACULAR, WITH SOME SCARY EXPOSURE ON ONE OR TWO CORNERS'

There's a lot packed into 100 miles on this ride. After a start that takes you through a long and beautiful valley, you visit old towns, climb a couple of mountains and end up riding through the cradle of the Industrial Revolution.

Much Wenlock is the start town, the place that gave its name to one of the 2012 Olympic mascots. It was done to honour a resident, Dr William Penny Brookes, who set up the Wenlock Olympian Games in 1850 and was one of the founding fathers of the modern Olympics.

The Wenlock Games had athletics, quoits, cricket, football and cycling on penny-farthings, as well as fun events such as wheelbarrow races, and even a race for grannies. Dr Brookes became involved with the Zappas Olympics in Greece and helped form the International Olympic Committee (IOC) and organise the first modern Games in 1896.

Corve Dale lies between two areas of high ground, the Wenlock Edge and the Clee Hills. It's a beautiful valley that runs straight towards Ludlow, while the River Corve meanders through lush pastures in the valley bottom. You follow the Corve until Beambridge, then climb over a low shoulder of the Wenlock Edge to Craven Arms.

There's a discovery centre at Craven Arms, in case you want to know more about Shropshire and have time to look. Otherwise push on into the Clun valley and follow the river downstream to where it joins the Teme, which you follow upstream to the frontier town of Knighton.

Knighton stands on Offa's Dyke, an earthwork that formed the ancient border between the English kingdom of Mercia and the Welsh kingdom of Powys. Offa was the King of Mercia, and the dyke

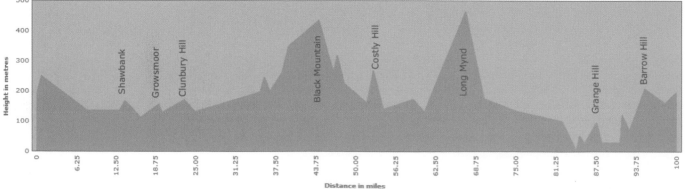

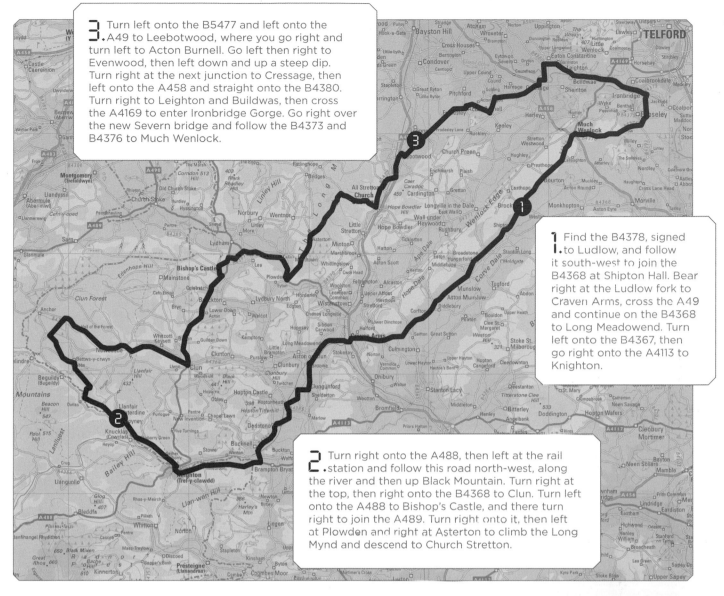

3. Turn left onto the B5477 and left onto the A49 to Leebotwood, where you go right and turn left to Acton Burnell. Go left then right to Evenwood, then left down and up a steep dip. Turn right at the next junction to Cressage, then left onto the A458 and straight onto the B4380. Turn right to Leighton and Buildwas, then cross the A4169 to enter Ironbridge Gorge. Go right over the new Severn bridge and follow the B4373 and B4376 to Much Wenlock.

1. Find the B4378, signed to Ludlow, and follow it south-west to join the B4368 at Shipton Hall. Bear right at the Ludlow fork to Craven Arms, cross the A49 and continue on the B4368 to Long Meadowend. Turn left onto the B4367, then go right onto the A4113 to Knighton.

2. Turn right onto the A488, then left at the rail station and follow this road north-west, along the river and then up Black Mountain. Turn right at the top, then right onto the B4368 to Clun. Turn left onto the A488 to Bishop's Castle, and there turn right to join the A489. Turn right onto it, then left at Plowden and right at Asterton to climb the Long Mynd and descend to Church Stretton.

can be traced from the Dee estuary in the north to the River Wye in the south. As well as a defence it seems to have been a political statement. The dyke uses natural ridges, but where a ditch was dug the earth was always piled on the Mercian side, and where it encounters hills it's always on their west slope, so the Mercians had the higher ground and looked down on Powys.

You follow the new Welsh border next as far as Black Mountain, a tough climb to over 430 metres. It's hard at the beginning, with 137 metres gained in the first 1.7 kilometres, so that's an 8.5 per cent average but with a very steep upward kick at Redgate. It gets a lot easier after that.

You descend to Clun, where there's a Norman castle and other interesting buildings, then head for Bishop's Castle, from where even on a dull day you'll see the second big climb. Long Mynd is from the

Welsh for Long Mountain, and it's a high one with steep sides. There are several ways up, so I picked the hardest — sorry. The climb is 3.9 kilometres long at 6 per cent average gradient and it reaches 487 metres at the top, right next to Pole Bank, the ridge high spot at 516 metres. The first kilometre is brutal as well, be warned.

It is a gorgeous hill, though, and the descent into Church Stretton is spectacular, with some scary exposure on one or two corners. Once down in the quaint little spa town, which was dubbed Little Switzerland by the Victorians, you head north-east to begin the final leg of the ride, a short run along the Ironbridge Gorge. This is where industry began in the late 17th and early 18th centuries, with all sorts of mining and iron smelting and allied trades. You even pass the original iron bridge, built in 1779, the first in the world.

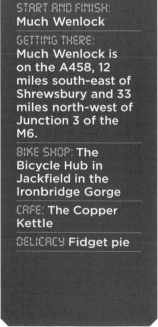

START AND FINISH:
Much Wenlock

GETTING THERE:
Much Wenlock is on the A458, 12 miles south-east of Shrewsbury and 33 miles north-west of Junction 3 of the M6.

BIKE SHOP: The Bicycle Hub in Jackfield in the Ironbridge Gorge

CAFE: The Copper Kettle

DELICACY Fidget pie

NORTHAMPTONSHIRE

RIDE FACTS

Rating
Medium

Total climbing
900 metres

Killer climb
Laughton Hills

Northamptonshire is big and it's difficult to do justice to it in one ride. It's landlocked, surrounded by eight other counties – its border with one, Lincolnshire, being the shortest in the UK at 19 metres (63 feet). It's largely farmland, but there's a contrast in the north. That's why I focused on the northern half of the county and didn't visit the far south, where Silverstone and some surrounding towns have made Northamptonshire a world centre for motor sport.

Not that you'll be deprived if you're a closet petrol head. The start town, Oundle, has a motor-racing circuit, and ten miles into the ride you pass Rockingham Motor Speedway. It's not only Europe's fastest oval banked track, and the first built in Britain since Brooklands, but it also has a road circuit within the oval that hosts car and motorbike racing.

The track's in a part of Northamptonshire called the Rockingham Forest. Only

pockets of woodland remain of the original 200 square miles, but they are sufficient, along with the rolling landscape, to provide a contrast to the rest of the county, which is mainly farmland.

You skirt the northern edge of Corby, a town built on steel production that made use of iron deposits here that had been worked on a small scale for over 100 years. Corby was still called a village in 1939 when its population was 12,000, swelled by an influx of Scottish steelworkers, and it continued to grow. It became a town in 1950, but when the steel industry was rationalised in 1979, Corby missed out. The resulting unemployment disaster led to difficult times for the town, but a lot of work went into the recovery, and Corby has come through successfully. The ride follows the line of hills south of the Welland valley, with villages on top of each one. In contrast the town of Market Harborough lies in a dip, but the hilly theme resumes with some tough climbs on a saw-tooth section called the Laughton Hills. This extends west then south to Husbands Bosworth. To reach the village you ride over a 1,066-metre tunnel through which the Grand Union Canal passes.

You've briefly crossed over into South Leicestershire, but the excursion ends at Stanford on Avon, as you head south through Crick to Daventry. This is where the BBC put one of their first broadcasting stations. It was 1925 and Daventry was chosen because it gave maximum contact

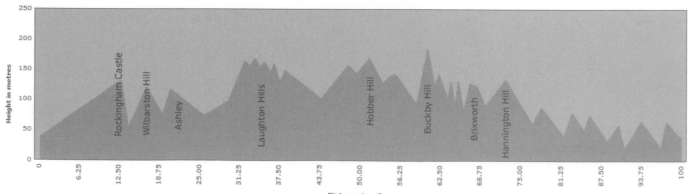

Height in metres / Distance in miles

Rockingham Castle · Wilbarston Hill · Ashley · Laughton Hills · Hobber Hill · Buckby Hill · Brixworth · Hannington Hill

2. Continue to Lubenham, where you turn right then left, then go right to Mowsley, then left, and left again onto the A5199. Turn right at Husbands Bosworth onto the A4304 and left at North Kilworth to Stanford on Avon. Continue south over the A14 and turn right in Yelvertoft to ride through Crick and over the M1. Turn right onto the A5 and first left onto the A361 to Daventry.

1. Head west on the A427. Turn right then left at Upper Benefield. Turn right onto the A43 and take the first left. Ride past the Speedway and around the north of Corby to take the A6003 north. Turn left in Rockingham onto the B670 (note the amazing colour of the local stone in the buildings here). Turn right onto the A427 and right to Wilbarston, and keep right to Ashley. Then turn left onto the B664 and join the A4304 to ride through the centre of Market Harborough.

3. Follow the ring road east and turn left onto the B4036 to Long Buckby. Turn right onto the B5385 and cross the A428 to Ravensthorpe, Teeton, Spratton, Brixworth and Holcot. There, turn left and first right to Hannington, then Little Harrowden and Isham, where you go right on the A509 to Wellingborough. Turn left on the ring road, then left on the A510 and first right to go left onto the B571. Follow this road over the A6 to Great Addington. Turn right to Ringstead and left to Denford, Thrapston and Islip, where you go right onto the A6116, and first right off it to Aldwincle, and continue to Oundle.

with England and Wales. Then in 1932 Daventry became the centre of the Empire Service, now known as the BBC World Service, and the call sign 'Daventry Calling' rang out across the globe.

The next quarter of the ride is hilly, and quite exciting, too, when you cross the causeway between the two halves of Pitsford Reservoir. This leads to the final, flatter section, around Wellingborough and along the Nene valley. The valley wasn't created by the river you see today; it's too wide to have been formed by it. Ice did the work, or rather the massive amount of water released at the end of the Ice Age, which found its way through here to the North Sea. The water brought tonnes of gravel with it, which was extracted, and today there are water-filled pits reaching almost all the way back to Oundle.

'THE HILLY THEME RESUMES WITH SOME TOUGH CLIMBS ON A SAW-TOOTH SECTION CALLED THE LAUGHTON HILLS'

START AND FINISH: Oundle

GETTING THERE: Oundle is on the A605, 12 miles south-west of Junction 17 of the A1(M).

BIKE SHOP: Oundle Bikefix in Lutton

CAFE: Beans on New Street

LOCAL DELICACY: Towcester cheesecakes

NORTH COTSWOLDS

RIDE FACTS

Rating
Medium

Total climbing
1250 metres

Killer climbs
The Dover's Hill and Broadway Hill combo

The North Cotswolds are difficult to put in a region. This ride starts where I reckon the Cotswolds divide into north and south. But it reaches out towards Banbury, which I'd put in southern England, then the Vale of Evesham, which is the Midlands, and finally Cheltenham, which I'd have to say was in the west or south-west for the purposes of this book.

The Cotswolds are great for cycling, a hilly upland area with open views and roads that seem to roll on for ever. Climbing onto the Cotswolds from the north and west is tough, but the views over the flatlands beyond make the struggle worthwhile. You make that climb twice on this ride, while visiting a string of Cotswold villages. Some are busy tourist traps, but a mile away there'll be a place just as pretty that seems undiscovered. The villages have streams and ponds, village greens and deep-windowed thatch cottages made from ochre-coloured stone that looks as warm as toasted teacakes.

The first leg goes north-east past Chipping Norton to a part of the Cotswolds that seems to attract people who can afford to live anywhere. Pop stars and politicians, celebrated artists and just plain celebrities – there are more per square mile here than anywhere outside London. This is partly because it's fashionable, but the Cotswolds' beauty must also be a factor because they've been recorded in words, songs and pictures.

Chipping Campden is far more old Cotswolds. It stands on the northern edge, a former big player in the wool trade that still carries a whiff of the farmyard and indulges in its own 'Olimpick Games'.

'THE COTSWOLDS ARE GREAT FOR CYCLING, A HILLY UPLAND AREA WITH OPEN VIEWS AND ROADS THAT SEEM TO ROLL ON FOR EVER'

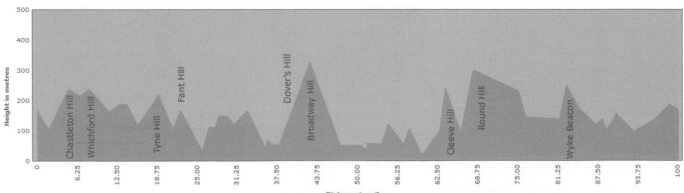

Height in metres

Chastleton Hill · Whichford Hill · Tyne Hill · Fant Hill · Dover's Hill · Broadway Hill · Cleeve Hill · Round Hill · Wyke Beacon

Distance in miles

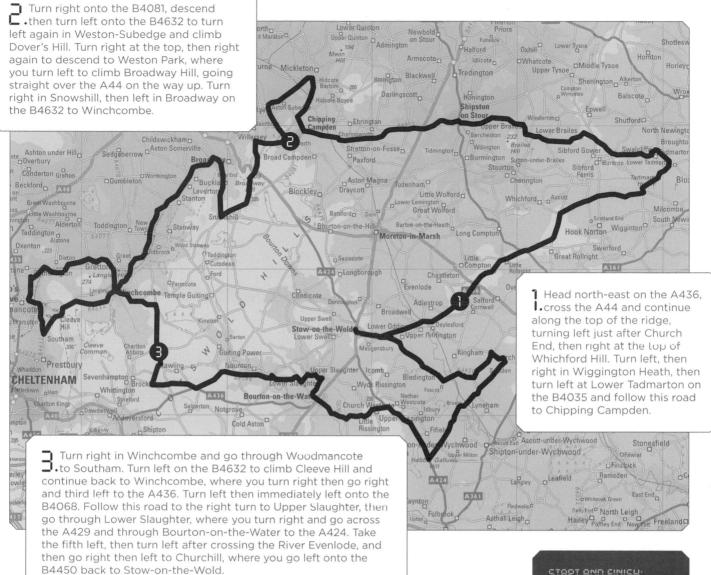

2. Turn right onto the B4081, descend then turn left onto the B4632 to turn left again in Weston-Subedge and climb Dover's Hill. Turn right at the top, then right again to descend to Weston Park, where you turn left to climb Broadway Hill, going straight over the A44 on the way up. Turn right in Snowshill, then left in Broadway on the B4632 to Winchcombe.

1. Head north-east on the A436, cross the A44 and continue along the top of the ridge, turning left just after Church End, then right at the top of Whichford Hill. Turn left, then right in Wiggington Heath, then turn left at Lower Tadmarton on the B4035 and follow this road to Chipping Campden.

3. Turn right in Winchcombe and go through Woodmancote to Southam. Turn left on the B4632 to climb Cleeve Hill and continue back to Winchcombe, where you turn right then go right and third left to the A436. Turn left then immediately left onto the B4068. Follow this road to the right turn to Upper Slaughter, then go through Lower Slaughter, where you turn right and go across the A429 and through Bourton-on-the-Water to the A424. Take the fifth left, then turn left after crossing the River Evenlode, and then go right then left to Churchill, where you go left onto the B4450 back to Stow-on-the-Wold.

These started in 1612 as a bit of healthy fun and competition for farm workers, although they include the punishing sport of shin kicking, which can't be much fun to lose at.

The Games are still going, held as they always were on Dover's Hill, named after their founder Robert Dover, and there's still shin kicking, as well as dwile flonking (you'll have to look that up as it's too complicated to explain) and modern sports such as motorcycle scrambling. The route climbs Dover's Hill, which is a regular venue for cycling's national hill-climb championships.

The climbing continues, although less steeply, to the top of Broadway Hill, where the views north over the Vale of Evesham, and west over Tewkesbury and the Malverns are worth stopping to see. Don't stop too long, though, or

you could get cold and stiffen up on the long descent towards Cheltenham, and you'll need warm legs for another steep ascent of the Cotswold Edge. This climb is a pass between Cleeve Hill, the highest point in the Cotswolds at 317 metres, and Nottingham Hill.

The final section descends steadily then crosses an undulating section to Stow-on-the-Wold. It goes through Upper and Lower Slaughter and Bourton-on-the-Water, places that are good examples of what I said about tourist villages lying right next to less visited ones. Bourton-on-the-Water is beautiful but packed with people, whereas Upper and Lower Slaughter have everything Bourton has – the water, the thatched cottages and the wonderful flower gardens – but this seems to be known only to the locals.

START AND FINISH: Stow-on-the-Wold

GETTING THERE: Stow-on-the-Wold is 16 miles north-east of Cheltenham on the A40 and A429. There's a rail link from Worcester to Moreton-in-Marsh, five miles north of Stow-on-the-Wold.

BIKE SHOP: The nearest bike shop is Bourton Cycles on the industrial estate in Bourton-on-the-Water.

CAFE: Stow-on-the-Wold's youth hostel in The Square has a cafe.

LOCAL DELICACY: Slow-roast hogget (it's lamb)

RIDE FACTS

Rating
Medium

Total climbing
950 metres

Killer climb
Ankerdine Hill

'THE ABBERLEY HILLS PROVIDE A GREAT WARM-UP FOR TODAY'S KILLER CLIMB, ANKERDINE HILL'

This ride starts and ends in the market garden of England, the Vale of Evesham, and circles the county town of Worcester by linking together old spa towns, areas of outstanding beauty and that great outlier of the Welsh mountains, the Malvern Hills.

Evesham is on a loop of the River Avon, and as you ride north out of town you pass the battlefield where in 1265 Simon de Montfort and his men were trapped, hemmed in by the river, and slaughtered by King Henry III's men, led by his son Prince Edward. It must have been terrible.

The first part of the ride is marked by massive greenhouses, a sign of the area's fruit and vegetable industry. The route gets hillier as it rolls towards Bromsgrove, passing an incredible feat of engineering on the Worcester and Birmingham Canal at Stoke Wharf. You are 60 metres above sea level on the canal bridge, but to the east a series of 35 locks lifts the canal up to 136 metres in about 2.5 miles. It's one of the longest flights of locks in Europe.

Skirting around the western edge of Bromsgrove you head south to Droitwich Spa. Any name in England with 'wich' in it means salt, and in Droitwich's case it refers to mining going back to Roman times. The huge masts you see on your left as you enter town are the BBC's central long-wave transmitter, located here because the salt underground provides a good earth and boosts power.

The Abberley Hills lie to the west of Droitwich and provide a great warm-up for today's killer climb, Ankerdine Hill, which is a regular venue for local hill climbs. Luckily the route climbs the north side, which is easier, but that means the descent is steep, so take care.

The climbing continues all the way to Great Malvern, the town standing in tiers up the eastern slope of the Malvern Hills, a stubborn chain of 680-million-year-old rock. Their high spot is the Worcestershire Beacon at 435 metres (1395 feet), and several other peaks break the 1000-foot barrier along their north to south run.

The Malverns are truly beautiful. Edward Elgar, a local and a very keen cyclist, was inspired by them to write *Pomp and Circumstance*. George Bernard Shaw lived and walked here, as did C. S. Lewis. The scenery also inspired the 14th-century poet William Langland, author of one of the oldest classics of English literature, *Piers Plowman*, which begins: 'On a May morning on a Malvern hillside, as I lay and leaned and looked on the water, I slumbered and slept, so sweetly it murmured.'

The hills are much lower when you descend from the Malverns to cross the River Severn. The route does nearly a complete circuit of Bredon Hill to arrive at historic Elmley Castle, near a hill known locally as Besscaps because Queen Elizabeth I was presented with a hat when she visited. It's five miles from there back to Evesham.

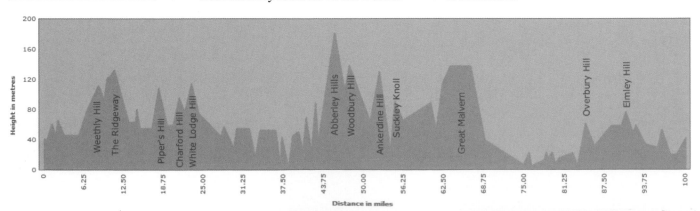

2. Go south straight through town and turn right onto the A38 town bypass and turn left onto the A4133 to Holt Heath. Now the route gets hilly. Turn right onto the B4196 and then turn left onto the B4194 and left again to Dunley. There, turn left onto the A451 and turn right to Abberley. Turn left onto the B4202 and left again onto the A443 to Great Witley, where you go right onto the B4197 and follow it south over Ankerdine Hill to the A44. Turn right and go first left, then left again and right. Go south, through Suckley, and turn left onto the A4103 and right onto the B4219 to Great Malvern.

1. Go north from the town centre and pick up the B4088 and follow it to the A422. Cross the A422 and follow the A441 north, then turn left onto the B4090 to Hanbury. There, turn right onto the B4091 to Bromsgrove, crossing the A38 just before entering town and turn right to the town centre. Turn left onto the A448 and left on the first road after the M5. Turn right then keep left to Cooksey Corner. Continue south to Droitwich Spa.

3. Turn right onto the A449, which is the town's main street and has plenty of cafes if you are flagging, and at Malvern Wells turn onto the B4209. Turn right onto the B4211 and left onto the A4104 at Upton-upon-Severn. Follow the A4104 to Defford and go right onto the B4080 and left just before Bredon and keep left to Kemerton. Turn right at Conderton and left at Beckford to Ashton under Hill. Turn right in Elmley Castle, left after Netherton and right onto the B4084 to Evesham.

START AND FINISH: Evesham

GETTING THERE: Evesham is on the A46, 14 miles south-east of Worcester via the A44.

BIKE SHOP: Vale Cycles in Port Street

CAFE: Word of Mouth Cafe in Vine Street

LOCAL DELICACY: Vale of Evesham fruit and vegetables

HEREFORDSHIRE

'THE LAST PART OF THE RIDE WINDS ALONG SOME DELIGHTFULLY QUIET AND TINY LANES'

Herefordshire likes bikes. It's full of back lanes and rivers, winding past woods and fields, hills and orchards. Sitting in the lap of England but snuggled up to Wales, with just a single short stretch of motorway, Herefordshire is less travelled, less rushed and in closer tune with two wheels than much of the rest of Britain.

This ride starts in the city of Hereford and heads north over the River Lugg, then north-east past several of the orchards that supply Hereford's cider industry and on to Bromyard. The undulating terrain continues to Tenbury Wells, a town with a crazy-looking spa. Architecturally it's said to be Chinese Gothic, but it looks more Disney to me. It's just in Worcestershire and you cross over into Shropshire just north of the River Teme.

There's a reason for this county hopping, and it's called Clee Hill. The view from the road that the route uses is good, but just behind Clee Hill is the higher Titterstone Clee Hill. There's a road to the top and if you're feeling strong it's worth making the effort to climb it because the view is fantastic. In the west you can see nothing but mountains from Snowdonia to the Brecon Beacons; to the south there's the Malvern Hills; the West Midlands sprawl into the east, and it's said that you can see the Staffordshire Moorlands in the north, but I can't vouch for that.

The ride route heads west to Ludlow. With its fine castle it's a Marcher town from when the Welsh borders, or Marches

as they were called, were ruled by the March Lords from just after the Norman Conquest until the 16th century. Ludlow is a beautiful place, one that time seems to have diverted around, and one that's dedicated to food. After that the route rambles on into Wales at Presteigne, then back into Herefordshire and south to Kington, from where it follows the gorgeous River Arrow to Leominster.

It was in Leominster that the last recorded ordeal by ducking stool was inflicted, when a lady called Jenny Pipes

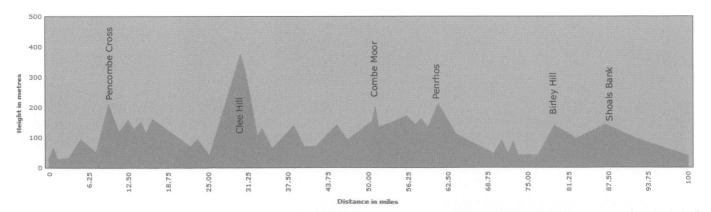

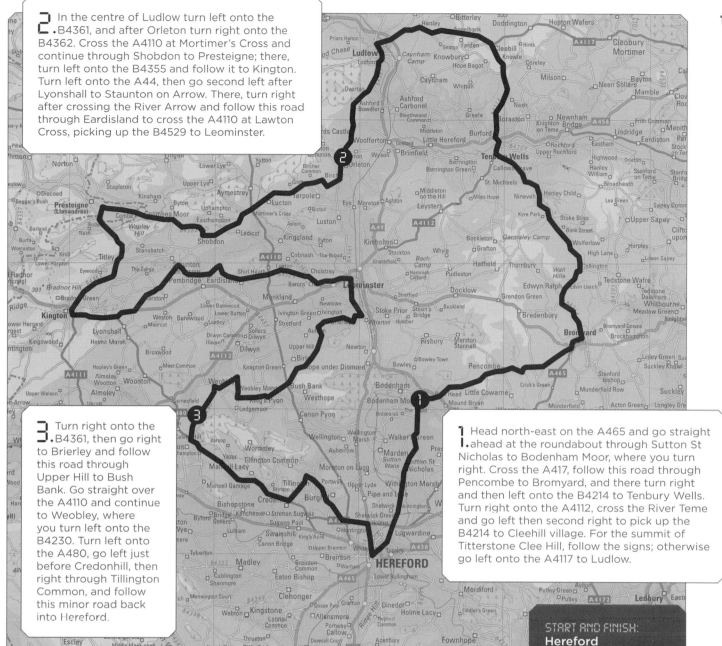

2. In the centre of Ludlow turn left onto the B4361, and after Orleton turn right onto the B4362. Cross the A4110 at Mortimer's Cross and continue through Shobdon to Presteigne; there, turn left onto the B4355 and follow it to Kington. Turn left onto the A44, then go second left after Lyonshall to Staunton on Arrow. There, turn right after crossing the River Arrow and follow this road through Eardisland to cross the A4110 at Lawton Cross, picking up the B4529 to Leominster.

3. Turn right onto the B4361, then go right to Brierley and follow this road through Upper Hill to Bush Bank. Go straight over the A4110 and continue to Weobley, where you turn left onto the B4230. Turn left onto the A480, go left just before Credonhill, then right through Tillington Common, and follow this minor road back into Hereford.

1. Head north-east on the A465 and go straight ahead at the roundabout through Sutton St Nicholas to Bodenham Moor, where you turn right. Cross the A417, follow this road through Pencombe to Bromyard, and there turn right and then left onto the B4214 to Tenbury Wells. Turn right onto the A4112, cross the River Teme and go left then second right to pick up the B4214 to Cleehill village. For the summit of Titterstone Clee Hill, follow the signs; otherwise go left onto the A4117 to Ludlow.

(I kid you not) occupied the chair while being dunked into a pond as punishment for being a scold. The practice sounds medieval, and it was originally, but this was in 1808. The instrument of her torture is on display in the Priory Church, and there's a Ducking Stool pub in Leominster.

The last part of the ride winds along some delightfully quiet and tiny lanes threading between a series of pretty, wooded hills to Weobley, one of the 'black and white' villages, as they're called locally because of the number of old half-timbered houses. Charles I spent the night hiding here after he lost the Battle of Naseby in 1645.

From there you head to Hereford by sneaking around the back of Credenhill Barracks. This is the new headquarters of the SAS, who recently moved out of Hereford. Credenhill has been a military place since the Iron Age, when there was a fort on top of the hill that is covered by Credenhill Park Wood today. Bulmer's cider was first produced in Credenhill. Once back in Hereford it's well worth visiting the cathedral, where the *Mappa Mundi* is on display. Drawn around 1300, it's an amazing record of how scholars of the time saw the world not only in geographic but in spiritual terms.

START AND FINISH:
Hereford

GETTING THERE:
Hereford is 20 miles north-west of Junction 2 of the M50, reached by the A417 and A438. It also has good rail links with South Wales, the north-west of England and the Midlands.

BIKE SHOP: Climb On Bikes on Coningsby Street

CAFE: Diego's, near the cathedral

LOCAL DELICACY: Cider cake

ANGLESEY

'YOU PRESS ON TO THE END OF THE ROAD, LITERALLY, AT A HEADLAND THAT OVERLOOKS PUFFIN ISLAND'

Anglesey, or Ynys Mon (because three-quarters of the inhabitants speak Welsh), is an island separated from the rest of Wales by a narrow strip of water called the Menai Strait. There are two bridges across it: the Menai Bridge, Thomas Telford's 1826 suspension bridge, and the slightly newer Britannia Bridge. They both make magnificent entrances to Anglesey, but the suspension bridge is just that bit more elegant and spectacular.

Bangor, from where you start, is a beautiful university city on the mainland, and the bridge is not far from the city centre. I once crossed it by night and saw trails of bioluminescence, perhaps krill that had drifted in from the open sea, shimmering on the bow wave of a boat

passing below. The straits are steep-sided and narrow where the bridge is, and that steepness continues where the road goes right and runs along a shelf to Beaumaris and its beautifully preserved castle.

From there you press on to the end of the road, literally, at a headland that overlooks Puffin Island. It's a large lump of limestone 500 metres off the coast and it's home to thousands of sea birds – but hardly any puffins. In the late 19th century, brown rats were accidently introduced to the island, and they saw off nearly all the puffins before steps were taken to eradicate the rodents. Anglesey has a mixed-up geology; so much so that students go there on field trips because they see a lot for their money. There are

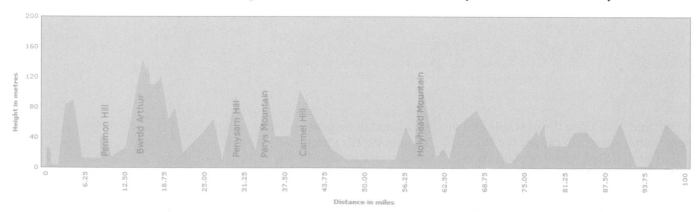

Height in metres — 200, 160, 120, 80, 40, 0

Penmon Hill · Bwrdd Arthur · Penysarn Hill · Parys Mountain · Carmel Hill · Holyhead Mountain

Distance in miles — 0, 6.25, 12.50, 18.75, 25.00, 31.25, 37.50, 43.75, 50.00, 56.25, 62.50, 68.75, 75.00, 81.25, 87.50, 93.75, 100

1. Start in upper Bangor, find the A5 and cross the Menai Bridge, turning right at the roundabout onto the A545. Continue straight through Beaumaris and join the B5109, then turn right in the direction of Penmon and Puffin Island. Retrace to the B5109, turn right and continue north, then turn left at Mariandyrys. Turn left to Llanddona, turn right then right again on the B5109. Turn right on the A5025 and follow this road all the way to Amlwch.

2. Turn left at the first roundabout onto the B5111 and climb over Parys Mountain. Turn right in Llannerch-y-medd onto the B5112, then turn right onto the A5 and left at the junction to do a loop south and north past Valley airfield. Turn left onto the A5, left onto the B4545, then left in Trearddur and follow this road all the way to South Stack. Retrace and turn first left to Holyhead.

3. Turn left onto the B4545, then left over the A55 to turn right onto the A5. Turn left at Valley onto the A5025. Turn right onto the B5109 and continue on this road to Llangefni. Turn right onto the A5114, left onto the A5 and right onto the B4419. Continue straight at Llangaffo on the B4421, then turn left onto the A4080 and follow this road to the A5 junction. Turn right onto the A5 and follow this road over the suspension bridge back to Bangor.

mountains there, too, but they are so designated with tongue in cheek. The first you climb, Parys Mountain, just outside Amlwch, is only 128 metres high and most of it has been lost to quarrying for copper ore.

The climb leads you inland and across the island, to RAF Valley. As well as being the RAF's Search and Rescue Force's HQ, RAF and Navy pilots are given fast-jet training here. Then you come across a surprise: there's another island tacked onto the end of Anglesey. It's Holy Island, where there's also another mountain, as well as Anglesey's biggest town.

Holyhead Mountain reaches 220 metres and is made of quartzite. First you go out and back along the west side of it to some cliffs, where you can see the North and South Stacks, which both have more puffins on them than Puffin Island, as well

as other sea birds. The changing colours as you look down each stack shows the layered geology of this part of Anglesey.

Holyhead is a busy port, with ferries going to and from Ireland, and it has recently become a place where cruise ships land. Aluminium was smelted here until 2009, an industry that saw the harbour used by huge cargo ships carrying bauxite. Now coaches can use the big jetties to pick up cruise passengers and take them away on day trips.

The rest of the ride uses a B-road that goes right down the middle of the island, almost back to the Menai Bridge. Just before the end there's a detour to Newborough Warren. This is a huge beach and dune system of over 20 square kilometres. It's a protected site, and so mature that Corsican pines grow on almost half of it.

START AND FINISH: Bangor

GETTING THERE: Bangor is just off the A55, 60 miles west of Chester. It's also 30 miles north-west of Llangollen on the A5. There's a rail link with Chester, and from there the national network.

BIKE SHOP: Evolution Bikes on the High Street

CAFE: Brazillia on Bridge Street

LOCAL DELICACY: Lobscow (it's a stew)

SNOWDONIA

'IT'S AN
IMPRESSIVE,
MUSCULAR
PLACE, AND
SO ARE ITS
TOWNS AND
VILLAGES'

Two distinct halves, three passes and a thorough exploration of stately Snowdonia all go into this 100-mile ride. It also visits the seaside twice, and one of the places is so extraordinary, so unexpected, that they made a cult TV series there. Snowdonia has everything, including a fair amount of rain, but that only makes the dark slate scenery shine a little more. They say that every cloud has a silver lining; well, in Snowdonia they do.

Snowdonia is mostly made of slate, with small outcrops of volcanic rocks. It's an impressive, muscular place, and so are its towns and villages. You begin this ride in what was the heart of the Welsh slate industry at Blaenau Ffestiniog. There were ten mines here once, when North Wales was chapel, strong beliefs, moral rectitude and closed pubs on a Sunday. Today it has re-branded itself as a tourist destination, either as a place for wild adventures, or for creativity. There is a concerted effort to promote the arts in Snowdonia.

The first half of the ride describes a wide arc down to Tremadog Bay, then goes around the western flank of the mountains up to Caernarfon. The route runs very close to Portmeirion, and it's worth turning off it to see the Italianate village designed and built by Sir Clough Williams-Ellis between 1925 and 1975. It has featured in many films and TV programmes, but is best known for a slightly weird 1960s spy drama called *The Prisoner* that even today has a huge following.

You get a really good look at the bay when the road crosses the sands to Porthmadog. Then you go inland to ride along the feet of the mountains, with the wide open Lleyn peninsula on your left, bound for the sea at Caernarfon. This is one of the oldest places in Wales. A Celtic tribe, the Ordovices, some of the original Welsh people, lived here. It also guards the entrance to the Menai Strait, with access to huge mineral deposits in Anglesey and Snowdonia, so Caernarfon was a Roman stronghold. Caernarfon Castle, completed in 1330, secured the town and still dominates it today.

Caernarfon is where the ride changes. You enter the mountains just outside town and climb up to Pit's Head before tackling the fearsome Pen-y-Pass, climbed via the Bwlch y Gwddel. Pen-y-Pass lies between Snowdon, which at 1085 metres is the highest mountain in Wales, and Glyder Fawr, which is one metre short of the 1000-metre mark. Several paths to the two peaks start at Pen-y-Pass, and there's a youth hostel and a cafe.

There's a long descent down the Pass of Llanberis, with two beautiful lakes lying near the bottom. Then there's a short flattish section to Bethesda, where the second major climb of this ride begins, the Nant Ffrancon Pass. Bethesda used to be famous for quarries; now it's famous for music. Several successful bands, including Super Furry Animals, come from the place known locally as

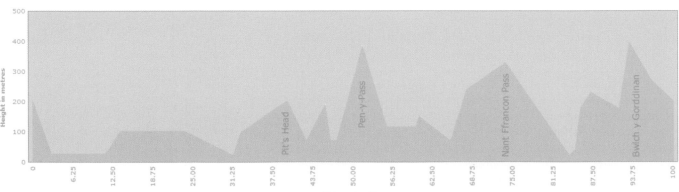

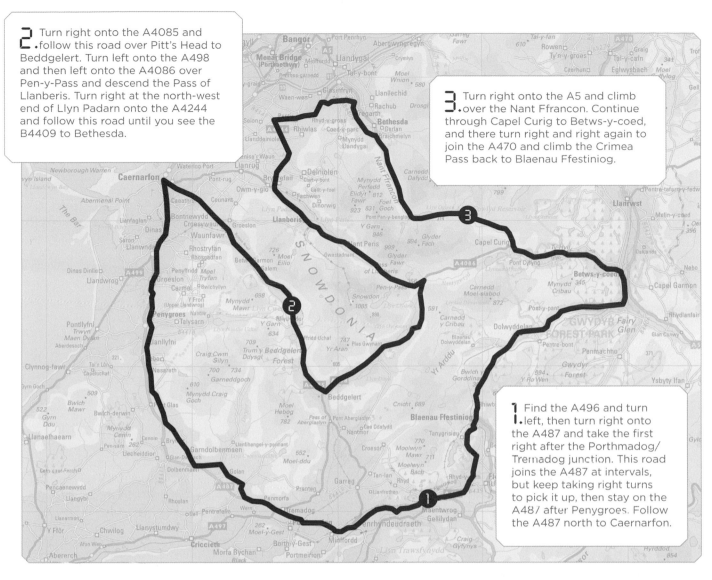

2. Turn right onto the A4085 and follow this road over Pitt's Head to Beddgelert. Turn left onto the A498 and then left onto the A4086 over Pen-y-Pass and descend the Pass of Llanberis. Turn right at the north-west end of Llyn Padarn onto the A4244 and follow this road until you see the B4409 to Bethesda.

3. Turn right onto the A5 and climb over the Nant Ffrancon. Continue through Capel Curig to Betws-y-coed, and there turn right and right again to join the A470 and climb the Crimea Pass back to Blaenau Ffestiniog.

1. Find the A496 and turn left, then turn right onto the A487 and take the first right after the Porthmadog/ Tremadog junction. This road joins the A487 at intervals, but keep taking right turns to pick it up, then stay on the A487 after Penygroes. Follow the A487 north to Caernarfon.

Pesda. Together they have created a music movement known as Pesda Rock.

Nant Ffrancon Pass tops out at just over 300 metres, and the descent goes through Capel Curig, where the forest on the opposite side of the road is part of Plas-y-Brenin, a mountain-adventure and mountain-bike centre. You continue past Swallow Falls to Betws-y-coed, then to the final climb, and the highest and hardest on the route, Bwlch y Gorddinan, or Crimea Pass in English, before a short descent back to Blaenau Ffestiniog.

START AND FINISH: Blaenau Ffestinlog

GETTING THERE: Blaenau Ffestiniog is 41 miles west of Llangollen using the A5 and A470.

BIKE SHOP: There isn't one at the moment, but a mountain-bike trail centre is planned and that should have a shop.

CAFE: The Bridge Cafe on Church Street

LOCAL DELICACY: Tawts Pum Munud (it's another kind of stew, cooked on top of the stove in an open pan and with smoked bacon in it)

BERWYN MOUNTAINS

RIDE FACTS

Rating
Hard

Total climbing
2100 metres

Killer climb
World's End

The Berwyns may not be as steep as the Clwydian Range but they are higher, they cover a wider area and they feel far more remote. They can even look forbidding; indeed, just seeing them caused King Henry II to give up on his planned invasion of Gwynedd in 1165. They are still a wild and empty place, where raptors circle the skies, their gimlet eyes scouring the thick heather below.

The ride opens with a pretty wild climb. World's End sounds ominous but it's a glorious hill. It starts hard with a double switchback across the faces of two very steep slopes, then eases over Esclusham Mountain, which is punctured with old mine shafts. The last bit, which goes through a small stand of conifers where a stream sometimes floods the road, is very steep.

The long descent has a very steep upward section just before halfway, and it takes you into the Vale of Llangollen. For a short stretch into town the River Dee flows on one side of the road, while the Llangollen Canal, a feeder branch taking water from the Dee to the Shropshire Union Canal, is on the other. Llangollen is on the A5, so in coaching days it was a stop on the London–Holyhead route. It's also at the bottom of an important pass on the way to the North Wales coast.

The Horseshoe Pass is one of those climbs every cyclist should ride. It has a long race history, with hill-climb titles being decided there, and it's been part of a lot of big British road races. But it's not in this ride just for history; the road follows a beautiful line, especially where it does a huge left and right horseshoe-shaped bend near the summit.

A long section in the Dee valley follows, and then you must buckle up for the longest climb of the ride. Cwm Pydew is nearly five miles of 4.3 per cent average gradient and climbs to 490 metres. It's also the first true taste of the Berwyns, whose craggy peaks string out in a line to the north of you at the summit. This is where it's worth doing some bird watching, because the Berwyns are one of the few places in Britain you stand a chance of seeing a peregrine falcon.

Each Berwyn peak has a valley running away from it. You ride down the Tanant valley, then into the Rhaeadr, heading for the summit of Moel Sych at 827 metres,

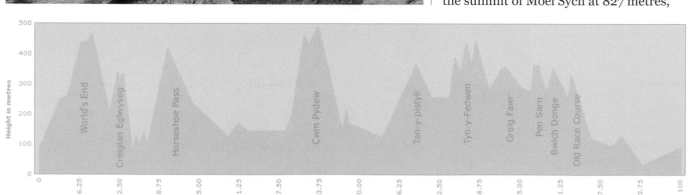

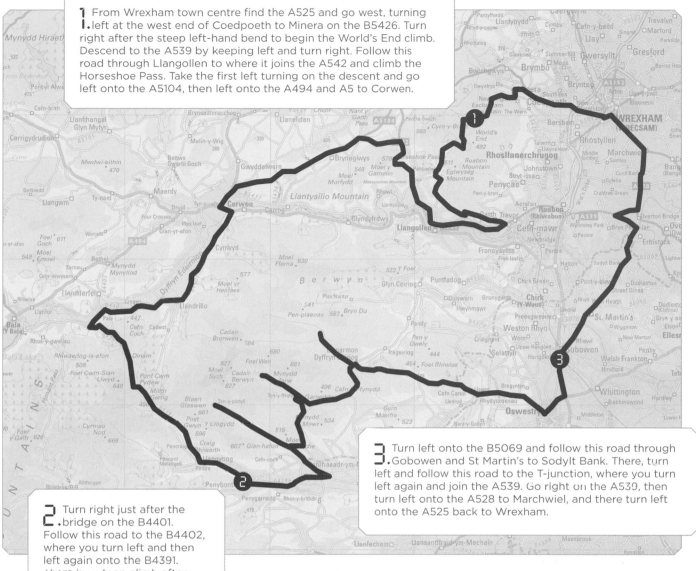

1. From Wrexham town centre find the A525 and go west, turning left at the west end of Coedpoeth to Minera on the B5426. Turn right after the steep left-hand bend to begin the World's End climb. Descend to the A539 by keeping left and turn right. Follow this road through Llangollen to where it joins the A542 and climb the Horseshoe Pass. Take the first left turning on the descent and go left onto the A5104, then left onto the A494 and A5 to Corwen.

2. Turn right just after the bridge on the B4401. Follow this road to the B4402, where you turn left and then left again onto the B4391. There is a steep climb after this junction. Follow the road to Penybontfawr and turn left onto the B4396 then left onto the B4580. Turn left in Llanrhaeadr-ym-Mochnant. Follow this road to Tan-y-pistyll and retrace to Commins, where you go left and second left then keep left to climb to Tyn-y-ffridd. Retrace, then keep left to Llanarmon Dyffryn Ceiriog, where you turn left and climb to the end of the road. Retrace through Llanarmon Dyffryn Ceiriog and continue on this road to the B4580, and turn left to Oswestry.

3. Turn left onto the B5069 and follow this road through Gobowen and St Martin's to Sodylt Bank. There, turn left and follow this road to the T-junction, where you turn left again and join the A539. Go right on the A539, then turn left onto the A528 to Marchwiel, and there turn left onto the A525 back to Wrexham.

over them just before what felt like an earthquake. The whole event threw the authorities into confusion, and the police and then RAF helicopters scoured the area for clues. It wasn't until later that geologists offered an explanation by suggesting that the lights were due to a magnitude 3.5 earthquake felt over a large area of North Wales. The lights might have been earthquake light, which is sometimes seen in areas undergoing tectonic stress, and they could have been meteors. However, UFO searchers took another view, some of them claiming that an alien spacecraft had crashed, and the *Sun* christened the incident 'Roswelsh'.

The last section of the ride leaves the Berwyns for more gentle terrain by nipping across the border into England. Then it goes through Oswestry, which has been in both countries, and crosses the River Dee again for the final run back to Wrexham.

but the road doesn't quite go up that far. It's the same in the next one, which heads towards Cadair Berwyn, and the final one, the Ceiriog valley.

The Berwyns made big news in 1974, when strange lights were seen hovering

START AND FINISH:
Wrexham

GETTING THERE:
Wrexham is on the A483 ten miles south of Chester. It has a rail links with Chester, and with Shrewsbury and the West Midlands.

BIKE SHOP: Bike Shop Wrexham on Stansty Road

CAFE: Kristina's Cafe on Chester Street

LOCAL DELICACY: Welsh cakes

WALES

CLWYDIAN RANGE

RIDE FACTS

Rating
Very hard

Total climbing
2350 metres

Killer climb
Moel Arthur

There are hardly 100 consecutive metres of flat in 100 miles on this ride. The set-piece climbs come in quick succession, and some are very steep. This 100-miler is a challenge for anybody, but you need to be conditioned to riding successive steep hills before trying it. Do that, and you can take pride in conquering this ride's saw-tooth profile and doing something that's close to the edge of what is reasonable.

The Clwydian Range runs in a long, thin, south-east to north-west line and in older times formed part of the walls of fortress Wales. The strategic importance of the mountains was amplified by a geological fault running behind them, making their west side incredibly steep.

However, although the Clwydians are a significant lump of geography, they aren't big enough to contain a 100-mile ride, at least not without doing a lot of retracing, so the first part of this one explores some of the mountains behind them. You start in Ruthin, which means Red Fort, at the southern end of the wide, flat valley created by the Clwyd fault, the Vale of Clwyd.

The first section runs along the edge of Clocaenog Forest, a forbidding place at the best of times, so try not to think about the fate of a poor man who handcuffed himself to a tree here in 2002 and threw away the keys. They only discovered his skeleton in 2005. It's a huge place, and one you enter again after the very steep climb up Mynydd Poeth.

The road trends generally upwards after passing Llyn Brenig, a large lake built to help regulate the flow of the River Dee through its tributary the Alwen. A lot of rain falls here, so without the Llyn Brenig acting as a safety valve, the Dee would flood a lot. The long climb takes you to the pass just below Tan-y-graig mountain, and at 464 metres it's the highest point of the ride.

The road trends downhill from here to Llansannan, then there's a series of steep hills, all touching the 300-metre contour, before you reach Denbigh and some respite. They are tough climbs with sections above 10 per cent, and sometimes well above it. The respite comes as you cross the Vale of Clwyd, but it's short because at Waen you start the first true Clwydian climb, Penycloddiau.

Descend that and you almost double back to climb Moel Arthur, which is named after the peak that's just to the north when you reach the top. A hill fort was built there 2500 years ago, but flints and ancient tools have been found in caves here that date back 40,000 years.

'THE DESCENT OF BWLCH Y-PARC IS QUITE STEEP AND VERY TECHNICAL WITH SOME FEARSOME BENDS'

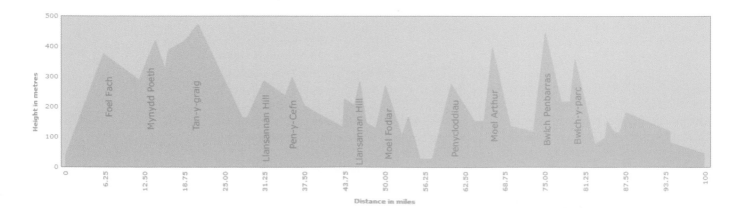

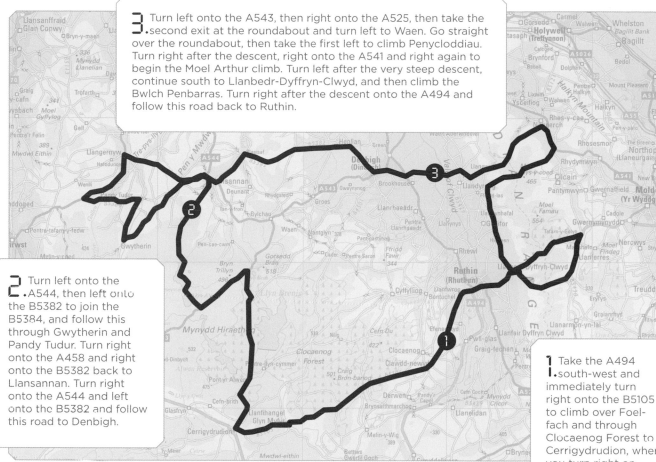

3. Turn left onto the A543, then right onto the A525, then take the second exit at the roundabout and turn left to Waen. Go straight over the roundabout, then take the first left to climb Penycloddiau. Turn right after the descent, right onto the A541 and right again to begin the Moel Arthur climb. Turn left after the very steep descent, continue south to Llanbedr-Dyffryn-Clwyd, and then climb the Bwlch Penbarras. Turn right after the descent onto the A494 and follow this road back to Ruthin.

2. Turn left onto the A544, then left onto the B5382 to join the B5384, and follow this through Gwytherin and Pandy Tudur. Turn right onto the A458 and right onto the B5382 back to Llansannan. Turn right onto the A544 and left onto the B5382 and follow this road to Denbigh.

1. Take the A494 south-west and immediately turn right onto the B5105 to climb over Foel-fach and through Clocaenog Forest to Cerrigydrudion, where you turn right on the B4501. Continue through the forest past Llyn Brenig; at the Sportsman's Arms turn left onto the A543, and turn right just after a bridge to start the difficult section to Llansannan.

START AND FINISH: **Ruthin**

GETTING THERE: **Ruthin is on the A525, 17 miles north-west of Wrexham.**

BIKE SHOP: **Cellar Cycles on Town Street**

CAFE: **Annie's Café, just off St Peter's Square**

LOCAL DELICACY: **Leek soup**

Take heart, there are only two more climbs to go now. You ride along the western edge of the range, below the highest peak, Moel Famau, then go left for Bwlch Penbarras. This is very steep to start with, especially between the cattle grid and Halfway House, and it eases only slightly after that. You are climbing up the drop of a fault line, so it was once much steeper. A long descent leads to the last and much easier climb. However, this ride can still bite you, because you'll be tired now and the descent of Bwlch-y-parc is quite steep and very technical with some fearsome bends. It's an A-road too, so there will be traffic. Take care and you'll return to Ruthin without scaring yourself.

NORTH CAMBRIAN MOUNTAINS

RIDE FACTS

Rating
Hard

Total climbing
1350 metres

Killer climb
Bwlch y Groes

'IF YOU RIDE UP THE BWLCH YOU NEED NEVER FEAR A HILL AGAIN'

This could be rated very hard, but I've reserved that for rides that have a succession of hard hills throughout their entire length. This ride consists of 40 miles of hills and 60 miles of gently rolling roads, but the three hills in that 40-mile stretch are tough; and the first one used to hurt the legs and break the spirits of some of the fittest bike racers in the world, when it was a feature of the testing Milk Race. Its name is Bwlch y Groes.

I've chosen Machynnleth for the start because it's far enough away to get your legs warmed up before the Bwlch, but close enough to it for the prospect of it

not to ruin your ride. You head up the wide lower Dovey valley on a minor road that tracks the river, and through Dinas Mawddwy, where the river changes character.

The Dovey shares a watershed with the River Dee, but it's very short, so a lot of water flows down it all at once. Where it had some wriggle room during the early part of the ride, now the river is constricted by mountains and it becomes a torrent. The valley opens up again briefly at Llanymawddwy, and the river can breathe while meandering along a small flood plain.

This is beautiful; you are riding along in a valley bottom, steadily gaining height and surrounded by mountains. Then you begin to puzzle, because there's no obvious way out. It looks as if you are riding towards a dead end; your way is blocked by mountains. Then the road switches right and goes up – welcome to the Bwlch.

There used to be a race called the Milk Race. It was a Tour of Britain, and it had been called that before the Milk Marketing Board took over its sponsorship. The race was famous for its route, for seeking out the hardest climbs and most dramatic scenery in England and Wales. Scotland had its own Milk Race.

The organisers loved the Bwlch, but this was back in the days when bikes had ten or 12 gears, and a 42 or later maybe a 39 was the smallest chainring. Many top international racers had to walk up the

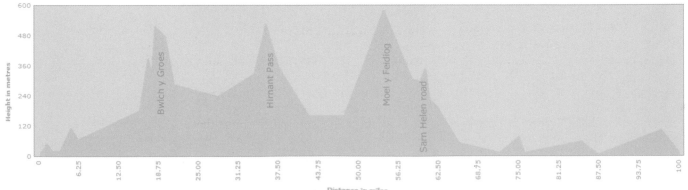

2. Turn left onto the B4403 before Bala and stay on it to ride along the south-east side of the lake. When you reach the A494, turn right and first left. Follow this road until the T-junction and turn left to begin the Moel y Feidiog climb. Stay on this road through the ski centre to the A470, and turn left to Dolgellau.

1. Go north on the A487 and turn right after the Dovey bridge onto the B4404. Follow the road on the north side of the Dovey to Minllyn, and there go left onto the A470 and first right at Dinas-Mawddwy. Turn right and continue on the north side of the Dovey until Pont y Pennant, where you cross it. In half a mile you start the Bwlch y Groes climb. Turn right just before the summit and descend to Lake Vyrnwy. Turn right and do a circuit of the lake until the right-hand turn at Alltforgan, where there's a car park. This is the Foel y Geifr climb to Bala.

3. Turn right onto the A493 just before Dolgellau and follow this road to Bryncrug, where you turn left onto the B4405. Follow this road past Tal-y-llyn Lake to Dol-ffanog, and there turn right up a short but very steep climb to the A487. Go right and follow this road back to Machynlleth.

Bwlch. And just to emphasise how hard the climb is, it was known as Hellfire Pass in the motor industry, where it was used for racing and to test hill performance.

The Bwlch rises to 554 metres, making it the highest road in Wales, but the crux is what happens after the right switchback: you gain 342 metres in 2.5 kilometres, so an average of 13.7 per cent with stretches of 25 per cent. I recommend a bottom gear of 34 x 28 and try to spread your effort up the climb; don't go too hard early on or you'll pay for it.

The circuit of Lake Vyrnwy is a contrast to what you've just been though. It's a soft, sylvan place, where an ornate tower is reflected on the surface of its long, glassy waters. The next climb starts at the end of the lake, but it's not as severe as the Bwlch; nothing is. But as well as its sheer beauty, you can take this fact from the ride: if you ride up the Bwlch you need never fear a hill again.

The last climb comes after Lake Bala, and is longer and less steep than the first two. Its descent takes you over the old Sarn Helen Roman road and eventually to Dolgellau, where the final leg of the ride begins.

This is a circuit of Cadair Idris, first riding out to the coast, then inland to Machynlleth. Cadair is Welsh for chair, and Idris is a mythical giant who is said to have used the mountain, one of the highest in Wales, as a chair to relax in and gaze up at the stars. It looks like a chair too, with its craggy summits forming the back behind a huge lake in a bowl scooped out by ice.

START AND FINISH: Machynlleth

GETTING THERE: Machynlleth is 29 miles north-west of Newtown via the A489 and A470. It has a rail link through Welshpool with Shrewsbury, and from there with the national network.

BIKE SHOP: The Holey Trail on Maengwyn Street

CAFE: The Quarry Cafe, also on Maengwyn Street

LOCAL DELICACY: Cawl (a stew made with lamb and leeks)

WALES

MID WALES

RIDE FACTS

Rating
Hard

Total climbing
1800 metres

Killer climb
The Arch

'IT'S A HARD
RIDE, AND
A WILD ONE
IN PLACES,
BUT FULL OF
BEAUTY AND
SURPRISES'

This ride crosses the mountain spine of Wales twice, journeying to the sea past the sources of two of Britain's best-known rivers, the Severn and the Wye, and returning through the Ystwyth and Elan valleys. It's a hard ride, and a wild one in places, but full of beauty and surprises.

You start in Llanidloes, a place with a busy past and a quirky present. It was a centre for lead and silver mining years ago, when it buzzed with trade and at times with civil unrest. Now it has wholefood shops and a Green Fair, while exotic men and women of a certain age dressed in cheesecloth and feathers lend its streets a distinct flavour. Llanidloes carries a whiff of patchouli oil and, occasionally, other exotic substances. It's so other-worldly that some locals call it Planet Idloes.

The town stands on the confluence of the River Clywedog and the Severn, about 20 miles from its source up on Plynlimon. You follow the river out of town, its source being on the other side of Hafren Forest, Hafren being Welsh for Severn. But then the route goes around the forest and into the upper Wye valley, very close to the Wye's source on the same mountain.

The climb to Eisteddfa Gurig goes over a shoulder of Plynlimon, which is the highest point of the Cambrian Mountains. Technically, all of upland Wales is Cambrian, but the name has come to mean the mid part of the country between the Brecon Beacons in the south and Snowdonia in the north. These places tend to take people away from Mid Wales, and

in doing so give this place a lonely majesty that makes cycling here such a treat.

You start to feel the pulse of these mountains on the lonely stretch from Ponterwyd to Talybont. The road climbs some of the hills, winds around others, and goes around a stunning reservoir, the Nant-y-moch. Then you ride through a dark and mysterious forest, up and then down a long descent to Talybont.

The downhill theme continues to the coast at Aberystwyth, the halfway house of Wales. This is where north meets south, where people from both places have traditionally come on holiday, and where several national offices and archives are based, including the Welsh Library. It's currently trying to brand itself as a cycling town, with family-friendly rides and an annual professional circuit race.

The town takes its name from the Ystwyth river, and you dip in and out of its valley now, following it up to a flat, boggy piece of land called Gors Lwyd. The water here helps augment the Ystwyth, while the infant River Elan tumbles off Esgair Elan into Gors Lwyd and emerges flowing in the opposite direction.

And you go with it, past the series of four reservoirs it fills. I should mention that a lot of rain falls in this part of Wales; it's one of the most important watersheds in Britain, so it could rain during this ride. Hopefully not enough to trouble you on the last climbs from Rhayader, where red kites rule the skies, and back to the sweet mellow vibe of Planet Idloes.

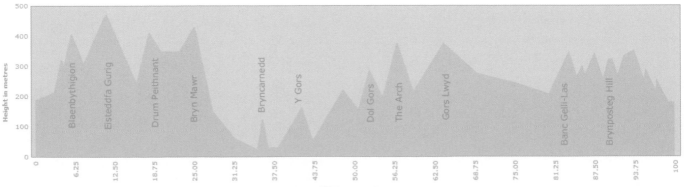

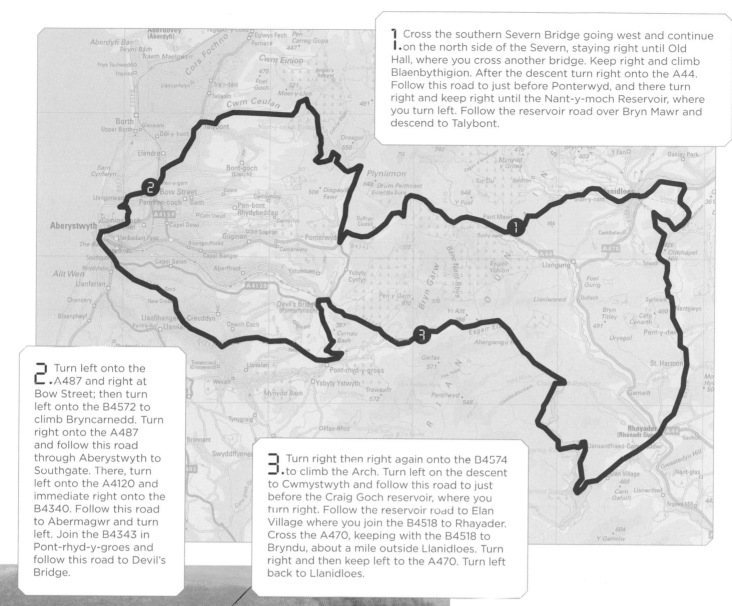

1 Cross the southern Severn Bridge going west and continue on the north side of the Severn, staying right until Old Hall, where you cross another bridge. Keep right and climb Blaenbythigion. After the descent turn right onto the A44. Follow this road to just before Ponterwyd, and there turn right and keep right until the Nant-y-moch Reservoir, where you turn left. Follow the reservoir road over Bryn Mawr and descend to Talybont.

2 Turn left onto the A487 and right at Bow Street; then turn left onto the B4572 to climb Bryncarnedd. Turn right onto the A487 and follow this road through Aberystwyth to Southgate. There, turn left onto the A4120 and immediate right onto the B4340. Follow this road to Abermagwr and turn left. Join the B4343 in Pont-rhyd-y-groes and follow this road to Devil's Bridge.

3 Turn right then right again onto the B4574 to climb the Arch. Turn left on the descent to Cwmystwyth and follow this road to just before the Craig Goch reservoir, where you turn right. Follow the reservoir road to Elan Village where you join the B4518 to Rhayader. Cross the A470, keeping with the B4518 to Bryndu, about a mile outside Llanidloes. Turn right and then keep left to the A470. Turn left back to Llanidloes.

START AND FINISH: Llanidloes

GETTING THERE: Llanidloes is on the A470, 14 miles south-west of Newtown, and 22 miles north-west of Llandrindod Wells via the A44 and A470. The nearest rail station is Caersws, eight miles north-east.

BIKE SHOP: No bike shop, but some cycling equipment and accessories carried at Idloes Motor Spares

CAFE: The Great Oak Cafe on Great Oak Street

LOCAL DELICACY: Bara birth (a sweet bread with currants and candied peel)

WALES

CARMARTHENSHIRE AND CEREDIGION

'THE NAME MEANS BALD OR BARREN HILL, AND MOELFRE IS BOTH, BUT ALSO BEAUTIFUL IN ITS SYMMETRY'

This ride travels through three landscapes: the foothills of the Cambrian Mountains, the craggy coast of Ceredigion and, glimpsed early on, the fertile Towy valley, which is known as the Garden of Wales.

Dylan Thomas described Carmarthen as a 'timeless, mild, beguiling island of a town'. It's the same today, with Thomas's favourite bar in Brown's Hotel still there and still sprinkled with a little Dylan dust. Carmarthen is also one of the oldest towns in Wales, founded in the Iron Age by one of the original Welsh tribes, the Demetae, who were among the country's true Celtic ancestors.

The route starts in the wide-bottomed Towy valley, but the hills start after six miles and do not let up for the next 94.

None of the climbs are super hard but there are a lot of them, and three go just over the 1000-feet mark.

The first, Bryn Gareg, is a pass between Mynydd Pencarreg and higher ground to the north-west. On the way to the summit you cross Sarn Helen, an old road built by the Romans. Running 160 miles as straight as possible between Conwy and Carmarthen, it linked the north and south of Roman Wales. Often it crossed quite high ground, which must have been pretty inhospitable 2000 years ago. The old road is remembered today by a mountain-bike trail that follows it, and by Super Furry Animals, who wrote a song called 'Sarn Helen'.

The descent leads to lovely Lampeter, a small town of around 3000 people that

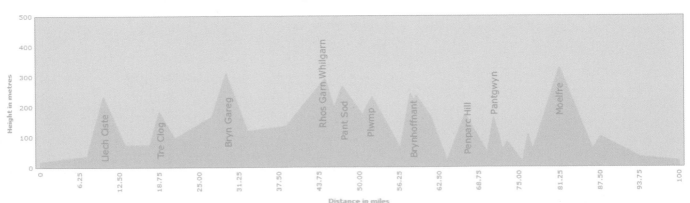

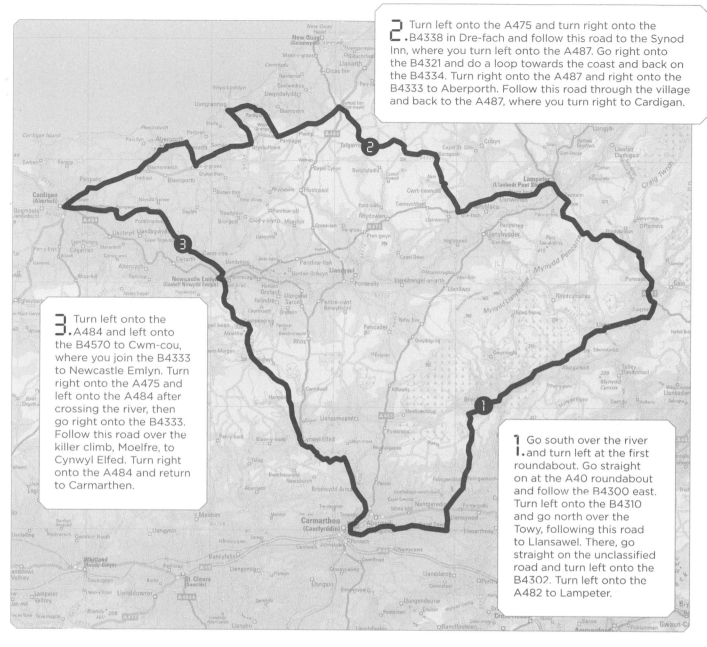

2. Turn left onto the A475 and turn right onto the B4338 in Dre-fach and follow this road to the Synod Inn, where you turn left onto the A487. Go right onto the B4321 and do a loop towards the coast and back on the B4334. Turn right onto the A487 and right onto the B4333 to Aberporth. Follow this road through the village and back to the A487, where you turn right to Cardigan.

3. Turn left onto the A484 and left onto the B4570 to Cwm-cou, where you join the B4333 to Newcastle Emlyn. Turn right onto the A475 and left onto the A484 after crossing the river, then go right onto the B4333. Follow this road over the killer climb, Moelfre, to Cynwyl Elfed. Turn right onto the A484 and return to Carmarthen.

1. Go south over the river and turn left at the first roundabout. Go straight on at the A40 roundabout and follow the B4300 east. Turn left onto the B4310 and go north over the Towy, following this road to Llansawel. There, go straight on the unclassified road and turn left onto the B4302. Turn left onto the A482 to Lampeter.

has an old university. The University of Wales, Trinity St David, to give its full name, dates back to 1882 and was created to train clergy, but it now awards a wide range of degrees in the arts and social sciences.

You are in Ceredigion now, named after Ceredig, a fifth-century writer. Ceredigion has some of the best beaches in Britain, with five Blue Flag, four Green Coast and 14 Seaside Awards given in 2011 alone. It is also one of only two permanent summer habitats in the UK of the bottlenose dolphin.

The dolphins go about their lives just off Aberporth, and at 60 miles the ride drops into and out of this amazing village. The beach is studded with rock pools, and each one is a watery jewellery box, while out to sea killer whales, basking sharks and sunfish have been seen, as well as the resident dolphins.

From there the route heads to Cardigan on the Teifi estuary, then does a loop in the hills north of the river to meet it again in Newcastle Emlyn. Newcastle is an old town with a ruined castle and a rather vindictive dragon legend. The dragon, or wyvern as they were called in Wales, only wanted to kip on the castle walls and somebody killed it while it was asleep.

Newcastle is also the start of the final climb, this ride's killer, Moelfre. The name means bald or barren hill, and Moelfre is both, but also beautiful in its symmetry. The descent ends in the Gwili valley for a fantastic final 12 miles of tree-lined twists and turns to Carmarthen.

START AND FINISH:
Carmarthen

GETTING THERE:
Carmarthen is on the A48, 16 miles from the western end of the M4.

BIKE SHOP: **Beiciau Hobbs Bikes on Old Langunr Road**

CAFE: **Cafe at 4 Queen Street**

LOCAL DELICACY: **Laverbread (it's made from seaweed)**

BRECON BEACONS

RIDE FACTS

Rating
Very hard

Total climbing
2100 metres

Killer climb
Rhiw Wen

The SAS don't do anything by halves. One of their mottos is 'Train hard, fight easy', so when they were picking a place to do their basic training they looked for somewhere that would test every fibre of their recruits' fitness and resolve. That place is the trackless and forbidding Brecon Beacons.

This ride is tough, there are no flat sections in it and nine significant climbs. It starts in Brecon under the shadow of Pen y Fan, the place where SAS recruits end their first of four weeks of basic training with a test, after doing a mountain march every day with loads. They call it the Fan Dance, and it comprises 15 miles from one side of Pen y Fan, over the top, down the other side and then back again, carrying a 56-pound pack and a rifle.

You pass the Fan Dance halfway checkpoint in the Taf Fechan Forest, where the route runs along the east side of the Brecon's highest mountain. It's halfway for the recruits but only an eighth of the way into your test, but at least you have the ride's first big climb, Torpantau, in your legs. Plus the scenery at road level is beautiful and it's far more benign than the gaunt mountain above you.

The ride continues past Pontsticill Reservoir, brushing the outskirts of Merthyr Tydfil, then it runs alongside one of the two River Taff tributaries, before spearing off west over the pass below Cefn Sychbant. This is a quite empty place today but was settled in prehistoric times, and there are many signs of old burial mounds and vestigial villages.

You are in the middle of one of the hardest sections of the ride now. Hill after hill culminates with two severe climbs, Bryn Melyn and Bwlch Bryn-rhudd. The first climbs a lonely valley carved out by the River Llia, and it has a wickedly steep descent with two hairpin bends that require extreme care. Bwlch Bryn-rhudd has a steep climb just before it, and then you join the main road up to the pass, where cuttings forge a way between the steep valley sides and the road follows a major geological fault line.

There's a long descent now down the Tawe valley to Ystradgynlais, where you climb up another valley to the start of the killer climb in Brynamman. The top of Rhiw Wen is 493 metres, the highest on this ride and sixth highest in Mid Wales. The pass is over a section of the Brecon Beacons called the Black Mountain, which is an escarpment. Doing this ride clockwise you climb its shallower dip

'THE SCENERY AT ROAD LEVEL IS FAR MORE BENIGN THAN THE GAUNT MOUNTAIN ABOVE YOU'

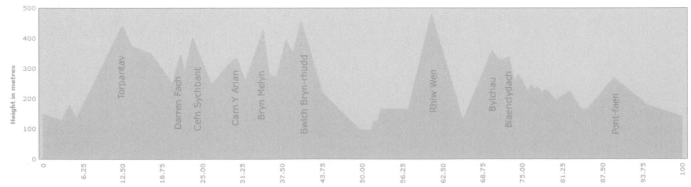

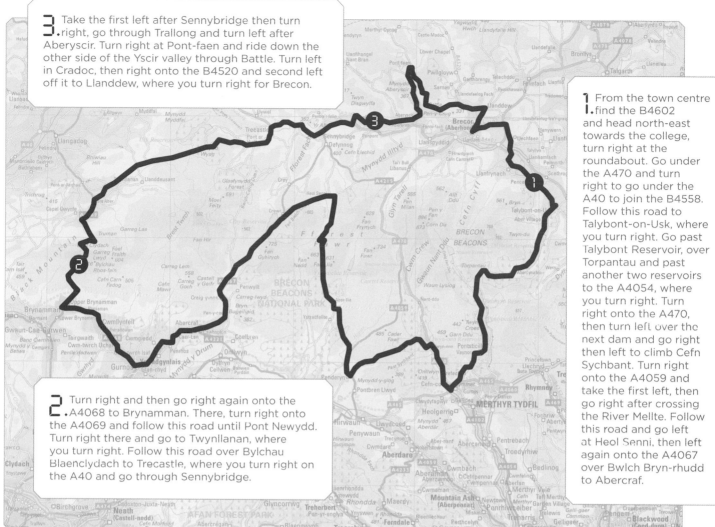

3. Take the first left after Sennybridge then turn right, go through Trallong and turn left after Aberyscir. Turn right at Pont-faen and ride down the other side of the Yscir valley through Battle. Turn left in Cradoc, then right onto the B4520 and second left off it to Llanddew, where you turn right for Brecon.

1. From the town centre find the B4602 and head north-east towards the college, turn right at the roundabout. Go under the A470 and turn right to go under the A40 to join the B4558. Follow this road to Talybont-on-Usk, where you turn right. Go past Talybont Reservoir, over Torpantau and past another two reservoirs to the A4054, where you turn right. Turn right onto the A470, then turn left over the next dam and go right then left to climb Cefn Sychbant. Turn right onto the A4059 and take the first left, then go right after crossing the River Mellte. Follow this road and go left at Heol Senni, then left again onto the A4067 over Bwlch Bryn-rhudd to Abercraf.

2. Turn right and then go right again onto the A4068 to Brynamman. There, turn right onto the A4069 and follow this road until Pont Newydd. Turn right there and go to Twynllanan, where you turn right. Follow this road over Bylchau Blaenclydach to Trecastle, where you turn right on the A40 and go through Sennybridge.

slope, rather than the much steeper scarp on the north side. It does mean you have to take care on the switchback descent, though, as it is a main road.

Now you are on the north side of the Brecons, with Bylchau Blaenclydach to climb, past the Usk Reservoir, which pools most of the high tributaries of the River Usk. The rest of the ride follows the young Usk's valley through Sennybridge and then throws in a loop up and down the Yscir valley. This is partly because it's beautiful and partly because I was getting back to Brecon well short of 100 miles. However the Yscir is a Special Area of Conservation (SAC) for lamprey,* twaite shad* and the European bullhead,* and you wouldn't have known that if I had been better at map reading.

*They're fish

START AND FINISH: Brecon

GETTING THERE: Brecon is 20 miles north-west of Abergavenny on the A40. Abergavenny is also its nearest rail link.

BIKE SHOP: Brecon Cycle Centre in the middle of town

CAFE: The Bridge Cafe on Bridge Street

LOCAL DELICACY: Pant-ysgawn, which is goat's cheese

BLACK MOUNTAINS

RIDE FACTS

Rating
Very hard

Total climbing
1800 metres

Killer climb
The Tumble

The Black Mountains are shaped like a rugby ball, with its sides along the English border and the Brecon Beacons, and its points facing north and south to Hay-on-Wye and Abergavenny. The range covers a quite small area, so 100 miles allows a thorough exploration, during which you not only ride around the mountains but delve into their hidden valleys.

Starting in Abergavenny does two things: it gets the killer climb out of the way early, and it allows you to experience two sides of Wales, the rural and the industrial. The climb is the Tumble, another bike-racing favourite that has an incredibly tough hairpin bend early on; and after a short descent you enter industrial Wales in Blaenavon.

Blaenavon is a World Heritage Site. It grew up around the ironworks, parts of which have been preserved as an attraction. The Big Pit, the Welsh mining museum, is also here. But there's no air lock between the two sides of the Tumble, no steady transition. To the north, where the Black Mountains dominate the horizon, it's all fields and farms and cottages. To the south are the Welsh Valleys, with old pit spoil heaps, boarded-up shops and rows of neglected houses. Once a hub of industry, pride and hardworking tradition, now the Valleys are largely ignored and in need of deeper regeneration than a few bits being turned into museums.

You cross the Heads of the Valleys road near Brynmawr and go north over a high pass, then descend to Llangynidr in the green Usk valley. This is the Black Mountains proper. You cross a well-preserved 17th-century bridge into Crickhowell, then follow a tributary of the Usk up into its U-shaped valley.

Six rivers are born on the layered sandstone plateau in front of you, and there's a wonderful description of their geography in a book by the academic and writer Richard Williams, called *The People of the Black Mountains*. In it he says that if you place the heel of your right hand on the plateau, with your middle

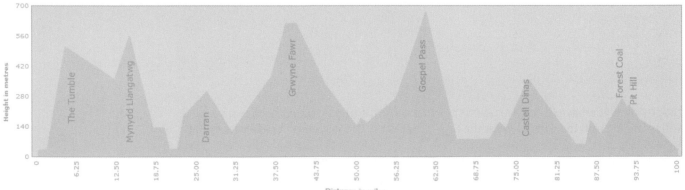

3. Keep left of the new bypass to climb to Pengenffordd, where you join the A479. Follow this downhill and turn left onto the A40 to Crickhowell, where you turn left at the end of town to Llangenny. Turn left and follow this road around the north side of the Sugar Loaf and keep right back to Abergavenny.

2. Continue north-east and go left up and retrace in each of the next two valleys. Turn left after the final one and left at Stanton then go north in the Vale of Ewyas to climb the Gospel Pass and descend to Hay-on-Wye. Turn left onto the B4530, left onto the A438, and then go left onto the A4078 to Talgarth.

1. From the town centre go west on the A40 then turn left at the roundabout to Llanfoist, where you join the B4246 going west. Turn left at the next junction and climb the Tumble over to Blaenavon, where you turn right on the B4248. Go straight ahead at the two roundabouts in Brynmawr. Turn left on the main road and right in Beaufort on the B4560. Head north over Cefn Onneu and turn right after the descent onto the B4558. Turn left to Crickhowell.

finger pointing south-east, then gently spread your other fingers and thumb, they denote the lie of the valleys. The one you are in, the Grwyne Fechan, will lie between your third and little fingers.

The next is the Grwyne Fawr, where the valley road runs almost to the top of the plateau, and the last couple of miles have a very rough surface. There's a bridleway beyond it, so an adventurous mountain biker could continue straight on, then down the steep slope of the Black Mountain's north face. But to experience that by road you have to retrace down the valley, then climb the Gospel Pass, the highest road in Mid Wales at 549 metres, which lies between two peaks, Hay Bluff

and Lord Hereford's Knob, or Twmpa, to give it its less snigger-provoking Welsh name.

The section from the bookish Hay-on-Wye to Talgarth runs along the Wye valley, then switches to a tributary to reach Talgarth, after which there is another tough climb to the Iron Age fort called Castell Dinas.

There's a long descent, another visit to Crickhowell, and you ride in a northern arc around the Sugar Loaf. Not quite as spectacular as its namesake in Rio, it has a conical summit that looks like a volcano, but isn't. The last climb crosses its eastern flank through the hamlet of Forest Coal Pit to Abergavenny.

START AND FINISH: Abergavenny

GETTING THERE: Abergavenny is on the A40, 16 miles east of Monmouth. It has rail links with Newport and Hereford.

BIKE SHOP: Gateway Cycles on Brecon Road

CAFE: For the Love of Cakes on Frogmore Street

LOCAL DELICACY: Welsh cakes

WALES

PEMBROKESHIRE

RIDE FACTS

Rating
Medium/hard

Total climbing
1700 metres

Killer climb
New Inn

'THE ROAD RUNS ALONG BEACHES AND CLIMBS OVER HEADLANDS'

Pembrokeshire has much in common with Cornwall. It's surrounded by the sea, two-thirds of its coast is pounded by the Atlantic, and its inland roads have a similar undulating nature. There are also lots of them, and you could spend years exploring Pembrokeshire's network of quiet lanes, but on this ride you visit the magnificent St Bride's Bay, the rugged north coast and a famous expanse of flat sandy beach in the south. The ride also gives a passing nod to Pembrokeshire's mountains, the Mynydd Preseli.

Haverfordwest, the county town, is a fine place, and an ideal one from which to begin exploring Pembrokeshire. The town isn't on the coast, but the coast almost comes to it because it's at the tidal head of the River Cleddau. Downstream, the Cleddau estuary is a drowned valley or ria, created during the Ice Age when sea levels were lower. Unaffected by ice, the Cleddan carved out a wide valley, but when ice located elsewhere melted, sea levels rose and the valley flooded, creating the fine natural harbour where a huge port and oil refinery was built at Milford Haven.

You get glimpses of the oil refinery on the south coast before the route swings north and switches your attention to the glorious wide sweep of St Bride's Bay. Pembrokeshire is called Gwlad Hud a Lledrith in Welsh, which means the land of magic and enchantment. You can see why here.

Just as in Cornwall, the road runs along

beaches and climbs over headlands, often with the nagging attention of strong sea breezes. The beaches are exciting, with surfing, power kites and sand-buggy racing all going on around the 2.5-mile Newgate Sands.

But then the coast changes, and beaches occupy tiny inlets set in spectacular cliffs. The route goes through

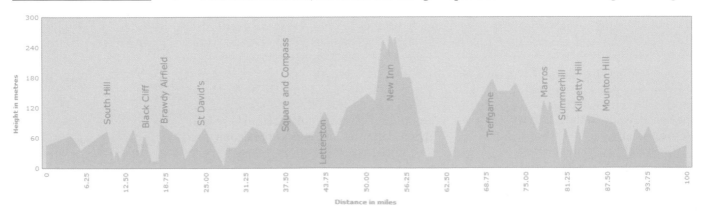

2. Turn left coming out of town on the B4583 and follow this road to Whitesands Bay. Retrace until the Burrows golf course, where you turn left. Follow this road to Llanrhian, and then turn right. Turn left in Croesgoch onto the A487 and then turn right onto the B4331 to Letterston. Turn right onto the A40 and take the second left off it. Follow this road to the B4329, where you turn left to New Inn. Turn right onto the B4313 to Maenclochog.

3. Follow the B4313 to Narberth, turn left onto the B4314 and follow this road to Pendine. Where the B4314 turns very sharply to the left at the top of the hill, carry straight on and follow this road to Amroth and Summerhill, where you turn right. Continue to Stepaside, turn right to Kilgetty Farm, and then left. Turn right onto the A478, left onto the A4115 and then right onto the A4075. Turn left onto the A40 and ride back to Haverfordwest.

1. Head out of town west on the B4341, then turn left onto the B4327. Turn right just before St Bride's and head for Little Haven. Continue north, keeping on the road nearest the sea, which eventually joins the A487, and follow that to St David's.

one of them, Solva, which used to be the main harbour of the St Bride's Bay area. It's another drowned valley, and when the tide is in, the steep valley sides rising straight out of the water look spectacular.

This peninsula is holy in Wales, as it was the home of their patron saint, St David, and you pass where he is buried in the grounds of St David's Cathedral. The route makes a final visit to Pembrokeshire's Atlantic coast at Whitsands Bay, just below St David's Head. It has been described as one of the best tourist beaches in the world, and it is a delightful place. A large rocky outcrop called Carn Llidi guards the north end of the beach, while to the south you can see Ramsey Island.

You now head inland towards Pembrokeshire's biggest hills. Mynydd Preseli is where the bluestones at Stonehenge were taken from. There are 43 of them 250 miles away in Wiltshire now, each weighing between two and four tonnes. How they got there is still a mystery. They were either carried by a glacier or by humans, and of the two theories the glacier one is becoming the less probable.

The final leg of the ride, before returning to Haverfordwest, visits Pendine Sands, a huge beach on the south coast. World records have been set on the seven-mile stretch of firm flat sand, including one by Sir Malcolm Campbell in 1927 of 174.22 mph. In 1933 Amy Johnson took off from here to fly the Atlantic. And in 2000 Malcolm Campbell's grandson, Don Wales, set an electric-car speed record of 137 mph.

START AND FINISH:
Haverfordwest

GETTING THERE:
Haverfordwest is 47 miles from the western end of the M4 using the A48 and A40. It has rail links with Swansea and Cardiff.

BIKE SHOP:
Mike's Bikes, 17 Prendergast

CAFE: Sands Cafe on Newgate Hill

LOCAL DELICACY:
Laverbread

WALES

THE VALLEYS

RIDE FACTS

Rating
Hard

Total climbing
1900 metres

Killer climb
The Bwlch

'THE PASS LIES BETWEEN TWO DEEP-GREEN FORESTS, AND THEN YOU PLUNGE DOWN THE OTHER SIDE'

The Welsh Valleys are beautiful. They may not be obviously beautiful, and I suppose what I see is coloured by the fact that not long ago this was a mining community similar to the one I come from. There's something about the contrast of mines with these valleys and mountains, about the rows of houses winding up the valleys, and about the stories they could tell. Sadly it's a melancholy appeal today, because the industry and the proud history it created is just history; there's been very little to replace it.

The start is in Llantrisant, and I've routed the ride around the western valleys because there's more traffic further east. You start out across the bottom of the Valleys, between them and the Vale of Glamorgan really, until you pick up the River Ogmore, turn inland and begin climbing its valley.

Cyclists call this climb the Bwlch. It's a long slog up to the switchback final slopes leading to a gaunt and craggy summit, which is the Bwlch y Clawdd pass. The Rhondda valley is ahead of you, and you descend into it at Treorchy, a focal point for one of the defining passions of the Valleys, male-voice choirs. The other is rugby.

The next big climb starts in Treorchy's neighbour Treherbert and it's spectacular. The Rhigos starts with two hairpin bends, then it climbs up the rocky face of Mynydd Ystradffernol. The pass lies between two deep-green forests, and then you plunge down the other side through more hairpins and past Tower Colliery.

Once the oldest continuous working coal mine in Britain, it's now sadly mothballed, but it could open again.

The route then slips around the Heads of the Valleys and into the Vale of Neath for a long downhill section, which ends by climbing Cimla Hill out of Neath town. This takes you into the Afan valley and comes out opposite Afan Argoed Country Park, which is an industrial heritage site and a mountain-bike centre with a very welcoming cafe serving home-made cakes. Well, they looked home-made to me.

The road leads back to the Bwlch, which is a three-way pass connecting the Afan, Ogmore and Rhondda valleys, but you turn off it at Cymer to climb up the side of Foel Fawr into the Lynfi valley. Then the route goes over sinuous Llangeinor Hill and straight across the Ogmore Valley into the Ogwr for a circuit of secluded Evanstown, tucked away in its own valley.

The Rhondda valley is Y-shaped, with the larger of two branches being the Rhondda Fawr, and the smaller the Rhondda Fach. Their suffixes come from the Welsh mawr, meaning large, and bach, as in the term of affection *dai bach*, meaning small. You've already been in the Fawr at Treorchy; now the route visits it again, briefly, before climbing the steep Myndd Ty'n-tyle and dropping into the Rhondda Fach.

The visit there is brief, too, as you climb the difficult Cefn Gwyngul,

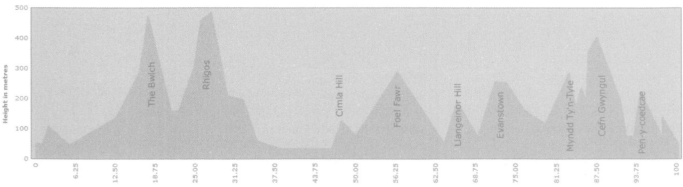

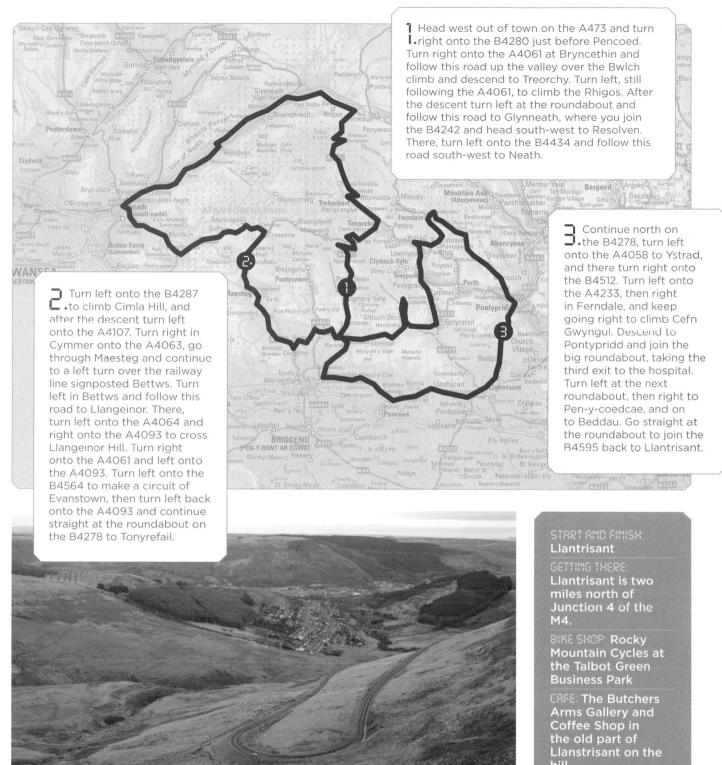

1. Head west out of town on the A473 and turn right onto the B4280 just before Pencoed. Turn right onto the A4061 at Bryncethin and follow this road up the valley over the Bwlch climb and descend to Treorchy. Turn left, still following the A4061, to climb the Rhigos. After the descent turn left at the roundabout and follow this road to Glynneath, where you join the B4242 and head south-west to Resolven. There, turn left onto the B4434 and follow this road south-west to Neath.

3. Continue north on the B4278, turn left onto the A4058 to Ystrad, and there turn right onto the B4512. Turn left onto the A4233, then right in Ferndale, and keep going right to climb Cefn Gwyngul. Descend to Pontypridd and join the big roundabout, taking the third exit to the hospital. Turn left at the next roundabout, then right to Pen-y-coedcae, and on to Beddau. Go straight at the roundabout to join the B4595 back to Llantrisant.

2. Turn left onto the B4287 to climb Cimla Hill, and after the descent turn left onto the A4107. Turn right in Cymmer onto the A4063, go through Maesteg and continue to a left turn over the railway line signposted Bettws. Turn left in Bettws and follow this road to Llangeinor. There, turn left onto the A4064 and right onto the A4093 to cross Llangeinor Hill. Turn right onto the A4061 and left onto the A4093. Turn left onto the B4564 to make a circuit of Evanstown, then turn left back onto the A4093 and continue straight at the roundabout on the B4278 to Tonyrefail.

START AND FINISH:
Llantrisant

GETTING THERE:
Llantrisant is two miles north of Junction 4 of the M4.

BIKE SHOP: Rocky Mountain Cycles at the Talbot Green Business Park

CAFE: The Butchers Arms Gallery and Coffee Shop in the old part of Llantrisant on the hill

LOCAL DELICACY: Glamorgan sausage

before descending to the Taff valley at Pontypridd and then on to the end at Llantrisant. If you see a big Swedish guy riding on the Cefn Gwyngul, it's the pro racer and 2004 Paris–Roubaix winner Magnus Bäckstedt. He lives in this area, having married a Welsh girl, and he uses this hill periodically to test his fitness.

EAST
ANGL

THE FENLAND 100

RIDE FACTS

Rating
Easy

Total climbing
It's flat, if you don't count bridges

Killer climb
None

'HERE, THE CHALLENGE TO THE CYCLIST IS FROM THE WIND NOT FROM HILLS, BUT THE FLATNESS CREATES A HUGE SKY AND AN OPEN HORIZON'

Years ago the Fens were marshes that flooded a lot, but when they were drained they became the most fertile land in Britain. They are flat, and here the challenge to the cyclist is from the wind not from hills, but the flatness creates a huge sky and an open horizon. They are also criss-crossed by a beguiling network of lanes, so many and so varied that as well as being a prescriptive route I hope this ride serves as an invitation to explore Fenland again later.

The start is in Wisbech, the capital of the Fens and once a wealthy port, as you can see from the grand houses lining the River Ouse. The town's history and wealth are based on Fen drainage, but there were

those who objected to it, known as the Fen Tigers. They feared that the drainage would change their way of life – which it did, but it was a hard and brutish life.

Holland had shown that drained marshland could be very productive, so the Earl of Bedford set Cornelius Vermuyden to work on draining vast areas of his land. The locals sabotaged much of Vermuyden's work during the Civil War, but when Oliver Cromwell took over the country at the end of the war he redoubled efforts to drain the Fens and created the landscape we see today.

The ride heads for the Wash, crossing the Ouse at Sutton Bridge, which can be busy with traffic, but then you return to the

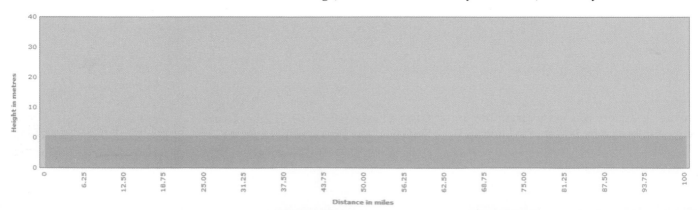

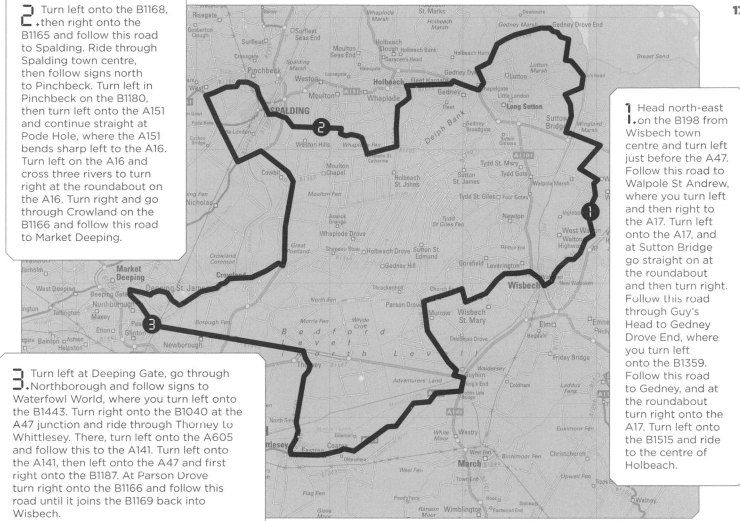

2. Turn left onto the B1168, then right onto the B1165 and follow this road to Spalding. Ride through Spalding town centre, then follow signs north to Pinchbeck. Turn left in Pinchbeck on the B1180, then turn left onto the A151 and continue straight at Pode Hole, where the A151 bends sharp left to the A16. Turn left on the A16 and cross three rivers to turn right at the roundabout on the A16. Turn right and go through Crowland on the B1166 and follow this road to Market Deeping.

1. Head north-east on the B198 from Wisbech town centre and turn left just before the A47. Follow this road to Walpole St Andrew, where you turn left and then right to the A17. Turn left onto the A17, and at Sutton Bridge go straight on at the roundabout and then turn right. Follow this road through Guy's Head to Gedney Drove End, where you turn left onto the B1359. Follow this road to Gedney, and at the roundabout turn right onto the A17. Turn left onto the B1515 and ride to the centre of Holbeach.

3. Turn left at Deeping Gate, go through Northborough and follow signs to Waterfowl World, where you turn left onto the B1443. Turn right onto the B1040 at the A47 junction and ride through Thorney to Whittlesey. There, turn left onto the A605 and follow this to the A141. Turn left onto the A141, then left onto the A47 and first right onto the B1187. At Parson Drove turn right onto the B1166 and follow this road until it joins the B1169 back into Wisbech.

quiet, winding lanes. These wander around the Wash, where the salt marsh looks very much how the whole of the Fens used to be.

Today the Fens are about agriculture on an industrial scale, but what is grown here has changed in recent years. Holbeach and Spalding once produced vast quantities of cut flowers, tulips mainly, in a business that rivalled the Dutch and was celebrated each year with parades of floats decorated with tulips. The parades still go on, but with tulip petals, a by-product of bulb growing, which is the focus of the flower industry here now; and in some years, crêpe paper has to be used instead. The vast, colourful fields of May tulips have been replaced by sugar beet, potatoes, rapeseed and other staples.

The next section goes south towards Peterborough, but on your way look left to the network of tiny lanes east of the crescent formed by Boston, Spalding and Wisbech. I didn't put them in this ride because a route would be too complicated

to describe, but they are the true Fen roads. Narrow, straight, accompanied by water, they link the Fen villages and fields, a fine tracery on the map with just a few preserved windmills dotted around them.

Windmills operated the first drainage pumps before steam engines and diesel took over. Now electric-powered pumping stations keep the Fens relatively dry. Most fields are below the level of the roads, too, and in places they are below sea level. This happened because as the peaty soil dried, it shrank, and because it shrank below the level of some rivers, their embankments had to be built higher, leading to the classic Fen scenery.

It is scenery that has captured many minds, including those of authors such as Charles Kingsley, Dorothy L. Sayers and Philip Pullman, as well as local storytellers, in whom the flat landscape, mists and mystery inspired supernatural fantasies. The Fens are full of ghosts, strange tales, and things half seen and half imagined.

START AND FINISH:
Wisbech

GETTING THERE:
Wisbech is on the A47, 19 miles north-east of Peterborough. It has a rail link with Peterborough through March, and with Cambridge through March and Ely.

BIKE SHOP: The Bike Shop on Market Street

CAFE: The Marina Cafe in Harbour Square

LOCAL DELICACY: Fenland celery

EAST ANGLIA

NORTH NORFOLK

EAST ANGLIA

RIDE FACTS

Rating
Easy

Total climbing
500 metres

Killer climb
Dam Hill

'USUALLY YOU'LL GET A TAILWIND ALONG THIS SECTION, SO OVERALL THIS IS A GOOD ROUTE FOR A FIRST 100-MILER'

North Norfolk is a beautiful and quite rarely visited part of the country. It's full of quiet roads and delightful villages, and time marches slightly slower here, so it's a great place to relax and play. It also seems to have its own climate. It can be sunny along this coast when the rest of the country is blanketed by cloud. Heck, the Queen has a house here, and she's got the whole country to choose from, so it must be good.

You start in Cromer, a great little seaside resort famous for its seafood, and the first section of the ride is east along the length of the North Norfolk Coast. I've put in a loop to the sea front in Sheringham as part of the route, but it's worth seeing the sea in lots of other places. The beaches are amazing. Blakeney and Wells-next-the-Sea are interesting for their saltwater marsh, and the sands at Stiffkey are over a mile wide at low water.

Keep an eye out on the tall reed beds, because that's where you might see, or more probably hear, one of Norfolk's famous bittern population. The reeds are the bittern's natural habitat. They are very shy wading birds with an unmistakable booming cry.

The grounds of Holkham Hall come next, where you ride through the deer park to Burnham Overy Staithe. Horatio Nelson, the admiral whose column stands in Trafalgar Square, was born in Burnham Thorpe, about a mile inland, and Burnham Overy Staithe is where he learnt

to sail. Richard Woodget, the captain of the famous clipper *Cutty Sark*, lived here too. Sailing is in this place's blood.

The final part of the opening leg is along Brancaster Bay to Hunstanton, which sits at the corner of the North Sea and the Wash. The Stump, Boston's church tower, can be seen across the water from here on a fine day. This is the last coastal section, because the route turns inland just south of Hunstanton at Heacham, and it becomes slightly hillier. There's nothing too major, just regular undulations of around 40 to 60 metres of height difference. Usually you'll get a tailwind along this section, so overall this is a good route for a first 100-miler.

You ride past Fakenham at 50 miles, then head north to Little and Great Walsingham. The villages have been a place of pilgrimage for nearly one thousand years, after a Saxon noblewoman had a vision of the Virgin Mary here. An abbey was built, and although that is in ruins now, there are shrines in the Slipper Chapel at Houghton St Giles and in Little Walsingham.

A further loop through the countryside ends with a short stretch of main road to Holt, where Olympic rowing gold medallist Matthew Pinsent comes from. Holt isn't far from Cromer, but the route takes a southerly line through Aylsham, on the River Bure, one of the Norfolk Broads' rivers, before the final leg back north to Cromer.

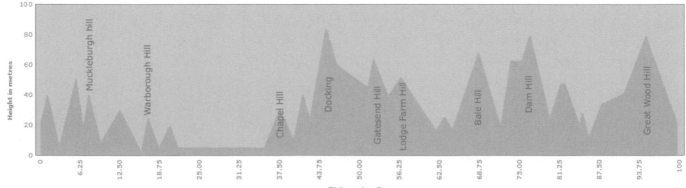

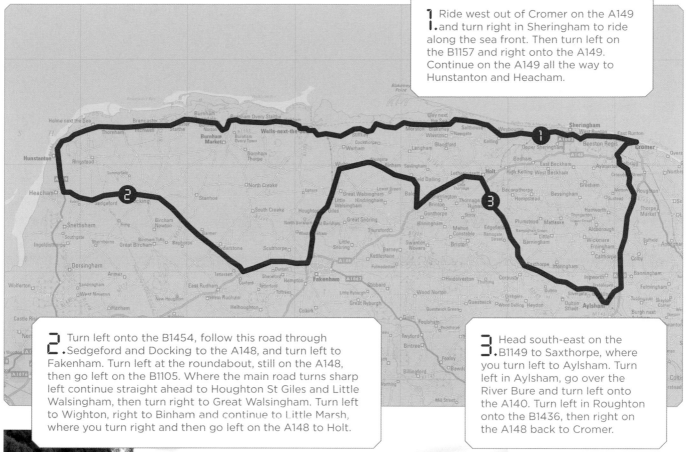

1. Ride west out of Cromer on the A149 and turn right in Sheringham to ride along the sea front. Then turn left on the B1157 and right onto the A149. Continue on the A149 all the way to Hunstanton and Heacham.

2. Turn left onto the B1454, follow this road through Sedgeford and Docking to the A148, and turn left to Fakenham. Turn left at the roundabout, still on the A148, then go left on the B1105. Where the main road turns sharp left continue straight ahead to Houghton St Giles and Little Walsingham, then turn right to Great Walsingham. Turn left to Wighton, right to Binham and continue to Little Marsh, where you turn right and then go left on the A148 to Holt.

3. Head south-east on the B1149 to Saxthorpe, where you turn left to Aylsham. Turn left in Aylsham, go over the River Bure and turn left onto the A140. Turn left in Roughton onto the B1436, then right on the A148 back to Cromer.

START AND FINISH:
Cromer

GETTING THERE:
Cromer is 25 miles north of Norwich on the A140. It has a rail link with Norwich on the Bittern Line.

BIKE SHOP: Pedal Revolution on West Street

CAFE: The Lifeboat Cafe is right next to the lifeboat gangway on the sea wall.

LOCAL DELICACY:
Cromer crabs

I hope you enjoy the ride. There's nothing dramatic about Norfolk; it's subtle, quite private and understated, and certainly impossible to get a feeling for on one visit. If you'd like to know more, and mix it with some self-deprecating humour that is very Norfolk, I recommend reading one of the Sid Kipper books by Norfolk's Chris Sugden, such as *Crab Wars*, which is set in Cromer.

CAMBRIDGESHIRE

Those who don't know it well tend to equate Cambridgeshire with its university city, which is an easy mistake. The university is highly regarded throughout the world, and we should all be very proud of that. But Cambridgeshire is not just Cambridge. It's a beautiful county, one as welcoming to cyclists as the city is, and it has two distinct faces. This ride looks at both of them.

Of course the university is a big influence. It's at the cutting edge of science and technology, and it's the reason for a phenomenon known as Silicon Fen. This is the area between Cambridge, Huntingdon, Ely and Newmarket, which also stretches south to Saffron Walden, and it's full of high-tech businesses.

You visit the Cambridge Fens on the first leg of this ride, as the route heads north through flat countryside from Cambridge to a holy island standing in a sea of dark soil. The island is made of Kimmeridge clay, which would have been relatively dry compared with the undrained marshes around it, so way back in the Bronze Age it provided a space for settlement. But Ely's glory is the cathedral. There was an abbey here in AD 673, and work began on the present building in the 11th century. Its star feature is a huge lantern at the top of the biggest tower. Getting it there must have been an immense feat back in 1340.

The route goes further into the Fens, crossing one of the key waterways in the original drainage project, the Hundred Foot Drain. Then the Fenland section ends; from Chatteris you head southwards to St Neots via Huntingdon, the birthplace of Oliver Cromwell.

You're running against the flow of the Great Ouse, and through a section dominated by water. The river has flooded old gravel pits either side of it, and Grafham Water, the eighth largest reservoir in Britain, lies just the other side of the A1 between Huntingdon and St Neots.

The terrain changes now, too. Rolling roads replace the flat ones of the Fens as the route slips past the south side of Cambridge. Grantchester on the banks of the River Cam is home to the greatest density of Nobel Prize winners anywhere in the world. The poet Rupert Brooke also once lived here, next to the Old Vicarage,

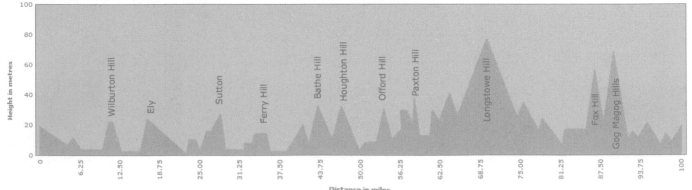

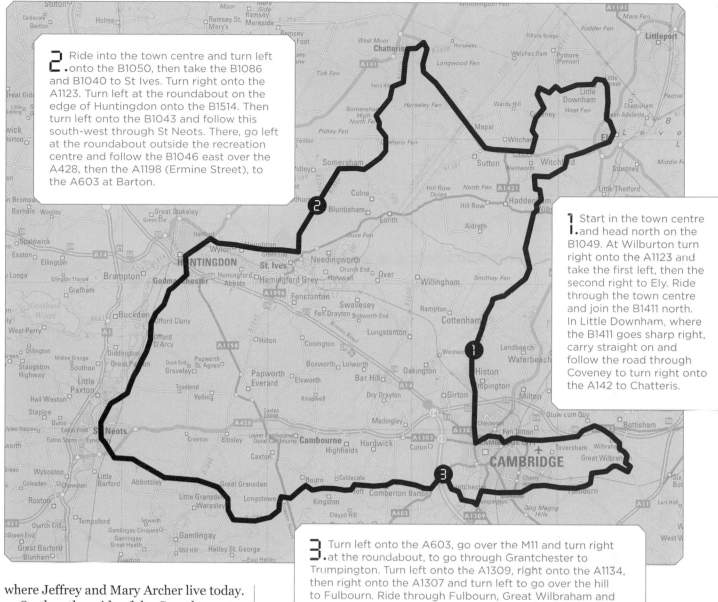

2. Ride into the town centre and turn left onto the B1050, then take the B1086 and B1040 to St Ives. Turn right onto the A1123. Turn left at the roundabout on the edge of Huntingdon onto the B1514. Then turn left onto the B1043 and follow this south-west through St Neots. There, go left at the roundabout outside the recreation centre and follow the B1046 east over the A428, then the A1198 (Ermine Street), to the A603 at Barton.

1. Start in the town centre and head north on the B1049. At Wilburton turn right onto the A1123 and take the first left, then the second right to Ely. Ride through the town centre and join the B1411 north. In Little Downham, where the B1411 goes sharp right, carry straight on and follow the road through Coveney to turn right onto the A142 to Chatteris.

3. Turn left onto the A603, go over the M11 and turn right at the roundabout, to go through Grantchester to Trumpington. Turn left onto the A1309, right onto the A1134, then right onto the A1307 and turn left to go over the hill to Fulbourn. Ride through Fulbourn, Great Wilbraham and Little Wilbraham to turn left onto the A1303. At the second roundabout head straight on into the centre of Cambridge.

where Jeffrey and Mary Archer live today.

On the other side of the Cam the route crosses the Gog Magog Hills. Gog and Magog are biblical names, which first appeared in the locality during the 16th century. There's nothing too steep in these round, chalky hills, and the highest point is around 75 metres.

The ride ends with a flatter loop east of the city and enters it past the airport, aiming for the city centre and the colleges. Cycling in Cambridge is a joy, which is why so many do it, and why I started and finished this ride in the heart of the city. I don't know if it's just because it's cheap transport for students, or because the city is flat, but cycling has flourished here and drivers tend to match their pace to it. But cycling is the right pace to enjoy this fine old city, and of course cycling gives you time to think, something that's very important here.

'IT'S A BEAUTIFUL COUNTY, ONE AS WELCOMING TO CYCLISTS AS THE CITY IS'

START AND FINISH: Cambridge

GETTING THERE: Cambridge is at the end of the M11, 43 miles north-east of London. It has direct rail links with London, the North and the Midlands.

BIKE SHOP: Ben Hayward Cycles on Trumpington Street

CAFE: Black Cat Cafe on Mill Road

LOCAL DELICACY: College pudding

EAST ANGLIA

BRECKLAND

RIDE FACTS

Rating
Easy

Total climbing
400 metres

Killer climb
None

Breckland is a gently undulating area of sandy heathland where the natural cover is gorse and Scots pine. It's one of the driest places in the UK, which is one reason why it's bike friendly; another is that it's neither heavily populated nor a major tourist destination, so the roads are fairly quiet. This is a great place for a first 100-mile ride, and one that has lots of connections with cycling, both ancient and modern.

Start in Bury St Edmunds in Suffolk, which shares Breckland with Norfolk. It's an old town now dominated by a huge sugar beet-processing plant. The route heads north from the centre through the Long Brackland part of town, where the man who won the first ever bike race was born.

His name was James Moore, and he won the race in May 1868 in a Paris park. Moore also won the first race on the open road, held one year later between Paris and Rouen. His original bike is on display in the Ely City Museum in Cambridgeshire. It's made from wood and has the pedals attached directly to its front wheel.

The first leg of the ride ends in Mildenhall, another place with a cycling connection. The grass-track race meeting held here each August Bank Holiday is one of the longest-running meetings in the country, and it's organised by Victoria Pendleton's father. Victoria rode some of her first races here, setting off on a path that would take her to nine world titles and the Olympic glory of two gold medals.

Like Lincolnshire, this part of the country has strong connections with the RAF. Mildenhall and the next place on the ride, Lakenheath, are both active air bases, although now they host American planes. Lakenheath hosts the 48th Fighter Wing, so you might see their F-15s in action as you pedal by. After Lakenheath the route dips into the Fens briefly before returning to Breckland at Feltwell and entering Thetford Forest.

The forest was planted just after the First World War to provide a strategic reserve of timber in case of further conflict. It was controversial, because it destroyed some of the natural heath. However, it's not the first change Breckland has been through. Its name means broken land, referring to the period in the Middle Ages when it was broken up for agriculture, before being returned to its natural heath

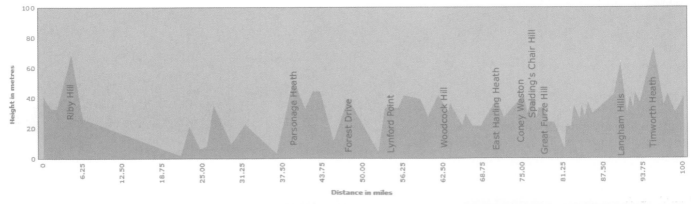

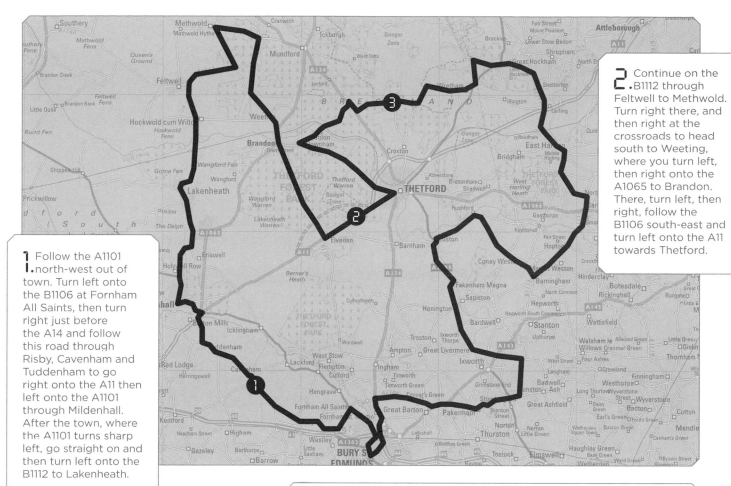

2. Continue on the B1112 through Feltwell to Methwold. Turn right there, and then right at the crossroads to head south to Weeting, where you turn left, then right onto the A1065 to Brandon. There, turn left, then right, follow the B1106 south-east and turn left onto the A11 towards Thetford.

1. Follow the A1101 north-west out of town. Turn left onto the B1106 at Fornham All Saints, then turn right just before the A14 and follow this road through Risby, Cavenham and Tuddenham to go right onto the A11 then left onto the A1101 through Mildenhall. After the town, where the A1101 turns sharp left, go straight on and then turn left onto the B1112 to Lakenheath.

later. Thetford Forest is one of the premier mountain-bike destinations in Britain. There are several prepared routes and over 100 miles of tracks for mountain bikes, as well as regular races.

The town of Thetford is just short of halfway round this ride. It's thought to have been the residence of Boudica, Queen of the Iceni tribe, who led an uprising against the Romans in AD 60. It's said that she led her army in a chariot with blades attached to its wheels; she certainly had a thirst for revenge on the Romans for their cruel treatment of her and her daughters after her father's death.

The second half of the ride visits a string of villages around the edge of the forest, and very pleasant they are too, with plenty of old churches, some thatched cottages and lots of tempting pubs. This is Greene King country, an independent brewer established by Benjamin Greene in 1779 and based in Bury St Edmunds. The company run over 2,000 pubs today, and produce several well-known brands, including Greene King IPA, Old Speckled Hen and Abbot Ale.

3. Turn right at the first roundabout going into Thetford, turn left on the A134, and go straight on at the roundabout and join the B1107. Turn right just before Brandon, left in Santon Downham and go right onto the A134, then left towards the Devil's Punchbowl. Turn left after the Devil's Punchbowl. Go left then right in East Wretham. Turn left onto the A1075 and first left off it. Turn right at Galley Hill, cross the A1075, ride through Great Hockham and turn right onto the B1111. Follow this road south to Barningham, where you turn right and keep left to the crossroads at Spalding's Chair Hill. Turn left onto the A1088 and go straight on at the roundabout north of Ixworth, then turn right and right in Stowlangtoft and follow this road to Pakenham and Great Barton. There, turn left onto the A143 and right onto the B1106 to Fornham St Genevieve, where you go left at the roundabout onto the B1106 back to Bury St Edmunds.

'THE SECOND HALF OF THE RIDE VISITS A STRING OF VILLAGES AROUND THE EDGE OF THE FOREST'

START AND FINISH: Bury St Edmunds

GETTING THERE: Bury St Edmunds is on the A14, 15 miles east of Newmarket and 28 miles east of Cambridge. It has rail links with Newmarket and Cambridge, too.

BIKE SHOP: Mick's Cycles on St John's Street

CAFE: Harriet's Cafe Tearooms, 57 Cornhill

LOCAL DELICACY: Red Pole beef

EAST ANGLIA

EAST SUFFOLK

RIDE FACTS

Rating
Easy

Total climbing
350 metres

Killer climb
Grange Farm

The Suffolk coast is fascinating and fragile. It has a nuclear power station, the charm of Southwold, and habitats for a wide range of plants and animals. A strip of natural heath lies just behind the coast, and as you go further inland East Suffolk becomes arable farmland. It also has some of the prettiest rivers in Britain.

This ride starts next to one of them, in the Waveney valley at Bungay. The valley is a lovely place with a bit of a reputation for alternative lifestyles. One set of Waveney characters that were definitely different were the coypus that thrived in the river until they became a problem during the early 1980s.

The coypu is a giant rodent, and a native of South America, but several escaped from a fur farm in the 1930s. River life suited them and they multiplied, leading to the setting up of Coypu Control, a band of trappers commissioned to get rid of them.

Their ensuing battles were given comic life by Mick Sparksman in a cartoon strip in the local newspaper, the *Waveney Clarion*. The hero, Coypu, was the laid-back leader of the Coypu Liberation Army, who had a taste for cider and root vegetables. His rag-tag band of followers led Coypu Control a merry dance while living out what seemed like one continuous party. There are some examples of the strip on www.waveneyclarion.co.uk.

The last coypu went in 1988, but not before two Coypu Control men caused a stir by reporting that they had seen the Waveney Monster, a ten-foot-long furry animal. The story got so much publicity and created such a stir that the holiday company Hoseasons offered £10,000 for a photograph of it. None has been produced so far, but take a camera in case – I think you'll know it if you see it.

At Harleston you leave the Waveney and Suffolk for a while and head into farm country, going north-west then south, on a long, straight road called the Heywood, to Diss. This is the southernmost town in Norfolk and the birthplace of Thomas Lord, creator of a well-known cricket ground in Marylebone.

From there the route goes east through Framlingham and Saxmundham to the coast at Aldeburgh. There's a beautiful sculpture on the beach here called *The*

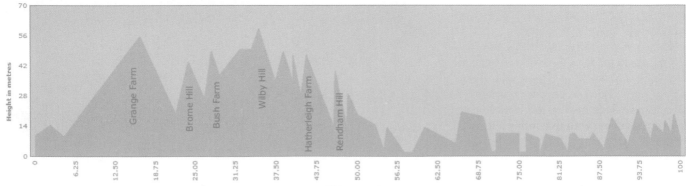

Height in metres — Grange Farm, Brome Hill, Bush Farm, Wilby Hill, Hatherleigh Farm, Rendham Hill

Distance in miles

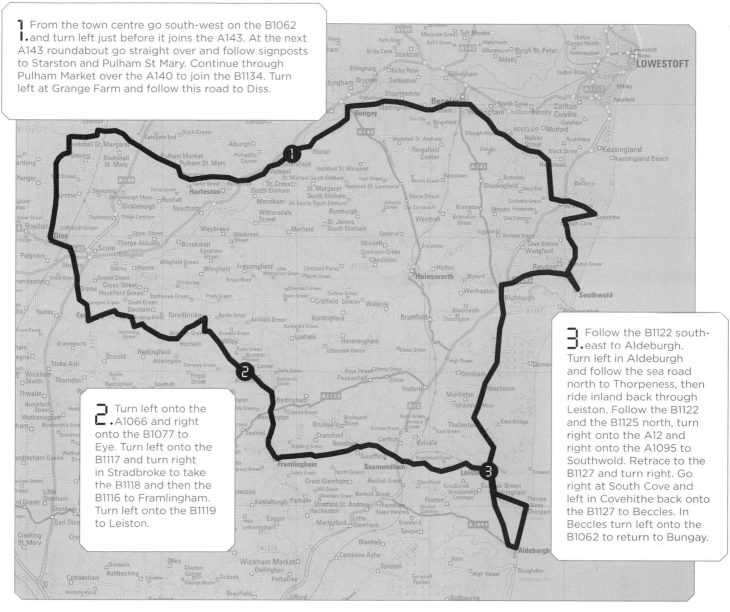

1. From the town centre go south-west on the B1062 and turn left just before it joins the A143. At the next A143 roundabout go straight over and follow signposts to Starston and Pulham St Mary. Continue through Pulham Market over the A140 to join the B1134. Turn left at Grange Farm and follow this road to Diss.

2. Turn left onto the A1066 and right onto the B1077 to Eye. Turn left onto the B1117 and turn right in Stradbroke to take the B1118 and then the B1116 to Framlingham. Turn left onto the B1119 to Leiston.

3. Follow the B1122 south-east to Aldeburgh. Turn left in Aldeburgh and follow the sea road north to Thorpeness, then ride inland back through Leiston. Follow the B1122 and the B1125 north, turn right onto the A12 and right onto the A1095 to Southwold. Retrace to the B1127 and turn right. Go right at South Cove and left in Covehithe back onto the B1127 to Beccles. In Beccles turn left onto the B1062 to return to Bungay.

Scallop. It was created to commemorate the composer Benjamin Britten, who lived in Aldeburgh, walked on this beach and helped create the Aldeburgh Festival.

The Suffolk coast is both gorgeous and interesting. From Thorpeness you can see the huge Sizewell B nuclear power station. Then after a loop inland behind the salt marshes, the route visits Southwold, which is stunning and has been the setting of many films and novels. Here, too, is the Adnams brewery, which is still the number one employer in town.

After one more view of the sea at Covehithe, where the marshes and lagoons to the north are hunting grounds of the marsh harrier, the route heads for Beccles. This means you are back in the Waveney valley, with five miles left in which to have a monster encounter and win that £10,000.

'AFTER A LOOP INLAND BEHIND THE SALT MARSHES, THE ROUTE VISITS SOUTHWOLD, WHICH IS STUNNING'

START AND FINISH: Bungay

GETTING THERE: Bungay is on the A143, 19 miles south-west of Great Yarmouth. It has rail links with Lowestoft and Ipswich.

BIKE SHOP: MG Cycles on Earsham Street

CAFE: The Willows Cafe at the Three Willows Garden Centre

LOCAL DELICACY: It's got to be Adnams. It was my best riding mate Pete Berman's favourite tipple. Pete was a victim of cancer and died too young.

WEST SUFFOLK

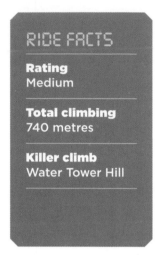

RIDE FACTS

Rating
Medium

Total climbing
740 metres

Killer climb
Water Tower Hill

This ride explores the gently undulating Suffolk countryside away from the coast. It's a very pleasant ride through very English scenery, where arable farming drives the economy, and it's notable for the number of hilltop farms you pass. Their location probably stems from using wind power many years ago. The hills are chalk, and this part of Suffolk is the northernmost reach of the chalk block that extends to the south coast between Dorset and Kent.

The ride starts and finishes in Stowmarket, once home to the pioneering DJ John Peel, after whom the local Arts Centre is named. Nowadays an annual music festival called StowFest is held there, celebrating local music of every genre from folk to reggae. Peel would have loved it.

After an opening climb to the radio mast at Cross Green, the route descends into the valley of the River Brett and then follows it to Lavenham, where the market square was the setting for John Lennon and Yoko Ono's 1970 film *Apotheosis*. The town is situated on one side of the Brett valley; you climb up its main street, and then keep climbing to the top of Likely Hill.

Now the road undulates past a series of hilltop farms, gaining altitude steadily

as it climbs a geographical feature called the Newmarket Ridge. The ride crosses it slightly north of its highest point, which is at Great Wood near Rede. Then you climb it again after descending to Newmarket.

Newmarket is the world centre of horse racing. Two classic races are held here, but more important is the money brought into the town and surrounding area by the famous stables. Breeding, training, sales, and the equine equivalent of sports science and injury treatment all take place in this centre of excellence.

It's also as far west in Suffolk as you can go, and the route follows the county border with Cambridgeshire south to Haverhill, which also borders Essex. Coming out of town you pick up the Stour and ride along its beautiful valley to Clare. This is the river that, further along its course in Dedham Vale, inspired the artist John Constable.

Clare is the start of your third ascent of the Newmarket Ridge, this time up Edmund's Hill. The prison you can just see over the fields to the west used to be called Edmund's Hill Prison; now it's Highpoint North. Notable inmates have included Myra Hindley.

The route trends down now into the River Glem valley, then crosses over

'IT'S A VERY PLEASANT RIDE THROUGH VERY ENGLISH SCENERY'

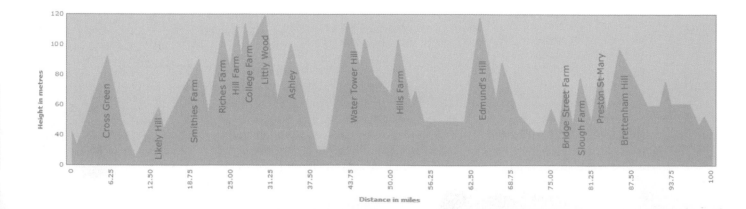

2. Turn left in the centre of Newmarket onto the A1304 and left onto the B1061. Follow the B1061 to the A143 junction and turn right to Haverhill. Follow the A143 through east Haverhill and turn left onto the A1092 to Clare. Turn left in Clare onto the B1063 to Stradishall, and there turn right and right again to Denston and Hawkedon, where you go straight on to the B1066 junction. Turn right onto the B1066 then left onto the A1092 to Long Melford. Turn left onto the A134 and turn right in Bridge Street to Lavenham.

1. Head west, then south out of town on the B1115. Follow this road to Bildeston, where you turn right on the B1078 to join the A1141 west to Monks Eleigh. Continue north through Lavenham on the A1141 to the A134, where you turn right and first left. Keep left until you see a signpost to Whepstead; turn right and keep right. Turn right in Whepstead and first left, then go left, then right to the A143, where you turn right, then left to Chevington. Continue straight through Chevington, Hargrave and Ousden to join the B1063 at the B1085 crossroads. Follow the B1063 to Newmarket.

3. Go down the hill in Lavenham and turn left just before the river and right to cross the river. Continue right, then turn left in Preston St Mary and follow this road through Brettenham to Hightown Green. Turn right, then left to Buxhall. Turn left to Rattlesden and then turn right towards the row of pylons. Continue uphill under them to Woolpit Green, where you turn right and right again to Woolpit Heath. Turn right in Borley Green, and left, then right to Harleston and Onehouse, and join the B1115 back to Stowmarket.

itself in Lavenham for the undulating last leg of Suffolk villages. They have a distinctive look, and throughout this ride you might have noticed a good number of pink cottages. Modern paint is used now, but the pink colour celebrates a tradition in which pig's blood was mixed with whitewash by some householders to provide a little variation in the streets.

One of the last villages you pass through before returning to Stowmarket is Woolpit, whose name refers to a pit dug to capture wolves. This is also where the legend of the green children originated. It's either a folklore story of imagined encounters with aliens, or it could be less fanciful and based on the persecution of Flemish immigrants in the 12th century.

START AND FINISH:
Stowmarket

GETTING THERE:
Stowmarket is 14 miles south-east of Bury St Edmunds on the A14.

BIKE SHOP: Barton's Bicycles on Marriott's Walk

CAFE: The Ossier Cafe in the grounds of the Museum of East Anglian Life

LOCAL DELICACY: Suffolk ham

EAST ANGLIA

BEDFORDSHIRE

EAST ANGLIA

RIDE FACTS

Rating
Medium

Total climbing
680 metres

Killer climb
Breakheart Hill

'THE SCENERY IS PLEASANT AND PRETTY; NOT SPECTACULAR, PERHAPS, BUT PERFECT FOR CYCLING'

Bedfordshire is the land of the Clangers. Not the little space creatures from the 1970s kids' TV series; a Bedford Clanger is a dumpling filled with meat and jam. It used to be such a staple in the county that 'Bedforders' were called Clangers by their neighbours. It's also a county of wide open rolling acres that nuzzles gently up to the Chilterns in its south-western corner.

Using Bedford as a hub, the ride heads north first to Kimbolton for a short stretch in Cambridgeshire, then west for another in Northamptonshire. This section goes through Poddington, close to the Santa Pod Raceway, the home of drag racing in Britain. The scenery is pleasant and pretty; not spectacular, perhaps, but perfect for cycling.

You cross the Great Ouse near Harrold going south, but it's a different-natured river to the one that flows through Cambridgeshire and the Fens. You are above the river's navigable limit now, so it's much smaller and meanders naturally through water meadows, unlike the straightened, man-made watercourse that it is further downstream.

The route passes through Cranfield, close to its university, which is just west of the village and is another British centre of excellence for technology. So is the Vehicle Proving Ground just past Millbrook Station. It's a 760-acre site built on the side of a steep ridge and has nearly 60 miles of roads and off-road tracks designed to test every aspect of motor vehicles.

Climbing up that ridge is quite tough on Breakheart Hill, the hardest of the ride. The ridge is formed by a rock called greensand, which is found all around the upper edges of the London Basin. It's sandstone that was deposited in a deep marine environment into which a lot of organic matter was washed, but where there was little oxygen present to help it decay. This accounts for its slight green tinge.

After the greensand section it's generally downhill as the route joins the valleys of the Flit and Ivel rivers to reach Biggleswade, birthplace of pioneer cyclist Dan Albone. Born in 1860, Albone was given a boneshaker bike for his ninth birthday, and by the time he was 13 he had designed his own bike, complete with suspension. He started the Ivel Cycle Works when he was 20 and won 180 races during the 1880s. His factory produced several groundbreaking bike models before a downturn in interest saw Albone turn to motor transport. Later he developed one of the world's first petrol tractors, the Ivel Agricultural Motor.

Bedfordshire has a lot of motoring history, with Vauxhall in Luton, and it also has history with air transport. There's Luton Airport, of course, which is all very modern; but towards the end of this ride you pass the huge hangars at Cardington, home of the *R101*. The *R101* was a massive airship, 223 metres long and the biggest flying craft in the world until the *Hindenburg* was built in Germany. It was designed to carry people long distances,

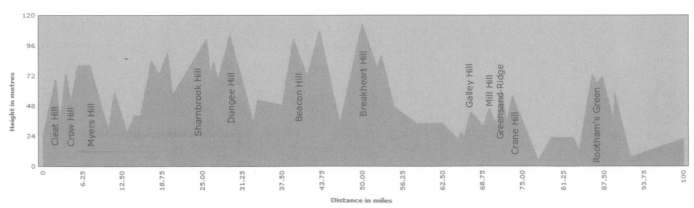

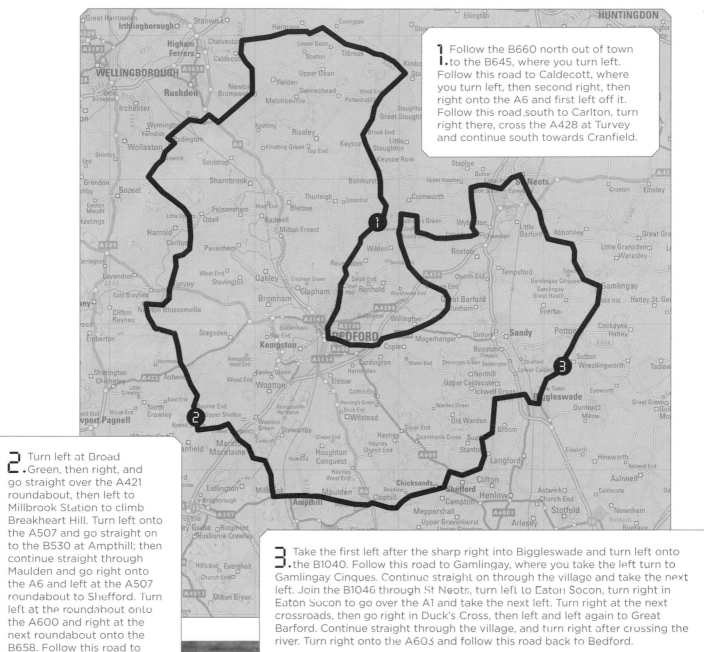

1. Follow the B660 north out of town to the B645, where you turn left. Follow this road to Caldecott, where you turn left, then second right, then right onto the A6 and first left off it. Follow this road south to Carlton, turn right there, cross the A428 at Turvey and continue south towards Cranfield.

2. Turn left at Broad Green, then right, and go straight over the A421 roundabout, then left to Millbrook Station to climb Breakheart Hill. Turn left onto the A507 and go straight on to the B530 at Ampthill; then continue straight through Maulden and go right onto the A6 and left at the A507 roundabout to Shefford. Turn left at the roundabout onto the A600 and right at the next roundabout onto the B658. Follow this road to Biggleswade.

3. Take the first left after the sharp right into Biggleswade and turn left onto the B1040. Follow this road to Gamlingay, where you take the left turn to Gamlingay Cinques. Continue straight on through the village and take the next left. Join the B1046 through St Neots, turn left to Eaton Socon, turn right in Eaton Socon to go over the A1 and take the next left. Turn right at the next crossroads, then go right in Duck's Cross, then left and left again to Great Barford. Continue straight through the village, and turn right after crossing the river. Turn right onto the A603 and follow this road back to Bedford.

but the development of airships ended for Britain in 1930 when the *R101* crashed in France on its maiden voyage, killing 48 of the 54 passengers, including the Air Minister. It ended in the rest of the world after the American airship *Akron* went down in 1933, killing 73, and the *Hindenburg* caught fire in 1937, killing 35.

START AND FINISH: Bedford

GETTING THERE: Bedford is eight miles from the A1's Sandy turn-off. It has a direct rail link to London, with King's Cross just 35 minutes away on the fast train.

BIKE SHOP: Transition Cycles on Castle Road

CAFE: The Jaffa Orchard, which is just off Castle Road

LOCAL DELICACY: The Bedfordshire Clanger, but done in a more modern way with shortcrust pastry, rather like a pasty

EAST ANGLIA

NORTH ESSEX

RIDE FACTS

Rating
Medium

Total climbing
1070 metres

Killer climb
Justice's Hill

'THERE'S NOTHING TOO REMARKABLE ABOUT THE ESSEX COUNTRYSIDE, BUT IT'S A GREAT PLACE TO RIDE A BIKE'

North Essex is hilly despite most of it lying beneath the 100-metres contour. That means there are no long climbs, and not many steep ones, but there are plenty of hills. It's what competitive cyclists call good racing country, and there used to be a very big race in this area, the Essex Grand Prix.

It started and finished in Halstead, and so does this ride. You even end it by riding up what was the finishing straight. It's the town's main street, and it's uphill. I counted 32 distinct climbs on this ride, some with names and some without, but that doesn't include the undulations in between or on top of some of them. You know it after you've ridden 100 miles in North Essex.

The ride heads south out of Halstead, then crosses the Colne valley, heading towards the River Stour to visit Dedham Vale and Flatford Mill in East Bergholt. The Stour is the Suffolk border here, and this is where John Constable did some of his finest paintings, including one called *Flatford Mill*.

You cross back into Essex at Bures, then head for Castle Hedingham, where the castle keep is one of the best-preserved examples of Norman building

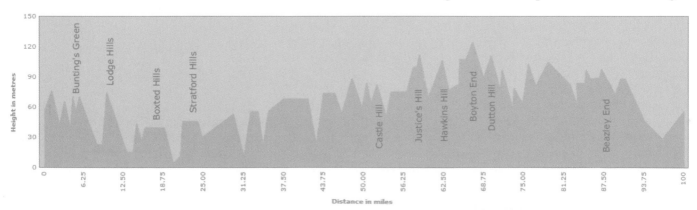

Height in metres

Bunting's Green
Lodge Hills
Boxted Hills
Stratford Hills
Castle Hill
Justice's Hill
Hawkins Hill
Boyton End
Dutton Hill
Beazley End

Distance in miles

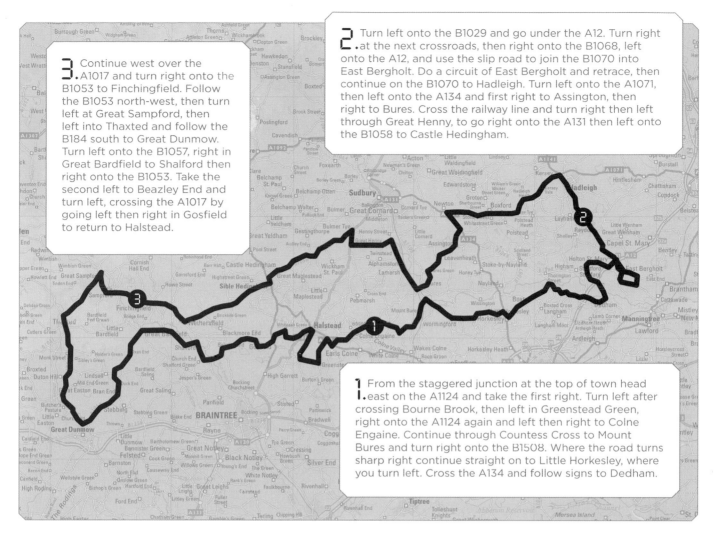

3. Continue west over the A1017 and turn right onto the B1053 to Finchingfield. Follow the B1053 north-west, then turn left at Great Sampford, then left into Thaxted and follow the B184 south to Great Dunmow. Turn left onto the B1057, right in Great Bardfield to Shalford then right onto the B1053. Take the second left to Beazley End and turn left, crossing the A1017 by going left then right in Gosfield to return to Halstead.

2. Turn left onto the B1029 and go under the A12. Turn right at the next crossroads, then right onto the B1068, left onto the A12, and use the slip road to join the B1070 into East Bergholt. Do a circuit of East Bergholt and retrace, then continue on the B1070 to Hadleigh. Turn left onto the A1071, then left onto the A134 and first right to Assington, then right to Bures. Cross the railway line and turn right then left through Great Henny, to go right onto the A131 then left onto the B1058 to Castle Hedingham.

1. From the staggered junction at the top of town head east on the A1124 and take the first right. Turn left after crossing Bourne Brook, then left in Greenstead Green, right onto the A1124 again and left then right to Colne Engaine. Continue through Countess Cross to Mount Bures and turn right onto the B1508. Where the road turns sharp right continue straight on to Little Horkesley, where you turn left. Cross the A134 and follow signs to Dedham.

in the country. The village is chocolate-box pretty, with some cottages dating back to the 15th century. Look for Buckley's Cafe halfway down the main street; it's very popular with Essex cyclists, and not just because it used to be a bike shop. You're just over halfway round the ride, so go on, have a breather; the carrot cake is excellent.

There are lots of big houses in the next section. Grave's Hall, Cust Hall, Gainsford Hall and Boyton Hall come within the next five-mile stretch of road. Weathersfield airfield on your left has been an RAF station, and an American air base, but is now a Ministry of Defence police-training facility.

After Finchingfield, where there's a restored post windmill, you cross the River Pant, which becomes the Blackwater further downstream, and follow it upstream to Great Sampford. The route swings southwards now to Thaxted. The composer of *The Planets*, Gustav Holst, lived here at The Manse between 1917 and 1925. The music to his hymn 'I Vow to

Thee, My Country', taken from that suite, is called *Thaxted*.

The route's southern corner is turned in Great Dunmow. It's the start of a section of tiny hamlets whose names have End as a suffix, as in Bran End and Duck End. Then you cross the Pant valley at Great Bardfield, where a collection of artists lived from the 1930s until the early 1970s. Their styles and their mediums varied, but they shared a love of this idyllic valley and the countryside around it. This is also where you will find the Blue Egg Cafe and farm shop, a favourite stop-off on his recovery rides for the world champion and Tour de France green-jersey winner Mark Cavendish, who lives in the area.

The final leg winds towards Halstead. There's nothing too remarkable about the Essex countryside, but it's a great place to ride a bike. The hills are enough to provide good views without inducing exhaustion, and the lanes wind through a wide variety of fields, farms and woodland. Essex isn't the only way, but it's a good way.

START AND FINISH:
Halstead

GETTING THERE:
Halstead is eight miles north-east of Braintree on the A131.

BIKE SHOP: The nearest shops are in Colchester, unless someone adventurous starts up before this is published.

CAFE: The Blue Egg in Great Bardfield is a great cafe, but there are also a couple on the High Street in Halstead.

LOCAL DELICACY: Wild strawberries

EAST ANGLIA

ESSEX CREEKS

Who doesn't like nosing about among boats and rivers, or doesn't relish the adventure of visiting an island? This ride has all of that, with plenty of wide open spaces, tranquil lanes and pretty villages thrown in.

You start in Colchester, the oldest town in Britain – there are places that are older but they were just settlements when Colchester was a fully working town. It was a key part of the Roman Empire, Camulodunum, the first Roman stronghold in Britain and the centre from which the south-east of England was ruled from around AD 10. It's an army town still, with the British military correction centre based there.

The first section of the ride heads south to Mersea Island, crossing by the Strood. This is an 800-metre causeway that's often covered by the high tide and is very old. In 1978 some oak piles were discovered during drainage work that revealed through dating that an early version of the causeway was built in Saxon times. The island was used as a burial ground by the Romans, and you climb over what are probably some of their remains three times getting on and off the island.

Back on the mainland – you'll need to consult local tide tables for this ride to make sure the Strood is clear to get on and off Mersea – the route heads around some of the creeks that empty into the Blackwater estuary to Maldon. This is the only place where you'll see Thames barges working, albeit in a tourism and education role. They are the last of the sailing barges that plied the Thames when London was an important port, doing the work of water-borne delivery vans.

Maldon is the gateway to the second part of this creeks experience, the Dengie peninsula, which lies between the Blackwater and Crouch estuaries. Both out-and-back sections here make great cycling. Flattish, well-surfaced roads, not much traffic, great views and all the time the salty tang of the sea in your nostrils.

You steadily work your way north-east along the peninsula towards Bradwell, then go south through Southminster to

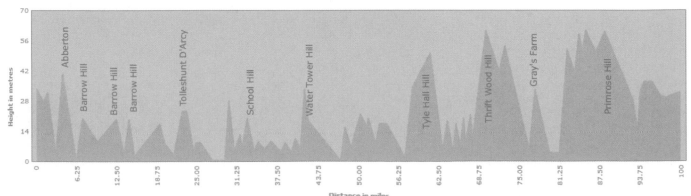

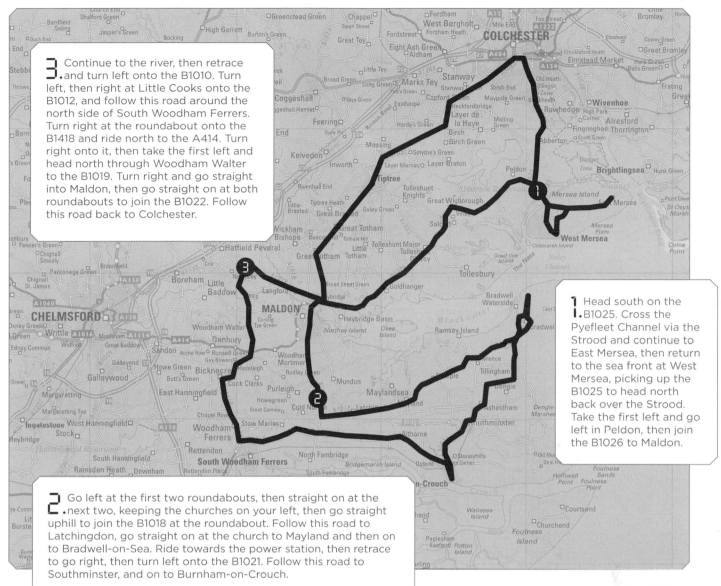

3. Continue to the river, then retrace and turn left onto the B1010. Turn left, then right at Little Cooks onto the B1012, and follow this road around the north side of South Woodham Ferrers. Turn right at the roundabout onto the B1418 and ride north to the A414. Turn right onto it, then take the first left and head north through Woodham Walter to the B1019. Turn right and go straight into Maldon, then go straight on at both roundabouts to join the B1022. Follow this road back to Colchester.

1. Head south on the B1025. Cross the Pyefleet Channel via the Strood and continue to East Mersea, then return to the sea front at West Mersea, picking up the B1025 to head north back over the Strood. Take the first left and go left in Peldon, then join the B1026 to Maldon.

2. Go left at the first two roundabouts, then straight on at the next two, keeping the churches on your left, then go straight uphill to join the B1018 at the roundabout. Follow this road to Latchingdon, go straight on at the church to Mayland and then on to Bradwell-on-Sea. Ride towards the power station, then retrace to go right, then turn left onto the B1021. Follow this road to Southminster, and on to Burnham-on-Crouch.

Burnham-on-Crouch. You'll see a lot of clapboard houses in the villages along this section; it's an old Essex style of building. The clap in clapboard comes from the Dutch word klappen, which means to split, referring to splitting logs. The Essex houses are weatherboarded rather than made from logs, but they help give the area a distinct look.

The empty flatlands to the east are Dengie Marshes, scene of an important bike race that mixes road with short off-road sections. The wind often blows in from the sea here, potentially making riding a slog, but it rarely is because the roads are never straight for long. Instead, what could be a straight road will have 90-degree kinks every few hundred metres, and on a map the roads look like steps. One section called Burnham Bends

goes for five miles in one direction but it's never straight for more than 300 metres.

Out of the peninsula the route heads north-east, back through Maldon, and into more rolling Essex countryside. Tiptree is on the route, one of the candidates for the title of Britain's biggest village. The countryside on this section is a little like Suffolk's hinterland, with arable farms mixed with patches of native heath.

'GREAT VIEWS AND ALL THE TIME THE SALTY TANG OF THE SEA IN YOUR NOSTRILS'

START AND FINISH:
Colchester

GETTING THERE:
Colchester is on the A12, 45 miles north-east of London, with which it has a direct rail link.

BIKE SHOP: Thomas's Cycle Revolution at the Peartree Business Centre in the Stanway area of Colchester

CAFE: Chapeau on Church Walk, a bike cafe and bike shop

LOCAL DELICACY: Mersea Island oysters

OXFORDSHIRE

Rating
Medium

Total climbing
830 metres

Killer climb
Windmill Hill

'HIGH ON ITS HILL, WITH ROLLING COUNTRYSIDE BEHIND IT, THE WINDMILL IS A JOY TO SEE'

This circuit of Oxfordshire looks first at the countryside east and north of the city, nipping into Buckinghamshire. Then it kisses the Cotswolds to the west, and follows a young and playful River Thames back to Oxford.

Oxford is a bike place. Thousands of cyclists commute and get about on two wheels here, and there's a definite bike vibe going on. It has existed for years, but Zappi's Cafe above the Bike Zone shop on St Michael Street helped bolster it. It's run by an Italian ex-professional racer, and inside you can taste the passion for cycling. The city is cycling infectious; people might come to Oxford as drivers or pedestrians, but they leave as cyclists.

I've started this route from the city centre, so you get some feel for cycling there, and you can drink in the atmosphere of the ancient colleges. Oxford is the oldest university in Britain, and one of the oldest in the world. The bricks and stones of the buildings here are steeped in learning and discovery. It's really worth riding among them for a few minutes.

Once out of the city, the route heads east through Thame, and then it dips into Buckinghamshire to visit the windmill in Brill. It's a fantastic feat of preservation. Some of the existing timbers date from the 1650s, and it was almost lost in 2000 when their decay had affected the building's structural integrity. The mill was saved by English Heritage and WREN, and we are all in their debt. High on its hill, with rolling countryside behind

it, the windmill is a joy to see. It's just far enough away from traffic to provide a direct link with the landscape some of our ancestors saw.

The ride heads back into Oxfordshire, and on the road to Bicester you will see a profusion of rail lines on your left. These are to do with the MoD's Ordnance Depot, which has its own rail system. You skirt the town, heading north then west across the Cherwell valley, where as well as the

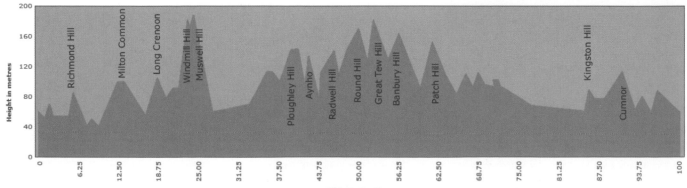

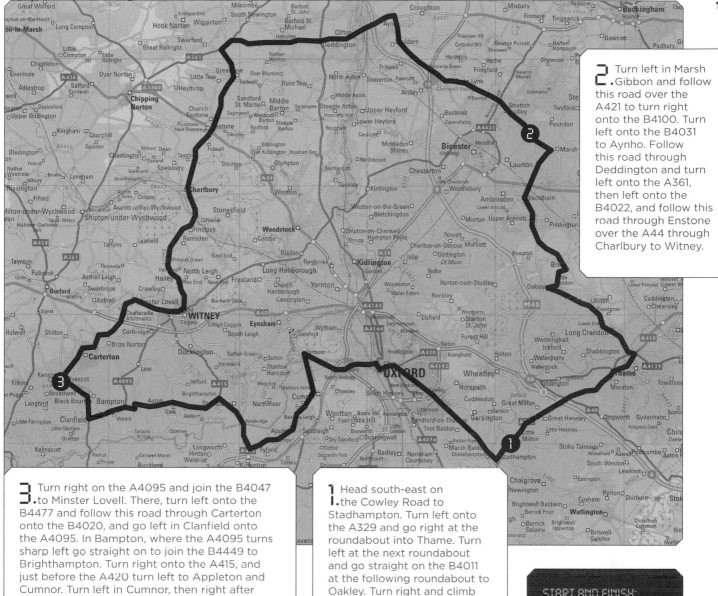

2. Turn left in Marsh Gibbon and follow this road over the A421 to turn right onto the B4100. Turn left onto the B4031 to Aynho. Follow this road through Deddington and turn left onto the A361, then left onto the B4022, and follow this road through Enstone over the A44 through Charlbury to Witney.

3. Turn right on the A4095 and join the B4047 to Minster Lovell. There, turn left onto the B4477 and follow this road through Carterton onto the B4020, and go left in Clanfield onto the A4095. In Bampton, where the A4095 turns sharp left go straight on to join the B4449 to Brighthampton. Turn right onto the A415, and just before the A420 turn left to Appleton and Cumnor. Turn left in Cumnor, then right after Farmoor Reservoir onto the B4044 to Botley. Follow this road back into Oxford.

1. Head south-east on the Cowley Road to Stadhampton. Turn left onto the A329 and go right at the roundabout into Thame. Turn left at the next roundabout and go straight on the B4011 at the following roundabout to Oakley. Turn right and climb up to Brill. Turn left in Brill and continue over Muswell Hill, then rejoin the B4011 and turn right in Blackthorn.

river you will see the Oxford Canal. This was built at the end of the 18th century to link the Thames, and therefore London, with the Midlands. It was a very important transport route until the more direct Grand Union Canal was built in 1805.

The other side of the valley signals the start of a hilly section of the ride, as the route goes south over the toes of the Cotswolds. Look for the Whiteways centre in Enstone, home of the Lotus F1 team, and previously Benetton. Charlbury is a lovely Cotswolds town, with Wychwood Forest just south-east of it, where members of an Oxford University history society do re-enactments of Saxon life.

There's a short stretch in the Windrush valley before a loop around Brize Norton. Then you enter the upper Thames valley, where the river is still only 20 miles from its source near Kemble in Gloucestershire. It's also called the Isis on this stretch and through Oxford.

Years ago the river was the Isis until it joined the River Thame south of Oxford. Then it became the Thame-Isis, and later the name was shortened to the Thames. The last section follows the Thames to Botley, where things get busy because this is an important artery into Oxford. Look for the cycle lanes and follow those back into the city.

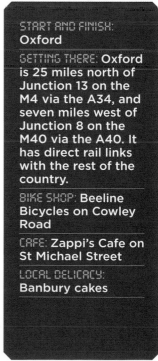

START AND FINISH: Oxford

GETTING THERE: Oxford is 25 miles north of Junction 13 on the M4 via the A34, and seven miles west of Junction 8 on the M40 via the A40. It has direct rail links with the rest of the country.

BIKE SHOP: Beeline Bicycles on Cowley Road

CAFE: Zappi's Cafe on St Michael Street

LOCAL DELICACY: Banbury cakes

HERTFORDSHIRE

RIDE FACTS

Rating
Medium

Total climbing
800 metres

Killer climb
Periwinkle Hill

South Hertfordshire, where this ride starts and finishes, is busy. It's very close to London, there are a lot of towns here, and you need to take great care on the main roads. Don't let this put you off, however; Hertfordshire is a great place to ride. The countryside is rolling and varied, with the west being higher and drier, the east lower with lots of little rivers, and one big one. This ride uses a network of quiet lanes to explore the county's two sides, visiting some historic sites as well as some modern ones.

Cheshunt is a typical Hertfordshire town in that it feels like the land of the eternal roundabout. Hertford and Stevenage have even more; they are both quite new towns and they were built for cars, not bikes. Cheshunt has one enviable place for family cycling, though. Lea Valley Park is where the town's double

track-cycling Olympic gold medallist Laura Trott learned to ride.

You are soon out in the countryside, passing the Royal Veterinary College just north of Potter's Bar. The route then shadows the A1(M) for a short while before heading around the north of St Albans. This was the second largest Roman town in Britain, called Verulamium, and is now a city with a cathedral dedicated to St Alban, who was executed by the Romans to become the first British Christian martyr. The first draft of the Magna Carta was drawn up in the cathedral, indicating the city's post-Roman importance.

From here the route heads north and then south, crossing some lovely open countryside on undulating roads to Welwyn. This is some of the best cycling in Hertfordshire, and it leads to Welwyn Garden City, a landmark in town planning. There's still a lot to be said for this concept that was developed back in the 1920s. The idea was to create new towns in the countryside with enough people to support industry but not so many that individuals lose their identity. The results were towns on a human scale where people could live and breathe, work and play, and never feel cowed by their surroundings. Welwyn is designed around the Parkway, a boulevard like the Champs-Elysées in Paris, although much more in keeping with the scale of an English provincial town. The route crosses the Parkway's northern end, so see what

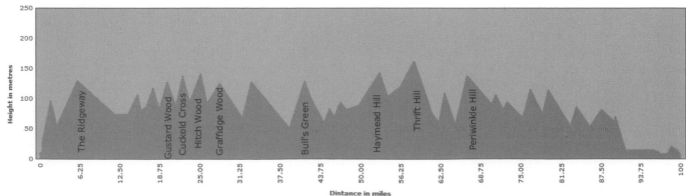

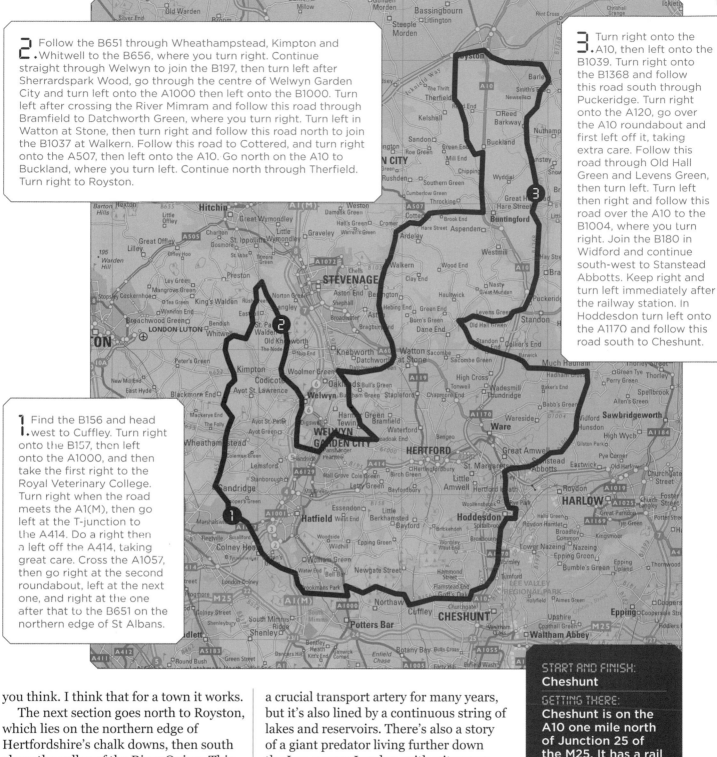

2. Follow the B651 through Wheathampstead, Kimpton and Whitwell to the B656, where you turn right. Continue straight through Welwyn to join the B197, then turn left after Sherrardspark Wood, go through the centre of Welwyn Garden City and turn left onto the A1000 then left onto the B1000. Turn left after crossing the River Mimram and follow this road through Bramfield to Datchworth Green, where you turn right. Turn left in Watton at Stone, then turn right and follow this road north to join the B1037 at Walkern. Follow this road to Cottered, and turn right onto the A507, then left onto the A10. Go north on the A10 to Buckland, where you turn left. Continue north through Therfield. Turn right to Royston.

3. Turn right onto the A10, then left onto the B1039. Turn right onto the B1368 and follow this road south through Puckeridge. Turn right onto the A120, go over the A10 roundabout and first left off it, taking extra care. Follow this road through Old Hall Green and Levens Green, then turn left. Turn left then right and follow this road over the A10 to the B1004, where you turn right. Join the B180 in Widford and continue south-west to Stanstead Abbotts. Keep right and turn left immediately after the railway station. In Hoddesdon turn left onto the A1170 and follow this road south to Cheshunt.

1. Find the B156 and head west to Cuffley. Turn right onto the B157, then left onto the A1000, and then take the first right to the Royal Veterinary College. Turn right when the road meets the A1(M), then go left at the T-junction to the A414. Do a right then a left off the A414, taking great care. Cross the A1057, then go right at the second roundabout, left at the next one, and right at the one after that to the B651 on the northern edge of St Albans.

you think. I think that for a town it works.

The next section goes north to Royston, which lies on the northern edge of Hertfordshire's chalk downs, then south along the valley of the River Quinn. This is where Hertfordshire changes from a dry upland chalk landscape to a wetter one with more streams and rivers.

The River Quinn flows into the River Rib, which you cross at Barwick, and then there's a short section in the Ash valley before the route meets the Lea just south of Ware. The Lea is a mass of water. It's a substantial river that joins the Thames in London's docklands, and as such was

a crucial transport artery for many years, but it's also lined by a continuous string of lakes and reservoirs. There's also a story of a giant predator living further down the Lea, nearer London, with witnesses claiming they have seen large geese dragged beneath the surface in seconds.

The route gets busy when it reaches Hoddesdon, with a sequence of roundabouts to be negotiated before returning to Cheshunt. Just take your time and take care. When I did this stretch most of the car drivers were bike aware, which is an increasing trend, but it only takes one who isn't.

START AND FINISH:
Cheshunt

GETTING THERE:
Cheshunt is on the A10 one mile north of Junction 25 of the M25. It has a rail link to Stratford in London.

BIKE SHOP: Hancocks on Cudmore Lane

CAFE: Fountain Cafe on Manor Croft Parade

LOCAL DELICACY: Braughing sausages

BERKSHIRE

RIDE FACTS

Rating
Hard

Total climbing
1450 metres

Killer climb
Lough Down

'IT'S A LONG PULL UP TO COOKLEY GREEN ON TOP OF THE CHILTERNS'

This ride looks at the western Chilterns, the section that's in Oxfordshire and only brushed by the Chilterns 100-mile ride. It also explores some of the adjoining and much more open Berkshire Downs, and the racehorse-training country around Lambourn. Finally, it pays homage to a classic 100-mile cycle race that used to be one of the most prized in Britain.

Reading is the start. It's a busy place, but after crossing the Thames you ride through the leafy suburb of Caversham. You also start climbing, because it's a long pull up to Cookley Green on top of the Chilterns, by which point you've gone from Thames level to well over 200 metres and mastered a steep intermediate bump called Shiplake Hill.

A sharp descent leads to Watlington, and then a gradual downhill trend ends in Wallingford for a run south by the River Thames. Jerome K. Jerome, author of *Three Men in a Boat*, lived near Wallingford. He must have known this stretch of the river well. You cross it in Goring, where the Thames flows through the Goring Gap, which separates the Chilterns from the Berkshire Downs.

That's where you're going next, up the killer climb of Lough Down and into an upland area very different from the Chilterns. Geologically they are the same, but there are more roads and settlements in the Chilterns and many more trees. Until 1974 the Berkshire Downs were all

in Berkshire, but now they're shared with Oxfordshire.

The Downs are a famous place for racehorse training, and you start passing their prepared gallops in the Compton area before a final dip into Oxfordshire at Wantage, where one of the greatest ever jockeys, Lester Piggott, was born. Hackpen Hill leads to where Piggott began his career, riding the horses his father trained at their stables at South Bank near Lambourn.

The Lambourn Downs are beautiful, wide open and laced with gallops. Seeing the horses training here is a joy. The Downs inspired J. R. R. Tolkien, and his descriptions of open hilly grassland in *The Lord of the Rings* are based on the landscape here. Your Berkshire Downs passage is interrupted by the River Kennet, and you follow it into Hungerford, where the Kennet and Avon Canal runs.

The route then does a loop south, squeezing between Newbury and the fearsome Inkpen Hill, on the edge of the Downs, to head through Thatcham and cross the A340 just south of Pangbourne. This was a hallowed place in cycling, one of the villages on the Bath Road 100 course, which ran from Reading to Abingdon, then south to the A4 – known as the Bath Road before it was given a number.

Until a transition period in the 1950s, time trialling was the mainstay of cycle racing in Britain. Riders competed over

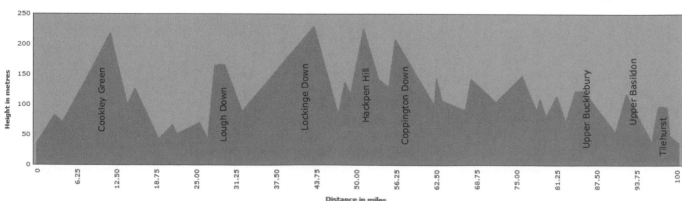

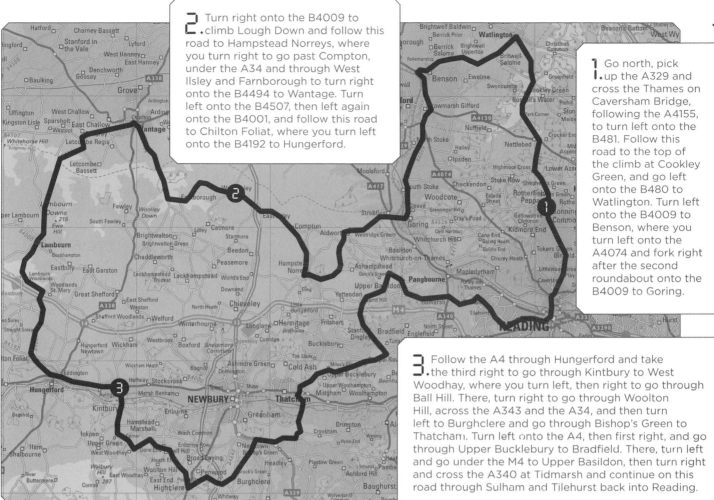

2. Turn right onto the B4009 to climb Lough Down and follow this road to Hampstead Norreys, where you turn right to go past Compton, under the A34 and through West Ilsley and Farnborough to turn right onto the B4494 to Wantage. Turn left onto the B4507, then left again onto the B4001, and follow this road to Chilton Foliat, where you turn left onto the B4192 to Hungerford.

1. Go north, pick up the A329 and cross the Thames on Caversham Bridge, following the A4155, to turn left onto the B481. Follow this road to the top of the climb at Cookley Green, and go left onto the B480 to Watlington. Turn left onto the B4009 to Benson, where you turn left onto the A4074 and fork right after the second roundabout onto the B4009 to Goring.

3. Follow the A4 through Hungerford and take the third right to go through Kintbury to West Woodhay, where you turn left, then right to go through Ball Hill. There, turn right to go through Woolton Hill, across the A343 and the A34, and then turn left to Burghclere and go through Bishop's Green to Thatcham. Turn left onto the A4, then first right, and go through Upper Bucklebury to Bradfield. There, turn left and go under the M4 to Upper Basildon, then turn right and cross the A340 at Tidmarsh and continue on this road through Sulham and Tilehurst back into Reading.

START AND FINISH:
Reading

GETTING THERE:
Reading is right next to the M4, served by Junctions 10 to 12. It also has good rail links with London and the rest of the country.

BIKE SHOP: AW Cycles on Henley Road in Caversham

CAFE: Caversham Cafe in St Mark's Precinct, just after the Thames bridge you cross going out of Reading

LOCAL DELICACY: Six Point Berk pork

standard distances of 25, 50 and 100 miles, and to see how far they could ride in 12 and 24 hours. The Bath Road 100 was a prized victory, a fact that saw the best compete in what were often very fast times by any standard. In 1958, Ray Booty of Nottingham, having cycled 100 miles from his home to Reading the previous day, became the first cyclist to go under four hours for 100 miles. He stopped the clock in Pangbourne Lane, which is just off the final part of this ride, at 3 hours 58 minutes and 28 seconds. Cycling wasn't as big then in Britain as it is nowadays, but in the cycling world Booty's performance was seen as being as important as Dr Roger Bannister's first ever sub-four-minute mile a few years earlier.

SOUTHERN ENGLAND

THE CHILTERNS

The Chilterns are one of Britain's little miracles. They are tucked into an armpit of motorways, right on the edge of our biggest city, and they are studded with its satellite towns, yet they seem miles away from the rush and push of the 21st century.

It's because this chalk upland lies under a network of byways and little lanes that form a connecting matrix between hamlets and villages, villages and towns, and all of them with each other. The network has grown over many years and reflects journeys seldom made now, but they allow cyclists to ride up a hillside with the roar of traffic from the M40 fading slowly under a flood of birdsong, while red kites wheel around in the sky above.

These are a Chiltern success story. The red kite is a large but elegant bird of prey that was once regarded as vermin. They were almost wiped out of the country by the 20th century, their only stronghold being a small area of Wales. Then attitudes changed, and the Welsh birds increased in numbers. Some of them, together with imported ones, were moved to different parts of the country, and five were let loose in the Chilterns in 1989. They multiplied steadily and are now an everyday but still striking feature of the landscape.

The route starts in Berkhamsted, where William the Bastard was offered the crown of England in 1066 and henceforth became known as William the Conqueror, which is a much catchier name. This is a hilly route, and you start uphill as soon as you leave town with the long ascent up to Ivinghoe Common.

You pass under the Whipsnade White Lion, cut into a chalk escarpment, and turn to climb over a shoulder of Ivinghoe Beacon. There's a long descent, then the route runs along the base of the Chilterns to Aston Clinton, which is the origin of the Aston in Aston Martin. Lionel Martin tested his first cars on Aston Hill. The route then continues to Watlington, with a couple of loops into the hills, including one to climb Whiteleaf Hill, a crucial climb in the Archer GP, a big bike race that has been forced into extinction by

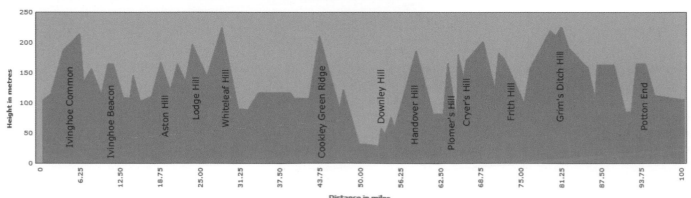

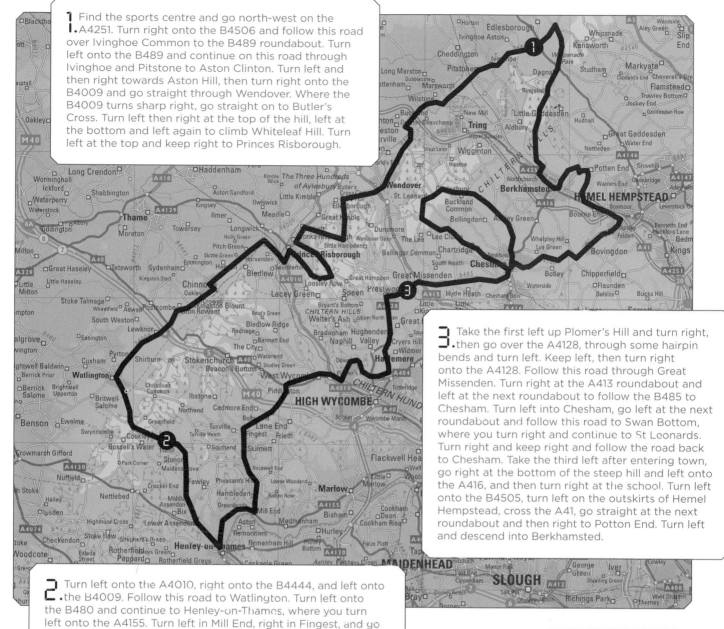

1. Find the sports centre and go north-west on the A4251. Turn right onto the B4506 and follow this road over Ivinghoe Common to the B489 roundabout. Turn left onto the B489 and continue on this road through Ivinghoe and Pitstone to Aston Clinton. Turn left and then right towards Aston Hill, then turn right onto the B4009 and go straight through Wendover. Where the B4009 turns sharp right, go straight on to Butler's Cross. Turn left then right at the top of the hill, left at the bottom and left again to climb Whiteleaf Hill. Turn left at the top and keep right to Princes Risborough.

3. Take the first left up Plomer's Hill and turn right, then go over the A4128, through some hairpin bends and turn left. Keep left, then turn right onto the A4128. Follow this road through Great Missenden. Turn right at the A413 roundabout and left at the next roundabout to follow the B485 to Chesham. Turn left into Chesham, go left at the next roundabout and follow this road to Swan Bottom, where you turn right and continue to St Leonards. Turn right and keep right and follow the road back to Chesham. Take the third left after entering town, go right at the bottom of the steep hill and left onto the A416, and then turn right at the school. Turn left onto the B4505, turn left on the outskirts of Hemel Hempstead, cross the A41, go straight at the next roundabout and then right to Potton End. Turn left and descend into Berkhamsted.

2. Turn left onto the A4010, right onto the B4444, and left onto the B4009. Follow this road to Watlington. Turn left onto the B480 and continue to Henley-on-Thames, where you turn left onto the A4155. Turn left in Mill End, right in Fingest, and go straight over the B482 and under the M40 to turn right onto the A40 to High Wycombe.

increased traffic counts and police costs.

The climb out of Watlington to Cookley Green Ridge is also hard. There's some respite from the hills as you descend to Henley-on-Thames and ride for three miles next to the river, but then they return with a vengeance. Downley Hill in High Wycombe is steep, and it's hilly when you drop into and climb out of the Hughenden Valley.

Towns come thick and fast, too. Great Missenden, where Roald Dahl lived, is followed by two visits to Chesham. But the towns are attractive and the countryside between them is stunning. Chiltern woods are gorgeous. They cover 01 per cent of

the land, making this the most heavily wooded area of England, and many are very old. There is evidence of woodland here from AD 1600.

One final loop in the hills north-east of Berkhamsted goes past a prehistoric structure called Grim's Ditch. There are Grim's Ditches, sometimes called Grim's Dykes, all over the chalk uplands of southern England. Archaeologists believe they may have marked out territories. However, the Chilterns' Grim's Ditch has different sections that appear to have different functions, one of which may have been as a saw pit, where wood was prepared for construction.

START AND FINISH:
Berkhamsted

GETTING THERE:
Berkhamsted is five miles west of Hemel Hempstead, which is at Junction 8 of the M1. It has direct rail links with London and the Midlands.

BIKE SHOP: Bike Knight on Church Road

CAFE: One Four Six on the High Street

LOCAL DELICACY: Aylesbury duck

SALISBURY PLAIN AND PEWSEY VALE

Salisbury Plain is high and wide, a place where you can breathe deeply, set your mind loose and really ride. The roads are good, and traffic mostly clusters along the A303 and around Stonehenge, both of which I've avoided, although the route passes the less well-known Woodhenge. This ride is a mental re-boot, a great place to think clearly and solve problems. Bikes are good for that. I can rack my brains for new ideas when sitting at my desk, then come back with three after a blast on my bike.

Where else would it start but Salisbury? The city is surrounded by some beautiful

little rivers and valleys, and I wanted this ride to explore some of them. The little Ebble comes first, then the route crosses over to the River Nadder, which like the others is a beautiful, clear chalk stream, with wreaths of water crowsfoot and brown trout nosing around in it. I love these rivers; they hold the same fascination as rock pools because you can see right into them.

You leave the river at Tisbury, a delightful village in the beautiful West Wiltshire Downs. There's a giant yew tree in the churchyard that's thought to be around 4000 years old. The road undulates upwards to Summerslade Down, the highest point on the ride at 230 metres. Then you descend to Warminster, which was once the UFO capital of Britain but for our purposes is the gateway to Salisbury Plain. It's a great place to make an entrance.

The route across the plain goes through Chitterne and Tilshead into the Vale of Pewsey. It's a lovely open road, but you have to watch out at the tank crossings. The military use Salisbury Plain a lot, but it also supports a quite specialised and diverse ecology, and although it's sparsely populated it has been populated for a long time. Salisbury Plain also had special significance as a religious or mystical centre, as Stonehenge suggests. More recently, though, the Plain has inspired people to write, paint and make music.

The Vale of Pewsey is special, too. It's a wide valley situated between the steep

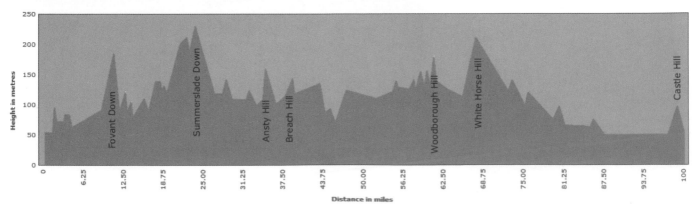

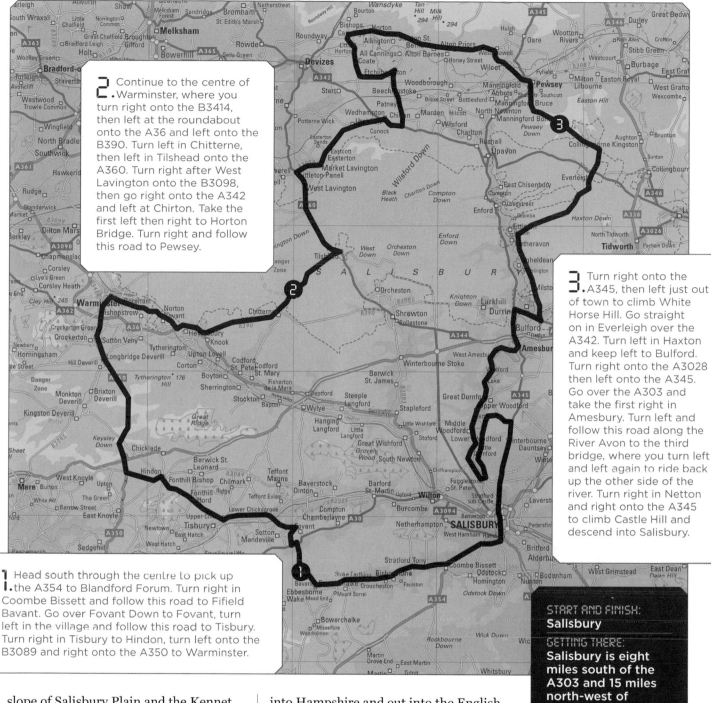

2. Continue to the centre of Warminster, where you turn right onto the B3414, then left at the roundabout onto the A36 and left onto the B390. Turn left in Chitterne, then left in Tilshead onto the A360. Turn right after West Lavington onto the B3098, then go right onto the A342 and left at Chirton. Take the first left then right to Horton Bridge. Turn right and follow this road to Pewsey.

3. Turn right onto the A345, then left just out of town to climb White Horse Hill. Go straight on in Everleigh over the A342. Turn left in Haxton and keep left to Bulford. Turn right onto the A3028 then left onto the A345. Go over the A303 and take the first right in Amesbury. Turn left and follow this road along the River Avon to the third bridge, where you turn left and left again to ride back up the other side of the river. Turn right in Netton and right onto the A345 to climb Castle Hill and descend into Salisbury.

1. Head south through the centre to pick up the A354 to Blandford Forum. Turn right in Coombe Bissett and follow this road to Fifield Bavant. Go over Fovant Down to Fovant, turn left in the village and follow this road to Tisbury. Turn right in Tisbury to Hindon, turn left onto the B3089 and right onto the A350 to Warminster.

slope of Salisbury Plain and the Kennet Downs. They are all chalk hills, and there's a white horse cut into them on both sides. You meet Pewsey's white horse as you climb back up to Salisbury Plain. Then there's another incredible stretch of open road before joining the Avon valley for the ride back to Salisbury.

There are five River Avons in England, and each is a tautology because Avon means river. This is the Hampshire Avon, despite most of it flowing through Wiltshire, and it carries the most diverse fish stocks in Britain. It rises east of Devizes and flows through Salisbury into Hampshire and out into the English Channel at Christchurch. The route swaps banks, following it almost to the city, then does a loop so you can enter Salisbury by Castle Hill, and see the cathedral's spire, the tallest in Britain, in all its glory.

Salisbury used to be called Sarum, and Castle Hill is the site of Old Sarum. The whole city was located here until overcrowding drove Bishop Poore to suggest relocating it in 1220. Legend has it that he shot an arrow into the air from Castle Hill that hit a deer, wounding it, and the new cathedral was built where the deer eventually died.

START AND FINISH:
Salisbury

GETTING THERE:
Salisbury is eight miles south of the A303 and 15 miles north-west of Southampton on the A36. It has rail links with London, the south coast and the Midlands.

BIKE SHOP:
Stonehenge Cycles on Fisherton Street

CAFE: Boston Tea Party on the High Street

LOCAL DELICACY:
Twinings teas from Andover

HAMPSHIRE

RIDE FACTS

Rating
Medium

Total climbing
1050 metres

Killer climb
Three Legs House Hill

Winchester in Hampshire used to be the capital of England, and it shows. The city was already the capital of Wessex, but it grew in importance after the Norman Conquest of 1066 when several smaller kingdoms were united into one England. It's still a very fine place, Winchester's cathedral is one of the largest in Europe, and inside the castle's great hall there is what was once thought to have been King Arthur's round table. Unfortunately it's not old enough, having probably been made around 1290 in the time of Edward I, but it's still impressive.This route starts in Winchester and it visits two of Hampshire's beautiful chalk rivers, the Test and the Itchen. Winchester is located on the latter. It also visits the hill country around Highclere, touches the western edges of the South Downs and goes through the Meon valley.

Hampshire's rivers are very special, and it doesn't share the Test or the Itchen with any other county. Both are world-renowned trout rivers, and are like the ideal river of your dreams, a sort of perfect combination of rivery things.

You join the Test just upstream of Stockbridge, a town with a long tradition of fishing, then follow it past a series

of splits and sluices, before taking the tributary valley of the Bourne Rivulet to start this ride's killer climb.

Don't be fooled by a summit after the first mile. The road descends sharply into a dry valley, but then climbs again to the real summit at Three Legs House. Highclere Castle, used as the setting for *Downton Abbey*, is below you in the next valley. The *Tatler* magazine recently christened this area Downtonia.

A long downhill section takes you back to the River Test in Whitchurch, then you ride a loop around its source, centred on Overton. You can just see the pond that the river flows out of in a field on your right, 200 metres after the Ashe junction. Soon the route goes south, over Popham Beacons, for no other reason than that it's pretty that way, before it passes beneath Hampshire's spaghetti junction, where the A303 joins the M3.

You cross the Itchen valley at New Alresford, which lays claim to being the watercress capital of the world. Watercress grows naturally in the Itchen, but commercial production is now done on farms, using large pools. The town has a Watercress Festival every May, and the approach through Old Arlesford past the ponds and the River Arle is a babble of

'THE APPROACH IS A BABBLE OF BROOKS, PLACID WATER AND LUSH GREEN MEADOWS'

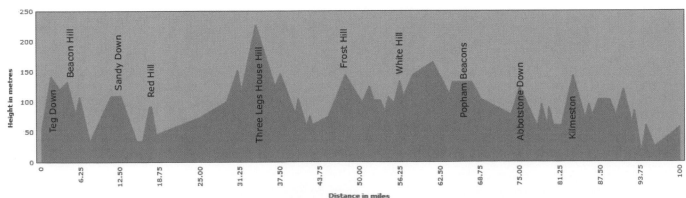

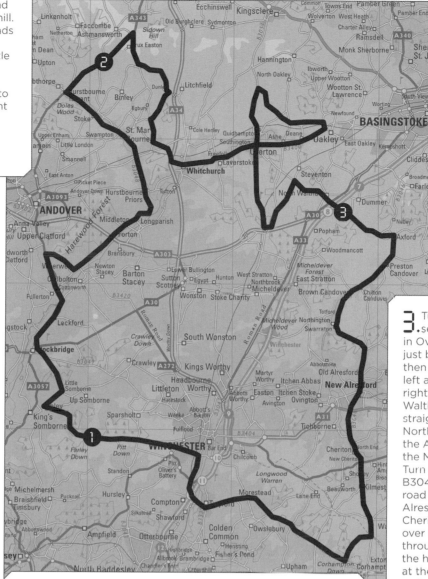

2. Turn right onto the A343 and turn right at the top of the hill. Turn left at the second crossroads then right at the bottom of the next hill and left at Egbury Castle Farm. Keep left to Whitchurch, where you turn left onto the B3400 to Overton. Turn left onto the B3051 and take the first right after Frost Hill Farm. Turn right under the railway bridge just before Oakley and follow the B3400 back to Overton.

brooks, placid water and lush green meadows.

Continuing south, you climb to the source of the Itchen just after Chcriton. You ride through Kilmeston to the top of the hill, then descend to Twyford and ride back into Winchester. The city wears its history well. The road you are riding on is a Roman one. On a hill to your left as you enter is Oliver's Battery, the site of an Iron Age earthwork that Oliver Cromwell used when laying siege to Winchester during the Civil War. There's another hill fort on your left, and as you approach the city centre you can see the original grid layout of Winchester, a city where history lives.

3. Turn left at the second crossroads in Overton and left just before the A303; then take the first left and go right and right again to North Waltham. Continue straight through North Waltham, cross the A30 and go under the M3 to Axford. Turn right onto the B3046 and follow this road through New Alresford to New Cheriton. Go straight over the A272, through Kilmeston up the hill and turn right at the top. Keep right, and turn right again after St Clair's Farm. Follow this road to Morestead, where you turn left to go through Twyford and take the B3335 back into Winchester.

1. Go west from the town centre on the B3040, take the first right after the hospital, cross the B3041 and follow this road west, almost to King's Somborne. Turn right just before the village, then turn left in Little Somborne, then left onto the B3049 to Stockbridge. There, you turn right onto the A3057, go north through Leckford and turn right onto the B3420. Where this road turns sharp right continue straight on the B3048. Follow this road to Hurstbourne Tarrant.

START AND FINISH: Winchester

GETTING THERE: Winchester is at Junctions 9 and 10 of the M3. It has a direct rail link with London.

BIKE SHOP: Hargroves Cycles on City Road

CAFE: The Corner House in the Market Place

LOCAL DELICACY: Watercress

BLACKMORE VALE

SOUTHERN ENGLAND

RIDE FACTS

Rating
Hard

Total climbing
1350 metres

Killer climb
Dungeon Hill

'AN ABSOLUTELY GORGEOUS COBBLED STREET OF OLD HOUSES MADE FAMOUS BY THE BOY-ON-A-BIKE HOVIS ADVERTS'

Blackmore Vale is a wide valley situated mostly in Dorset, and it's the flood plain of the River Stour and a number of its tributaries. The valley bottom is predominantly clay, so it's wet and milk production is the main farming activity in it. It's also why the Vale villages are built in strips, to coincide with strips of better-draining limestone that run across the wet clay. The surrounding hills are chalk, and this ride explores the Vale and the chalk uplands south of it.

This is Thomas Hardy country. *Tess of the d'Urbervilles* opens in Blackmore Vale, and Blandford Forum, where this ride starts, is Hardy's Shottsford Forum. The town stands inside a wide bend of the River Stour and opposite a beautiful example of a river cliff. It used to be terrorised by the Blandford Fly, a nasty biting insect that drew blood from its victims and often infected them. They bred in river vegetation, but the flies were greatly reduced when the authorities began waging biological warfare on them.

This ride is hilly, but you get an eight-mile warm-up beside the Stour, then go up a side valley before the first climb. This takes you over the flanks of Melbury Hill, and to the foot of the steep climb into Shaftesbury. Here you descend Gold Hill, an absolutely gorgeous cobbled street of old houses made famous by the boy-on-a-bike Hovis adverts.

From Shaftesbury the route tours both sides of Blackmore Vale, then does a loop to Sherborne and Yeovil. Sherborne is a lovely town full of interesting and well-preserved buildings, including an abbey.

The succession of hills eases slightly with a final crossing of the Vale to Glanvilles Wootton, but then intensifies as you enter the Dorset Hills. It's not as bad as it could have been, because Dorset roads tend to wriggle around hills instead of going straight over them.

Many of these round chalk hills, such as Dungeon Hill, have evidence of forts or other settlements on them; others might have been burial grounds. Dorset has been lived in a lot. There's evidence of Neolithic man throughout the county, which also had its own Celtic tribe. The Romans made extensive use of Dorset, and the first recorded Viking raid of Britain was made here in the eighth century.

After the hills around Alton Pancras the route enters the Piddle valley and drops with the stream to Piddletrenthide and Piddlehinton. It leaves the valley at Puddletown, just upstream of Tolpuddle, where the Tolpuddle Martyrs made history in 1832 by forming what was in effect the first trade union. They were transported to Australia for seven years for doing so, but were released after a public protest.

The last leg to Blandford Forum goes straight up a main road, and it's a tough slog over constant undulations, although there's usually a following wind. You enter Blandford by crossing the Stour close to a weir, where otters are often seen playing. They aren't shy and don't seem to mind even if they gather a crowd.

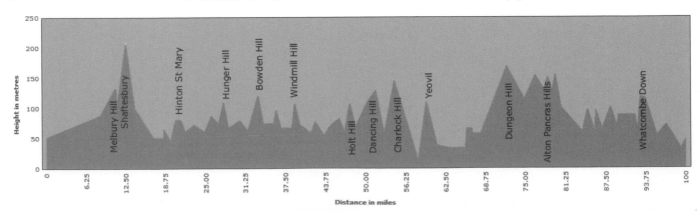

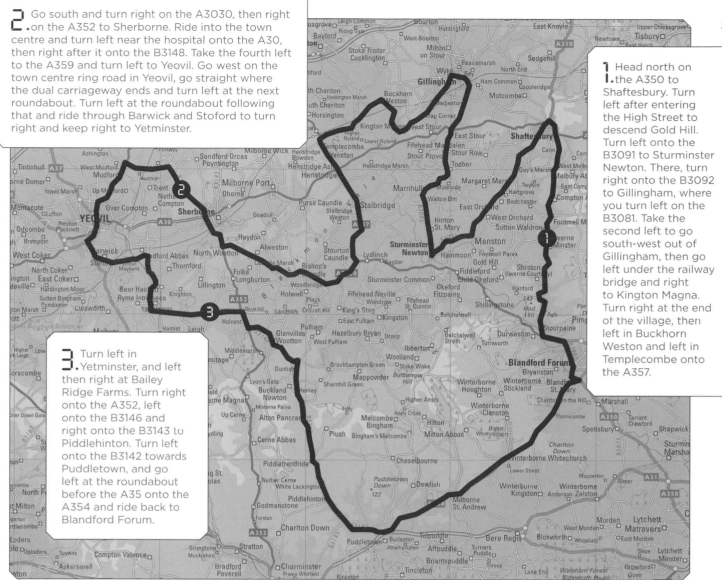

2. Go south and turn right on the A3030, then right on the A352 to Sherborne. Ride into the town centre and turn left near the hospital onto the A30, then right after it onto the B3148. Take the fourth left to the A359 and turn left to Yeovil. Go west on the town centre ring road in Yeovil, go straight where the dual carriageway ends and turn left at the next roundabout. Turn left at the roundabout following that and ride through Barwick and Stoford to turn right and keep right to Yetminster.

1. Head north on the A350 to Shaftesbury. Turn left after entering the High Street to descend Gold Hill. Turn left onto the B3091 to Sturminster Newton. There, turn right onto the B3092 to Gillingham, where you turn left on the B3081. Take the second left to go south-west out of Gillingham, then go left under the railway bridge and right to Kington Magna. Turn right at the end of the village, then left in Buckhorn Weston and left in Templecombe onto the A357.

3. Turn left in Yetminster, and left then right at Bailey Ridge Farms. Turn right onto the A352, left onto the B3146 and right onto the B3143 to Piddlehinton. Turn left onto the B3142 towards Puddletown, and go left at the roundabout before the A35 onto the A354 and ride back to Blandford Forum.

START AND FINISH:
Blandford Forum

GETTING THERE:
Blandford Forum is on the A354, 23 miles south-west of Salisbury. It has no rail links.

BIKE SHOP: Off Camber on Salisbury Street

CAFE: Scruples Coffee House on Barnack Walk

LOCAL DELICACY: Godminster Organic Brie

NEW FOREST

RIDE FACTS

Rating
Medium

Total climbing
750 metres

Killer climb
Longcross Plain

'THE VILLAGES STRETCH OUT TOWARDS EACH OTHER ALONG THE ROUTE AS IF THEY ARE TRYING TO HOLD HANDS'

The New Forest is part natural, part contrived, but as a place for people to visit and enjoy, it really works. It was created by William I as a hunting ground, but it wasn't new, as in newly planted, because there was already a forest here, occupied by an English tribe called the Jutes. William's men evicted them and wiped out their subsistence farming so he could have a place to play. He suffered for it, though, as two of his sons met untimely deaths in the New Forest.

Brockenhurst is one of the New Forest's bigger villages, but is fairly typical of them all. The grass on common land is kept short by New Forest ponies that wander free, and there's a pretty river, a ford and some posh hotels. These include Balmer Lawn, which was an army staff college during the Second World War and had many famous guests, including Winston Churchill and General Dwight D. Eisenhower.

The route goes straight into the forest past several 'inclosures', which are areas exempt from ancient rights of New Forest commoners. There are about 300 commoners today, with rights to graze

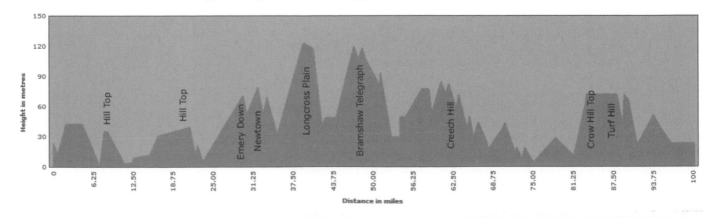

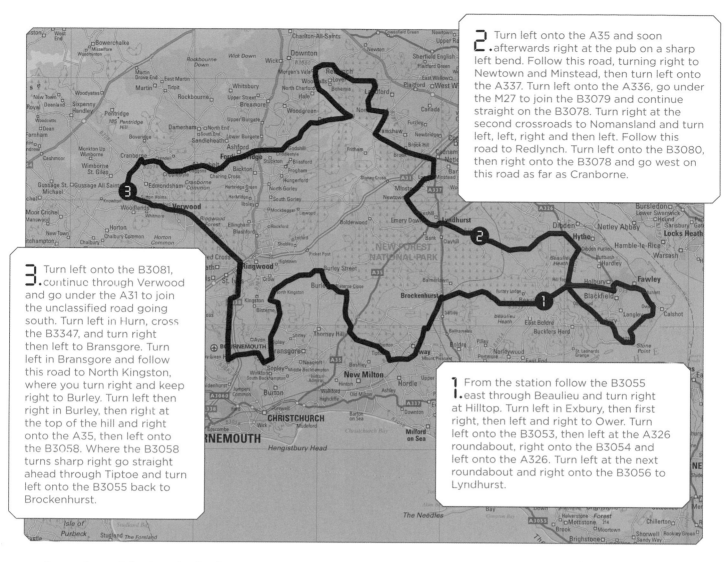

2. Turn left onto the A35 and soon afterwards right at the pub on a sharp left bend. Follow this road, turning right to Newtown and Minstead, then turn left onto the A337. Turn left onto the A336, go under the M27 to join the B3079 and continue straight on the B3078. Turn right at the second crossroads to Nomansland and turn left, left, right and then left. Follow this road to Redlynch. Turn left onto the B3080, then right onto the B3078 and go west on this road as far as Cranborne.

3. Turn left onto the B3081, continue through Verwood and go under the A31 to join the unclassified road going south. Turn left in Hurn, cross the B3347, and turn right then left to Bransgore. Turn left in Bransgore and follow this road to North Kingston, where you turn right and keep right to Burley. Turn left then right in Burley, then right at the top of the hill and right onto the A35, then left onto the B3058. Where the B3058 turns sharp right go straight ahead through Tiptoe and turn left onto the B3055 back to Brockenhurst.

1. From the station follow the B3055 east through Beaulieu and turn right at Hilltop. Turn left in Exbury, then first right, then left and right to Ower. Turn left onto the B3053, then left at the A326 roundabout, right onto the B3054 and left onto the A326. Turn left at the next roundabout and right onto the B3056 to Lyndhurst.

cattle, ponies and donkeys in the forest area, but not inside the inclosures.

You're heading for Beaulieu, home of the National Motor Museum. There's a scent of the sea here, Beaulieu River being tidal, and the next section of the ride heads onto Calshot Spit, where Southampton Water meets the Solent. Calshot was an RAF station used in the development of seaplanes, and today there's a velodrome in one of the hangars.

You return to the heart of the forest at Lyndhurst, then cross the M27 and A31 junction on a flyover. The A31 cuts the forest into north and south, and I've been careful to direct the route over or under it where it crosses, because it gets very busy. The northern half of the forest is more open, with as much heath as trees.

Heading south after a loop through Cranborne and Verwood, the route follows the River Avon downstream to Hurn, and then you cross the river to Bransgore. It was once thought the name came from a gruesome battle fought there, and that

Brans meant brains and gore was, well, gore, as in blood and gore. It's not true, because in Old English gore is a triangle of land. Presumably it was owned by someone call Bran, or Brand maybe.

The next section runs through some lovely lanes to Burley Street and Burley. As you climb out of Burley, the place on your left is Bisterne, where legend has it that a dragon lived. Burley also had a long connection with witches, but good ones. The last white witch of Burley, Sybil Leek, died in 1982. She was an astrologer as much as anything, but with an interest in the occult. She led a very interesting life and wrote several books, including *The Diary of a Witch*. You are quite near the end of the ride now, and quite near the coast; and the villages stretch out towards each other along the route as if they are trying to hold hands. They have some delightful names, too, like Tiptoe, Birchy Hill and Sway, from where you ride alongside the Lymington Flyer railway line back to Brockenhurst.

START AND FINISH:
Brockenhurst

GETTING THERE:
Brockenhurst is eight miles south of Junction 1 of the M27 on the A337. It has a direct rail link with Southampton.

BIKE SHOP: **Cycle Experience on Brookley Road**

CAFE: **The Buttery on Brookley Road**

LOCAL DELICACY:
Chocolate pigs and praline acorns from the Beaulieu Chocolate Studio

SOUTHERN ENGLAND

PORTLAND AND PURBECK

Rating
Medium

Total climbing
1050 metres

Killer climb
Whiteway Hill

This is a ride between two islands but you only cross one stretch of water to do it, and that comes right at the end of the ride. It explores Poole Harbour and the land behind it, Chesil Beach, the Isles of Portland and Purbeck, then ends with a nice little ferry ride. It starts and finishes in Poole, and on the outward and homeward stretches you get a good look at Poole Harbour.

Poole is one of the biggest natural harbours in the world, so big that there are eight islands inside it. The largest of them is Brownsea, on which there's a castle, some cottages and a church. In more warlike days this was an important place to own. The island was even industrialised during the 1850s when the owner exploited the china-clay reserves and built a pottery. The first ever scout camp was held on Brownsea, which continues to have strong connections with the scouting movement.

The route runs around the north end of the harbour to Wareham, from where it begins to climb up a long straight road through what was Dorset heath but is now a conifer plantation. You descend to cross the River Piddle then ride past Bovington Camp and its fascinating tank museum. My favourite is the Renault FT17, not so much va-va-voom as ba-ba-boom.

A section to Dorchester follows, along the River Frome. The ancient town was Thomas Hardy's Casterbridge, and its western end merges with one of Prince

> 'YOU GET GREAT VIEWS NORTH OVER AN AREA OF LAND WHERE GENERATIONS OF TANK COMMANDERS HAVE TRAINED'

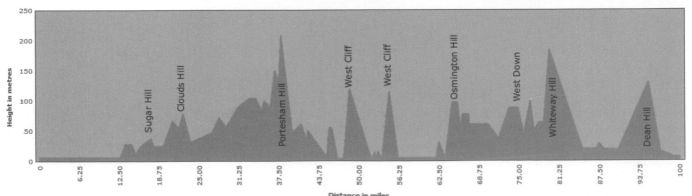

Distance in miles

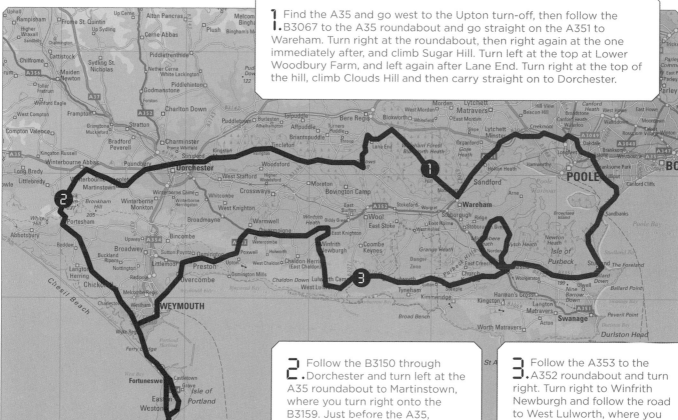

1. Find the A35 and go west to the Upton turn-off, then follow the B3067 to the A35 roundabout and go straight on the A351 to Wareham. Turn right at the roundabout, then right again at the one immediately after, and climb Sugar Hill. Turn left at the top at Lower Woodbury Farm, and left again after Lane End. Turn right at the top of the hill, climb Clouds Hill and then carry straight on to Dorchester.

2. Follow the B3150 through Dorchester and turn left at the A35 roundabout to Martinstown, where you turn right onto the B3159. Just before the A35, turn left to Portesham, where you turn left on to the B3157. Turn right onto the B3156 in Charlestown and go straight on at the roundabout, taking the A354 along Chesil Beach to the Isle of Portland. Turn right at the roundabout at the top of West Cliff and follow this road around the island, using the out-and-back road to visit Portland Bill, and rejoin the A354. Then follow the A354 until the third roundabout, where you turn right onto the A353 through Weymouth.

3. Follow the A353 to the A352 roundabout and turn right. Turn right to Winfrith Newburgh and follow the road to West Lulworth, where you turn left onto the B3070 to East Lulworth. Turn right just before entering East Lulworth and right again to climb Whiteway Hill. Turn right at the top and follow this road to Corfe Castle. There, turn left onto the A351 and then take the second right to do a right-turning loop back to Corfe Castle. Turn left onto the A3351 to Studland and continue on to the Sandbanks ferry. Cross Poole Harbour on the ferry and follow the B3369 back into Poole.

Charles's pet projects, the modern village built on older lines called Poundbury.

The character of the ride changes as the route wriggles between some of Dorset's lovely rounded hills and heads towards the coast. Start looking to your right after Portesham and you will catch glimpses of Chesil Beach. But after riding through Wyke Regis on the edge of Weymouth you get the full effect.

Chesil Beach is incredible; it's an 18-mile ribbon of shingle, an example of a barrier beach, but one that was pushed towards the coast as it formed. The shingle is perfectly sorted, from tennis ball-sized at the south-eastern end, where you cross over to the Isle of Portland, to pea-sized at the other. For part of its length the shingle piles up against the cliffs, but north-west of Weymouth there's a tidal lagoon behind Chesil Beach.

A swift circuit of the Isle of Portland sees the route go around Portland Harbour, where the sheltering effect of Chesil Beach is augmented by man-made barriers. Next comes Weymouth, and then at Furzy Cliff you climb into the Purbeck Hills. The hardest climb of the

ride, Whiteway Hill, comes after Lulworth Camp, and from the top you get great views north over an area of land where generations of tank commanders have trained.

The final part of the ride visits the impressive ruins of Corfe Castle before a circuit of a flat marshy heath where fingers of the sea encroach. Then you take a road that slowly climbs to the top of Dean Hill under the shadow of a taller ridge, before descending to Studland. Keep riding along the spit of land, with Poole Harbour on one side and the English Channel on the other, and you reach the Sandbanks ferry for the short trip back to Poole. You have to pay, but it was only one pound per bike when I did it.

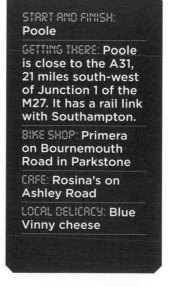

START AND FINISH: **Poole**

GETTING THERE: **Poole is close to the A31, 21 miles south-west of Junction 1 of the M27. It has a rail link with Southampton.**

BIKE SHOP: **Primera on Bournemouth Road in Parkstone**

CAFE: **Rosina's on Ashley Road**

LOCAL DELICACY: **Blue Vinny cheese**

NORTH DOWNS

SOUTH-EAST ENGLAND

RIDE FACTS

Rating
Hard

Total climbing
1500 metres

Killer climb
Leith Hill

The North Downs are the chalk uplands that run from Farnham in Surrey to the White Cliffs of Dover, but this ride focuses on a part of the North Downs that became world famous in cycling in 2012, the Surrey hills. The ride kicks off by going up Box Hill, which was on the Olympic road-race course. Then it stitches west, taking in several of the other Surrey hills before exploring the Downs' border with the Weald, and ends with another couple of classic Surrey hill climbs.

Dorking is right on Box Hill's doorstep. The hill is one side of the Dorking Gap, a space in the North Downs that the A24 and the River Mole thread through. Box Hill is a great climb; wooded, hair-pinned and steep at the bottom, it continues up an open grassy slope that was a grandstand during the Olympics, then it

hits the trees again at the top. Look for the cycling names painted on the road as you climb Box Hill.

A long descent takes you into lower, gently rolling Surrey countryside. The route then heads east to the southern edge of the Surrey hills and the beginning of a series of back-and-forth climbs. The first is the highest, Leith Hill. At 294 metres it's the second highest point in the whole of south-east England and the road climbs to 250 metres. On the way up you pass Leith Place, of which the pottery magnate Josiah Wedgwood and the composer Ralph Vaughan Williams were previous owners. There's a Gothic tower right on the summit of the hill, put there solely so that at the top you are standing at 1000 feet.

After a long descent you climb almost to the top of Leith Hill again, this time

'LOOK FOR THE CYCLING NAMES PAINTED ON THE ROAD AS YOU CLIMB BOX HILL'

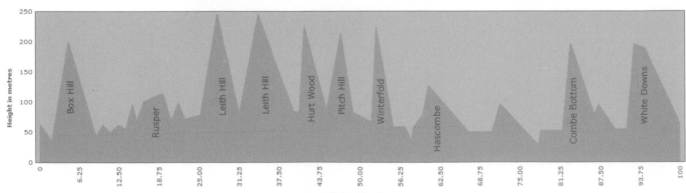

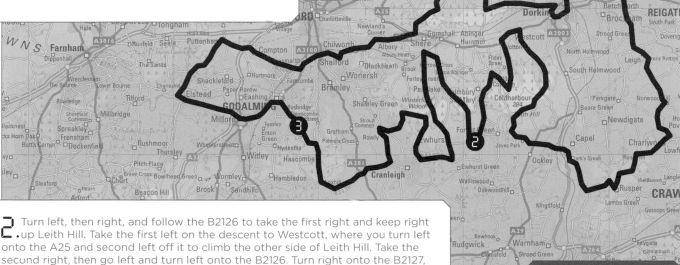

3. Turn right and climb Winterfold. Go left at the summit and keep left to descend to the B2128, where you turn left. Turn right at the roundabout and cross the A281 to join the B2130 to Godalming. Turn left onto the A3100 and keep right to cross the A3 flyover and follow the B3001 through Elstead, where you turn right after crossing the River Wey. Follow this road to Puttenham, and there turn right and right again to follow the B3000 over the A3 to the A3100 roundabout, where you turn left. Turn right at the next roundabout and follow the A248 through Shalford to its junction with the A25. Turn right onto the A25, then left to climb Combe Bottom, then turn right and then left to West Horsley. Turn right at the roundabout then left onto the B2039 and take the right fork in East Horsley to Effingham Junction, where you turn right just after the station and follow this road over the A246 and turn left at the next roundabout to Dorking.

1. Go east on the A25 and turn left at the roundabout onto the A24. Turn right at the second roundabout to climb Box Hill. Follow this road to Pebble Coombe, where you turn right onto the B2032. Cross the A25 roundabout and head south through Betchworth and Leigh to Norwood Hill. Turn right, then left, then turn right twice in Charlwood, then turn left and keep left to Rusper. Turn right, then right again onto the A24 and then turn left to Ockley.

2. Turn left, then right, and follow the B2126 to take the first right and keep right up Leith Hill. Take the first left on the descent to Westcott, where you turn left onto the A25 and second left off it to climb the other side of Leith Hill. Take the second right, then go left and turn left onto the B2126. Turn right onto the B2127, then second right to climb Hurt Wood. Go left in Peaslake, then turn left and right, then left in Burrows Cross. Take the next left to climb Pitch Hill and continue to Ewhurst, from where you follow the B2127 west to Cranleigh.

from the north side. A short descent through Holmbury St Mary leads to the start of the Hurt Wood climb, which has a couple of very steep corners about one quarter way up. There are two more to go in this section of quick-fire climbs: Pitch Hill and Winterfold.

The towns of Ewhurst and Cranleigh lie between the two. Ewhurst is real rock and roll: Eric Clapton lives in the hills just above town, Kenny Jones owns the Hurtwood Polo Park in Horsham Lane, and another resident is Procul Harum founder Gary Brooker.

With Winterfold's steep up and down behind you, the route crosses the Wey and Arun Canal, skirts Dunsfold Airfield, where you may be able to hear Jeremy Clarkson torturing a car for the BBC's *Top Gear*, and heads over a lower bit of the Downs to Godalming.

Charterhouse School is just outside Godalming, and there are three more public schools to the two state secondary schools in town. If TV or film producers want a nice English town they come to Godalming. And that name? It's wonderful, a name that many authors have played with over the years. The River Wey flows through Godalming and the route follows its valley to Elstead before heading north.

The Hog's Back rears up ahead of you here. It's a really impressive narrow ridge that's part of the North Downs and has the A31 running along the top of it. You ride up to its base at Puttenham, then head east for the last two Downs climbs. Combe Bottom is spectacular as it rises steeply away from Shere, a chocolate-boxy village that's another regular film location. The final section to Dorking crosses Ranmore Common before descending past Denbies vineyard.

START AND FINISH:
Dorking

GETTING THERE:
Dorking is on the A24, five miles south of Junction 9 of the M25. It has good rail links with London and the rest of the south-east.

BIKE SHOP: Head for the Hills on West Street

CAFE: The National Trust Cafe on Box Hill is so good it's worth going up the hill again to visit it after doing this ride.

LOCAL DELICACY: Whitedowns Cuvée NV bubbly, made from Denbies grapes grown in the Surrey hills

HIGH WEALD

RIDE FACTS

Rating
Hard

Total climbing
1400 metres

Killer climb
Camp Hill

If you expect the High Weald to be hilly you won't be disappointed. This is a hard ride in tough but beautiful terrain. Very few hills on it surpass the 200-metre mark, but there is almost no flat riding as the ride makes a complete circumnavigation of the High Weald, visiting some of its outstanding beauty spots.

It starts in Royal Tunbridge Wells, a place that earned renown when a chalybeate spring was discovered there in 1606. Chalybeate springs are full of minerals, particularly iron, and in the absence of much other medicine they were claimed to cure lots of diseases. In reality there wasn't much that drinking mineral-rich water could 'cure' but it would have made up for deficiencies and so made people feel better. Rich folk flocked to the wells and Tunbridge Wells hit boom time.

The hills start right outside town. The High Weald is good cycling country, full of quiet, tree-lined lanes, which this ride uses to good effect. You need a good sense of direction to follow it, but if you miss one turn another will be along in a minute.

Just after Penshurst and its vineyard you pass a great off-road cycling centre called PORC (Penshurst Off-Road Cycling). It's worth a separate visit here if you're into mountain biking. The trails are

great, there's a good cafe and, like all the best places, it runs on enthusiasm.

From there the ride threads along the northern edge of the High Weald past three castles, Chiddingstone, Hever and Bolebroke, bound for Forest Row and the Ashdown Forest.

This is Sean Yates country. Yates is a Tour de France stage winner and a yellow jersey who earned a reputation for forcing the pace at the head of the peloton for hour after hour. He was an invaluable asset to the teams he raced for, and he later became one of the world's best team managers. Yates was in the Team Sky car and in constant radio contact with Bradley Wiggins when he won the 2012 Tour de France. And despite the hundreds of thousands of miles he's ridden, Yates still loves bombing around the same High Weald roads that he trained on as a pro.

The hilly, tree-lined, country-lane character continues throughout this ride. Haywards Heath and Crowborough are the only towns on it, other than Tunbridge Wells. Crowborough and its approaches are the hilliest part of the route, with Crowborough Warren being the highest point of the whole High Weald at 248 metres. David Jason was born in Crowborough (sorry, I'm a fan), and so

'THE HIGH WEALD IS GOOD CYCLING COUNTRY, FULL OF QUIET, TREE-LINED LANES'

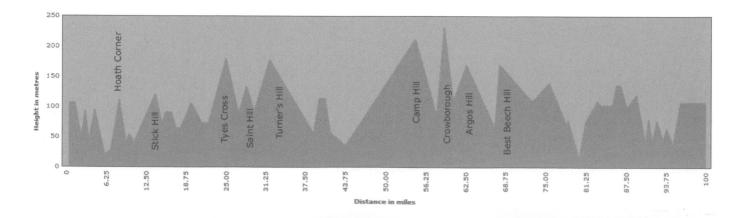

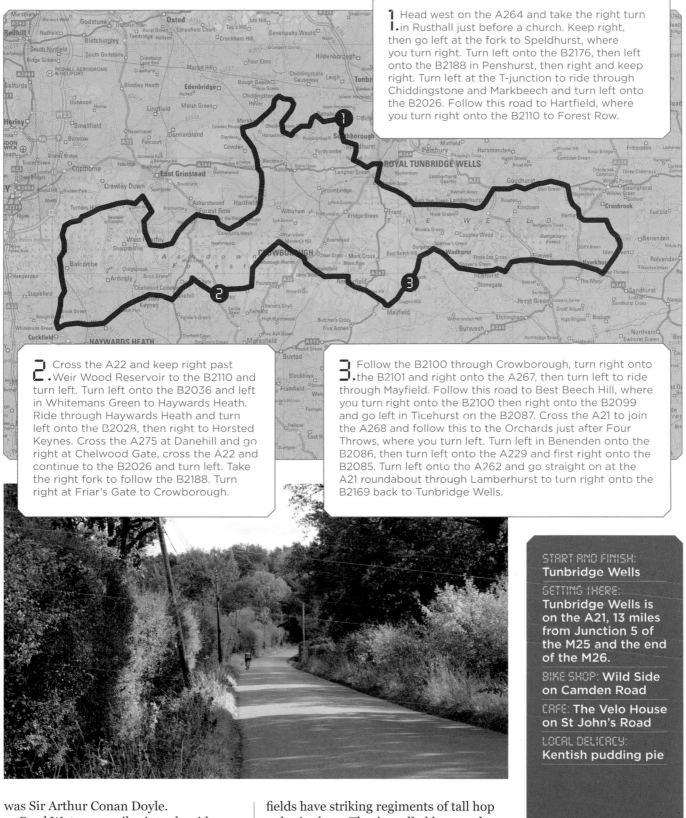

1. Head west on the A264 and take the right turn in Rusthall just before a church. Keep right, then go left at the fork to Speldhurst, where you turn right. Turn left onto the B2176, then left onto the B2188 in Penshurst, then right and keep right. Turn left at the T-junction to ride through Chiddingstone and Markbeech and turn left onto the B2026. Follow this road to Hartfield, where you turn right onto the B2110 to Forest Row.

2. Cross the A22 and keep right past Weir Wood Reservoir to the B2110 and turn left. Turn left onto the B2036 and left in Whitemans Green to Haywards Heath. Ride through Haywards Heath and turn left onto the B2028, then right to Horsted Keynes. Cross the A275 at Danehill and go right at Chelwood Gate, cross the A22 and continue to the B2026 and turn left. Take the right fork to follow the B2188. Turn right at Friar's Gate to Crowborough.

3. Follow the B2100 through Crowborough, turn right onto the B2101 and right onto the A267, then turn left to ride through Mayfield. Follow this road to Best Beech Hill, where you turn right onto the B2100 then right onto the B2099 and go left in Ticehurst on the B2087. Cross the A21 to join the A268 and follow this to the Orchards just after Four Throws, where you turn left. Turn left in Benenden onto the B2086, then turn left onto the A229 and first right onto the B2085. Turn left onto the A262 and go straight on at the A21 roundabout through Lamberhurst to turn right onto the B2169 back to Tunbridge Wells.

START AND FINISH:
Tunbridge Wells

GETTING THERE:
Tunbridge Wells is on the A21, 13 miles from Junction 5 of the M25 and the end of the M26.

BIKE SHOP: **Wild Side on Camden Road**

CAFE: **The Velo House on St John's Road**

LOCAL DELICACY:
Kentish pudding pie

was Sir Arthur Conan Doyle.

Bewl Water, 70 miles into the ride and straddling the border of Sussex and Kent, is an attractive reservoir made by damming the River Bewl. It has a glorious setting in the hills and you can see it almost all of the way along the road to Ticehurst.

Kent is orchard country, and many fields have striking regiments of tall hop poles in them. They're called hop gardens, and Kent is sometimes called the Garden of England. The hops used to be dried in round buildings with conical roofs called oast houses, many of which have been converted into desirable dwellings. You catch glimpses of one or two on the way back into Tunbridge Wells.

EAST KENT

'THIS RIDE IS HEADING FOR AN ICONIC BRITISH LANDMARK'

Starting from ancient and stately Canterbury, this ride visits Kent's north coast and the flatlands behind it. Then it climbs up onto the chalk cliffs and goes through one of the busiest passenger ports in the world before exploring the eastern edges of the North Downs. It's a ride that starts flat and ends hilly, and on one stretch you can see all the way across to France.

The first five miles climb out of Canterbury past the university to Tyler Hill, then trend down to the coast at Whitstable, famous for oysters, Somerset Maugham and the Maunsell sea fort. You might not be able to see the fort, it's nine miles offshore, but it's amazing up close. It was built during the Second World War and it looks like the machines the Martians used in *The War of the Worlds*. Six rusting hulks, each mounted on four stilt-like legs, toothless now but once heavily armed, were built to guard the approach to the Thames. They are a fascinating living-art project today; you can find out more on www.seafort.org.

You turn inland after a short leg along the seafront to Herne Bay, and cross the Great Stour River just east of Canterbury, then follow a spur of higher ground between it and the Little Stour. The Stour valley gets really marshy after the rivers join, but the scenery is fascinating. Look east over Ash Level, which is another place worth discovering some time if you get-chance; but this ride is heading for an iconic British landmark.

You climb over the White Cliffs of Dover after riding through Deal. Then there's a sharp descent to a hairpin bend and a short but steep climb to the Bleriot Memorial, commemorating the first cross-Channel flight in 1909. Lots of modern cross-Channel activity will be going on below, because you are right on top of the Port of Dover. It's busy; not as busy as it was, but it's still fascinating to see the ferries in mid-Channel with France behind them, or to watch the intricate manoeuvres as they dock to disgorge their cargo of vehicles.

The ride out of Dover goes up the Buckland valley onto the Downs, and then changes direction again to head for Folkestone. Look left near the end of the steep descent off the Downs and you might just catch a glimpse of the Channel Tunnel Terminal. The descent ends just over the M20, right next to the Eurostar rail tracks. Then you climb back up onto the Downs.

You are on Stone Street now, a Roman road that connected Canterbury – and one of the main Roman transport arteries in Britain, Watling Street – with Romney Marsh. The road goes straight, but you turn off to follow a lovely road that runs along a fold in the Downs to Bishopbourne, where you head back to the Roman road. The last section does a loop to the east of Canterbury, on which there's a beautiful flint church in Patrixbourne and the largest captive colony of gorillas in the world at the Howletts Wild Animal Park in Bekesbourne.

Height in metres

Tyler Hill · South Foreland · Dover Castle · Whitfield · Coldred Hill · Chapel Hill · Lyminge Hill · Cobb's Hill · Gorsley Wood · Petham Hill

Distance in miles

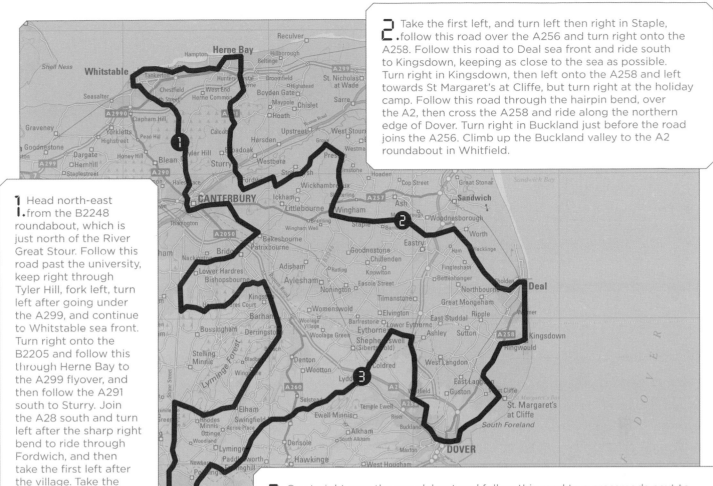

2. Take the first left, and turn left then right in Staple, follow this road over the A256 and turn right onto the A258. Follow this road to Deal sea front and ride south to Kingsdown, keeping as close to the sea as possible. Turn right in Kingsdown, then left onto the A258 and left towards St Margaret's at Cliffe, but turn right at the holiday camp. Follow this road through the hairpin bend, over the A2, then cross the A258 and ride along the northern edge of Dover. Turn right in Buckland just before the road joins the A256. Climb up the Buckland valley to the A2 roundabout in Whitfield.

1. Head north-east from the B2248 roundabout, which is just north of the River Great Stour. Follow this road past the university, keep right through Tyler Hill, fork left, turn left after going under the A299, and continue to Whitstable sea front. Turn right onto the B2205 and follow this through Herne Bay to the A299 flyover, and then follow the A291 south to Sturry. Join the A28 south and turn left after the sharp right bend to ride through Fordwich, and then take the first left after the village. Take the first right, then first left, then the second right and turn left in Frognall. Follow this road to Grove, where you turn right, then right again through Preston. Turn right onto the A257, and where that turns sharp right in Wingham join the B2046.

3. Go straight over the roundabout and follow this road to a crossroads next to the A256 and turn left to Eythorne. Turn left at the roundabout, then cross the A2 at the staggered junction, taking great care. Go through Lydden, then turn right then left. Follow this road over the A260 and turn left at Acrise Place to Etchinghill, where you turn right. Turn left at the crossroads, then join the A20. Follow the A20 to Junction 11 of the M20 and go straight on to the B2068, which is the third exit. Follow the B2068 north to Sixmile, and turn right. Go straight ahead at the crossroads, turn left, then keep right to Elham, where you turn left. Follow this road until a left sign to Kingston and take the first left after the village. Go left in Bishopsbourne and keep right to Upper Hardres Court, where you turn left. Turn right onto the B2068, then go right to Bridge and follow this road over the A2 to Patrixbourne, and turn left. Turn left after going under the railway, then turn left on the A257 back to Canterbury.

START AND FINISH:
Canterbury

GETTING THERE:
Canterbury is just off the A2, seven miles east of Junction 7 of the M2. It has direct rail links with London.

BIKE SHOP: Downland Cycles on St Stephens Road

CAFE: Julie's Cafe on North Lane

LOCAL DELICACY:
Whitstable oysters

SOUTH-EAST ENGLAND

SOUTH DOWNS

RIDE FACTS

Rating
Hard

Total climbing
1500 metres

Killer climb
Duncton Down

The South Downs are a chain of chalk hills that rise just east of Winchester and plough into the sea like the bow of a big white ship at Beachy Head near Eastbourne. Long and relatively thin, they lie south of the Low Weald, so this South Downs 100 has a bit of Low Weald in it, and the Low Weald 100 will include a bit of the South Downs.

You start in Billingshurst, which just to confuse things is in the Low Weald, but I chose this because riding towards the South Downs from the north is the best way to get a feel for them. They are an impressive sight, looking like a solid wall topped by undulating, round, green hills covered with short-cropped grassland.

The road south from Billingshurst is the Romans' Stane Street. It ran from London to Chichester straight over the North and South Downs, which long before the Romans came were one single dome of chalk. Erosion has now revealed the underlying clays of the High and Low Weald.

The route goes right at Pulborough, then climbs Duncton Down, which is impressive. The climb drags at first towards a steep wooded slope, then climbs it after a sharp right hairpin. It's steep and you're in among trees until a clearance on your right. It's worth stopping for a moment here, not just to get your breath back but for the view across the River Rother to Petworth Park.

The next section runs east just below the tops of the Downs on their south side. Then it heads south past Goodwood Racecourse and through Goodwood Park. When Britain hosted the world road-cycling championships for a second time, they were held here. It was in 1982 and

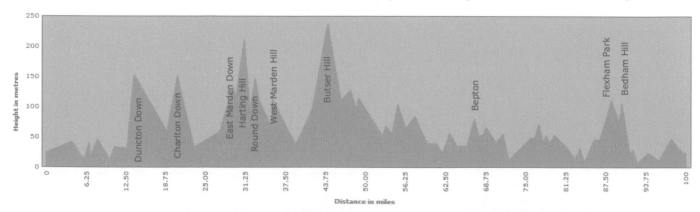

Height in metres

Duncton Down · Charlton Down · East Marden Down · Harting Hill · Round Down · West Marden Hill · Butser Hill · Bepton · Flexham Park · Bedham Hill

Distance in miles

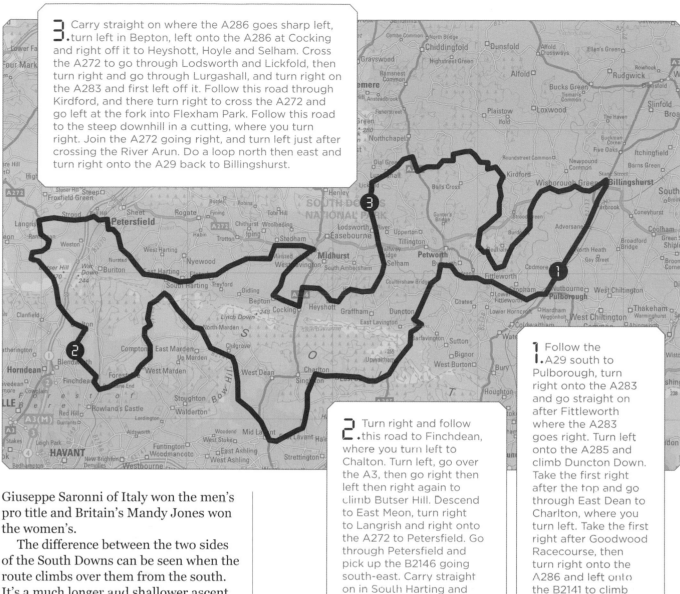

3. Carry straight on where the A286 goes sharp left, turn left in Bepton, left onto the A286 at Cocking and right off it to Heyshott, Hoyle and Selham. Cross the A272 to go through Lodsworth and Lickfold, then turn right and go through Lurgashall, and turn right on the A283 and first left off it. Follow this road through Kirdford, and there turn right to cross the A272 and go left at the fork into Flexham Park. Follow this road to the steep downhill in a cutting, where you turn right. Join the A272 going right, and turn left just after crossing the River Arun. Do a loop north then east and turn right onto the A29 back to Billingshurst.

2. Turn right and follow this road to Finchdean, where you turn left to Chalton. Turn left, go over the A3, then go right then left then right again to climb Butser Hill. Descend to East Meon, turn right to Langrish and right onto the A272 to Petersfield. Go through Petersfield and pick up the B2146 going south-east. Carry straight on in South Harting and follow this road to the A272, where you turn right. Turn right onto the A286 in Midhurst.

1. Follow the A29 south to Pulborough, turn right onto the A283 and go straight on after Fittleworth where the A283 goes right. Turn left onto the A285 and climb Duncton Down. Take the first right after the top and go through East Dean to Charlton, where you turn left. Take the first right after Goodwood Racecourse, then turn right onto the A286 and left onto the B2141 to climb Harting Hill. Turn left on the descent and climb Tower Hill to West Marden.

Giuseppe Saronni of Italy won the men's pro title and Britain's Mandy Jones won the women's.

The difference between the two sides of the South Downs can be seen when the route climbs over them from the south. It's a much longer and shallower ascent than any northern one. Just to emphasise the difference, you ride down a sharp descent that ends halfway up the north side of Harting Hill. Then you almost do a double back to climb the top half of Tower Hill.

This is becoming a good workout. From Finchdean, again on the south side, there's a long climb almost to the top of Butser Hill. At 271 metres this is the highest point of the South Downs. There is an annual running race up and down Butser Hill, and it's a great hang-gliding venue. The famous hang-gliding scene in *Only Fools and Horses* was filmed here.

You leave the hills for a while at Langrish to explore the River Rother and the lovely villages in its valley. The route then ambles eastwards, dipping into the lower hills either side of the Rother, before following the River Arun north back to Billingshurst.

'THE SOUTH DOWNS ARE A CHAIN OF CHALK HILLS THAT PLOUGH INTO THE SEA LIKE THE BOW OF A BIG WHITE SHIP'

START AND FINISH: Billingshurst

GETTING THERE: Billingshurst is on the A29, 15 miles south of Dorking. It has a rail link with Horsham and then other south-east and London stations.

BIKE SHOP: Southwater Cycles in the Loxwood area of town

CAFE: Burdfields Country Market on the High Street

LOCAL DELICACY: Truffles (I kid you not, they have been found here but are very rare, and you need a dog or a pig to find them)

LOW WEALD

The Weald is the low-lying land between the North and South Downs. It divides into two areas with the Low Weald encircling the High Weald. The southern part of the Low Weald is slightly wider that the rest of it, so this ride goes around that section with a quick look at the Pevensey Levels and two 'must see' bits of the South Downs.

The ride starts in Uckfield, the town where Lord Lucan went missing, and heads east through a succession of woods. All the Weald was wooded once; Weald is a derivation of Wald, the German word for wood, which flags that the area was a Saxon settlement.

Saxon names and wood references are repeated throughout the ride. Herstmonceux, for example, comes from the Saxon word hyrst, meaning wooded hill. It's where you enter the Pevensey Levels, a plain formed just after the Ice Age. Sea levels were much higher when the ice melted and the Pevensey area became a tidal estuary. It dried out as the sea levels fell, and today it's a flat area of land with a number of rivers flowing through it. The Pevensey Levels are where the Norman invasion of England began in 1066.

The next section of the ride does a loop around Eastbourne to visit somewhere that is truly spectacular. The ride to Beachy Head is pretty good. You cross the Cuckmere River in Hailsham and ride along its valley for a while. This is the river that nearly every geography textbook features to explain oxbow lakes. It's the perfect example of a mature, meandering river.

The route climbs steeply away from the Cuckmere up South Hill, and from there it follows the last bit of the South Downs to Beachy Head. It's at the eastern end of the chalk-cliff formation called the Seven Sisters. Beachy Head is 162 metres high and a jaw-dropping sight. It's familiar from films and television, but the cliff is also a notorious suicide spot.

The view is mesmerising, but it's time to press on. Heading north you leave the Downs, then ride along the line where they meet the Low Weald to visit one of British cycling's famous hills. Ditchling

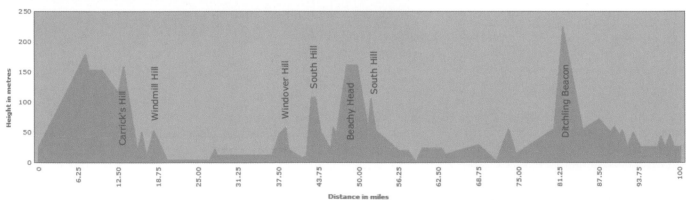

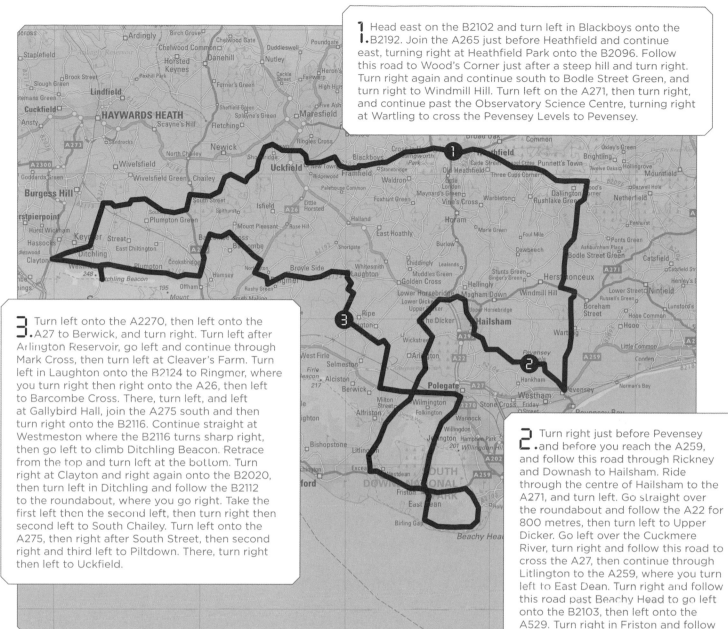

1. Head east on the B2102 and turn left in Blackboys onto the B2192. Join the A265 just before Heathfield and continue east, turning right at Heathfield Park onto the B2096. Follow this road to Wood's Corner just after a steep hill and turn right. Turn right again and continue south to Bodle Street Green, and turn right to Windmill Hill. Turn left on the A271, then turn right, and continue past the Observatory Science Centre, turning right at Wartling to cross the Pevensey Levels to Pevensey.

3. Turn left onto the A2270, then left onto the A27 to Berwick, and turn right. Turn left after Arlington Reservoir, go left and continue through Mark Cross, then turn left at Cleaver's Farm. Turn left in Laughton onto the B2124 to Ringmer, where you turn right then right onto the A26, then left to Barcombe Cross. There, turn left, and left at Gallybird Hall, join the A275 south and then turn right onto the B2116. Continue straight at Westmeston where the B2116 turns sharp right, then go left to climb Ditchling Beacon. Retrace from the top and turn left at the bottom. Turn right at Clayton and right again onto the B2020, then turn left in Ditchling and follow the B2112 to the roundabout, where you go right. Take the first left then the second left, then turn right then second left to South Chailey. Turn left onto the A275, then right after South Street, then second right and third left to Piltdown. There, turn right then left to Uckfield.

2. Turn right just before Pevensey and before you reach the A259, and follow this road through Rickney and Downash to Hailsham. Ride through the centre of Hailsham to the A271, and turn left. Go straight over the roundabout and follow the A22 for 800 metres, then turn left to Upper Dicker. Go left over the Cuckmere River, turn right and follow this road to cross the A27, then continue through Litlington to the A259, where you turn left to East Dean. Turn right and follow this road past Beachy Head to go left onto the B2103, then left onto the A529. Turn right in Friston and follow this road to Polegate.

Beacon was climbed in the Wincanton Grand Prix world cup races, and on stage six of the 1994 Tour de France, which finished in Brighton. Some of the best racers in the world have ridden up this hill, so I couldn't have you come here and not do it too. All the same, just ride to the top and ride back down, because any more time spent on the South Downs and this won't be a Low Weald ride.

The final section tops up the Low Weald's mileage with countryside that is typical of it. Lots of picturesque villages, woods, fields and copses make this one of those places that's as understated as the English character. However, like so many similar places, it still has stories to tell. Some are stories of success, while others are about human folly, like the Piltdown Man.

You ride through Piltdown just before returning to Uckfield. This is where Charles Dawson claimed in 1912 to have found skull and jaw fragments that belonged to a hominid missing link between apes and humans. Piltdown Man became famous, the fragments were exhibited in the British Museum and they were used to create drawings of what our ancestors looked like. It was 1953 before the hoax was revealed. The jaw fragments were only about 500 years old and from an orangutan, and the skull was a human one of medieval age into which fossilised chimpanzee teeth had been placed. The whole thing had been made to look older by staining with an iron solution and chromic acid.

START AND FINISH:
Uckfield

GETTING THERE:
Uckfield is on the A26, 13 miles south-west of Tunbridge Wells. It has a direct rail link with London.

BIKE SHOP: **In Gear on the High Street**

CAFE: **The Courtyard Coffee Shop**

LOCAL DELICACY:
Smoked ham from the Weald Smokery

ROMNEY MARSH

RIDE FACTS

Rating
Medium

Total climbing
720 metres

Killer climb
Lympne Hill

'IT'S AN ENCHANTING, HAUNTING PLACE. IT'S ALSO A GREAT PLACE TO RIDE A BIKE'

Romney Marsh is the collective name given to a group of marshes located behind the Kent and East Sussex coast. It has a distinctive look and an interesting history. This includes acting as a haven for smugglers, supporting a fishing industry and playing a crucial role in defending Britain in two world wars and in several earlier conflicts. Romney's history is also one of lost communities and battles with the sea. It's an enchanting, haunting place with many literary connections. It's also a great place to ride a bike.

There are no hills on the marsh part, but this ride visits some of the lower bits of the Downs and it crosses an inland island. It starts in Folkestone, the 'other' Channel port, and heads along the sea front to Hyde then Dymchurch. Have a look at the sea wall, because it's where the term Scott-free comes from. Back in the 1500s a tax called the Marsh Scotts was levelled through much of the marshes to maintain the Dymchurch sea wall, so all those living on the marsh borders were said to be living Scott-free.

This coast has always been heavily defended, and you can still see structures built during the First and Second World Wars, and some others called Martello Towers that date back to the Napoleonic Wars. There's a good example of a Martello Tower on the front in Dymchurch. You catch a glimpse just before the route turns inland.

The marsh section to New Romney is full of streams and ditches. It's not hard to

see why malaria was once a problem here. This is almost as far south as you can go in the UK; the summers are usually warm and the continent is just over the Channel.

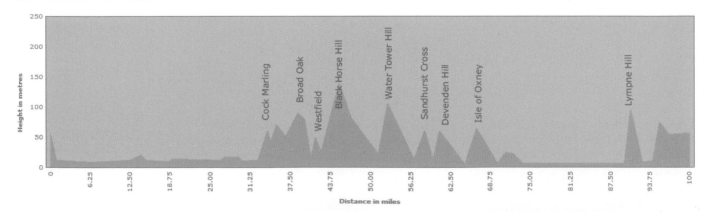

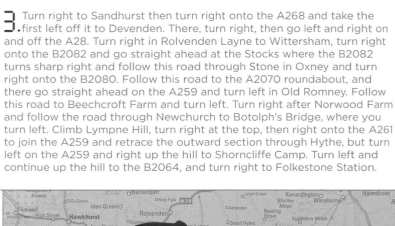

3. Turn right to Sandhurst then turn right onto the A268 and take the first left off it to Devenden. There, turn right, then go left and right on and off the A28. Turn right in Rolvenden Layne to Wittersham, turn right onto the B2082 and go straight ahead at the Stocks where the B2082 turns sharp right and follow this road through Stone in Oxney and turn right onto the B2080. Follow this road to the A2070 roundabout, and there go straight ahead on the A259 and turn left in Old Romney. Follow this road to Beechcroft Farm and turn left. Turn right after Norwood Farm and follow the road through Newchurch to Botolph's Bridge, where you turn left. Climb Lympne Hill, turn right at the top, then right onto the A261 to join the A259 and retrace the outward section through Hythe, but turn left on the A259 and right up the hill to Shorncliffe Camp. Turn left and continue up the hill to the B2064, and turn right to Folkestone Station.

1. Start near the railway station and descend to the sea-front. Turn right onto the A259, then take the Hythe sea-front road. Turn right in Hythe and left onto the A259. Turn right in Pennypot and follow this road to Dymchurch. Turn right in Dymchurch, then first left, then left to New Romney. Turn right onto the A259 and left onto the B2071, then go right at the sea front and follow this road through Lydd-on-Sea. Turn right, then turn left in Lydd onto the B2075. Follow this road through Camber to Rye.

2. Stay just north of the town centre and turn right on the B2089 to Broad Oak, where you turn left on the A28 to Hastings. Turn right on entering Hastings on the A2100 to Battle. The site of the Battle of Hastings is on your left between the B2204 and the abbey. Turn right at the roundabout on the A2100 and take the last right going out of Battle then turn left. Turn right after Whatlington, cross the A21 and turn left on the B2244. Turn right on the B2165 at Cripp's Corner, and in Staplecross where the B2165 turns sharp right continue straight to Bodiam.

People died of the disease here right up until 1806, when drainage was improved dramatically by the Royal Military Canal and the mosquito's habitat was restricted.

The next leg follows the coast towards Dungeness and onto the massive shingle of Denge Beach. Look out for some huge concrete structures after Greatstone; they are sound mirrors placed there in 1920 to detect the early approach of aircraft to Lydd airport. The beach has fresh and saltwater environments, and is home to an incredible diversity of plants and to significant numbers of coastal birds.

You leave the marsh at Rye, a charming town on the confluence of three rivers. It was an important place, part of the Cinque Ports confederation that played a key defensive role, but a lot of smuggled goods also passed through here. Rye is an arty place today, and it has played a key role

in literature. It's a gateway to the sea, but it's also a gateway to some hillier country behind it. That's where this ride goes next.

You ride along a ridge, cross the Brede Valley and skirt around Hastings then over Blackhorse Hill to the site of the 1066 battle and the town named after it. The abbey you pass on entering Battle was founded in 1095 to commemorate the beginning of Norman England. The high altar is said to be on the exact spot where the English King Harold died.

The route continues undulating north to Sandhurst – not the military academy one though, which is in Berkshire. Then it heads over the Isle of Oxney and back across Romney Marsh to climb Lympne Hill. This takes you up onto the Downs just outside Folkestone, where you have one more hill to climb through the town streets before the end of the ride.

START AND FINISH:
Folkestone

GETTING THERE:
Folkstone is right at the end of the M20 and has a direct rail link with London.

BIKE SHOP: **ACTiV Cycles on Sandgate Road**

CAFE: **The Hub on the High Street in Sandgate, which is one mile west of Folkestone and on this ride route. The Hub is also a bike shop.**

LOCAL DELICACY: **Samphire**

SOUTH-EAST ENGLAND

SOUT
WES
ENGL

SOUTH COTSWOLDS

Rating
Medium

Total climbing
1150 metres

Killer climb
Swift's Hill

This ride around the southern half of the Cotswolds starts in an ancient Roman city, looks at the Wiltshire Downs, then grapples with the Cotswold Edge, while playing hide and seek with the infant River Thames. Also, it clearly shows the contrast between the steep western edge and the shallower dip slopes of the eastern side of the Cotswolds.

Cirencester was Corinium to the Romans, and there's lots of evidence of their occupation in and around the town. The first section of the ride runs north-east along a ridge that is cut by streams and rivers, notably the Colne in Bibury.

The ridge runs to Burford, where the route changes direction, going south down a steep descent to enter the upper Thames valley at Lechlade-on-Thames. The river is navigable as far as here, and it's where David Walliams began his 140-mile Thames Sport Relief swim to Westminster in August 2011.

You ride past a section of the Cotswold Water Park, which has 147 separate lakes and covers 40 square miles in total. Then the route loops south past RAF Fairford, once host to USAF B-52s and stealth bombers, as well as being the only Space Shuttle abort runway in the UK. You pass

'THE TOWN SCRAMBLES UP THE HILLSIDES IN LAYERS LIKE THE TIERS OF A WEDDING CAKE'

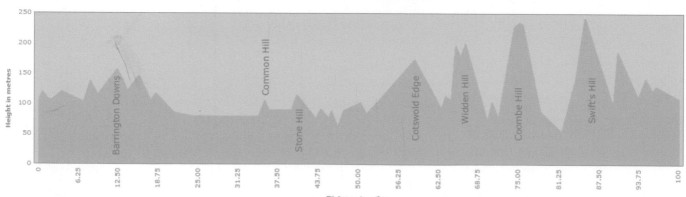

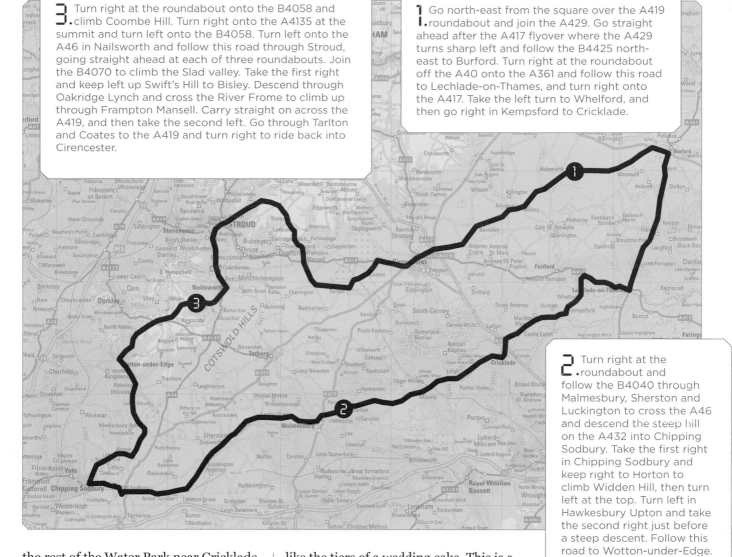

3. Turn right at the roundabout onto the B4058 and climb Coombe Hill. Turn right onto the A4135 at the summit and turn left onto the B4058. Turn left onto the A46 in Nailsworth and follow this road through Stroud, going straight ahead at each of three roundabouts. Join the B4070 to climb the Slad valley. Take the first right and keep left up Swift's Hill to Bisley. Descend through Oakridge Lynch and cross the River Frome to climb up through Frampton Mansell. Carry straight on across the A419, and then take the second left. Go through Tarlton and Coates to the A419 and turn right to ride back into Cirencester.

1. Go north-east from the square over the A419 roundabout and join the A429. Go straight ahead after the A417 flyover where the A429 turns sharp left and follow the B4425 north-east to Burford. Turn right at the roundabout off the A40 onto the A361 and follow this road to Lechlade-on-Thames, and turn right onto the A417. Take the left turn to Whelford, and then go right in Kempsford to Cricklade.

2. Turn right at the roundabout and follow the B4040 through Malmesbury, Sherston and Luckington to cross the A46 and descend the steep hill on the A432 into Chipping Sodbury. Take the first right in Chipping Sodbury and keep right to Horton to climb Widden Hill, then turn left at the top. Turn left in Hawkesbury Upton and take the second right just before a steep descent. Follow this road to Wotton-under-Edge.

the rest of the Water Park near Cricklade, where the route gets hilly again.

You are in Wiltshire now and the road undulates up through Malmesbury, then climbs back into Gloucestershire past Badminton, of Horse Trials fame, to the top of the Cotswold Edge. A steep descent takes you to Chipping Sodbury, where the route swings north. The various 'Chippings' in the Cotswolds come from the Old English word cepping, meaning market.

The hills get serious now. Widden Hill is tough, but Coombe Hill is harder. You climb from 73 metres in Wotton-under-Edge to 195 metres in two sinuous kilometres, so an average of 6 per cent. Then there's a long drag to the summit at 247 metres. There's also a long descent to Nailsworth, before what I think is one of the best bits of this ride.

Stroud is built up the steep sides of the valley of the River Frome, and the town scrambles up the hillsides in layers,

like the tiers of a wedding cake. This is a literary town, with many famous authors having lived or been born here. My favourite is the Reverend W. Awdry, who was vicar of Rodborough and the creator of the *Thomas the Tank Engine* children's books. The route passes his church just before starting its climb out of Stroud. Laurie Lee is another Stroud man.

The killer climb, Swift's Hill, comes soon after Stroud and lifts you out of the Slad valley, which is where Laurie Lee grew up. This is another winding climb that is quite spectacular. It has two very steep sections after two corners, one at a quarter of a mile up and the other exactly one mile into the climb.

There's a descent through Bisley, which ends in a very steep down and up into and out of the Frome valley, then the route trends downhill back to Cirencester. You pass the site of a Roman amphitheatre on your left as you enter the town, where the ride finishes in the square.

START AND FINISH:
Cirencester

GETTING THERE:
Cirencester is 14 miles north-west of Swindon on the A419. The nearest rail stations are in Stroud and Swindon.

BIKE SHOP:
Independent Bikeworks in Brewery Court

CAFE: Jack's Cafe right next to the museum

LOCAL DELICACY:
Chestnut soup

FOREST OF DEAN

RIDE FACTS

Rating
Hard

Total climbing
2000 metres

Killer climb
Hart Hill

The Forest of Dean is a beauty and a beast. It is an ancient wood with many secrets, both old and new, but its sylvan glades are draped over some very hilly terrain. That makes cycling hard here, but it brings rewards, and not just the satisfaction and glow of crossing hard terrain using your own power. The highest hills are clear of trees in places, so you see the forest undulating away all around you, and in the west there are views of the Welsh mountains.

The Forest is a leafy bridge between England and Wales. It lies west of the River Severn and east of the Welsh border. The ride has three main sections. The first is flatter and heads down the Severn. Then it visits the spectacular Wye valley, saving an exploration of the Forest for the final 50 hilly miles.

It starts in Cinderford, a former coal-mining town with terraced streets laid out as if they are in the Welsh Valleys. There has been a lot of industry in the Forest of Dean for a long time. Charcoal was made here even before the Romans came, and they had the locals mine coal for them and smelt iron. Iron and coal production grew here during the Industrial Revolution, and in later times steel was produced in the Forest. That has all gone now, but there are several interesting heritage sites that help support tourism here. A number of high-tech companies are also based in the 21st-century Forest.

The main purpose of the opening River Severn section is to ride across the old Severn Bridge. Every cyclist should do it, because the cycle path next to the road platform is high and spectacular. Just ride over, then head back to Chepstow, where you cross the River Wye by the old bridge near the castle.

The Wye valley is gorgeous. Winding, steep-sided and stacked with trees, it's a deferred pleasure for the moment as you climb Hart Hill towards St Brievels in order to make the best entrance, which as with any valley is from above.

You cross the Wye by Brockweir Bridge, with the spectacular Tintern Abbey in the valley bottom on your left. The route runs towards it, then climbs away in order to ride along the valley but above it for a short while, because it's just a better way to see it. You join the main valley road later to skirt Monmouth and begin your

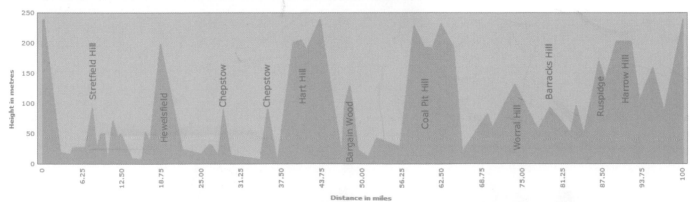

Height in metres

Stretfield Hill
Hewelsfield
Chepstow
Chepstow
Hart Hill
Bargain Wood
Coal Pit Hill
Worral Hill
Barracks Hill
Ruspidge
Harrow Hill

Distance in miles

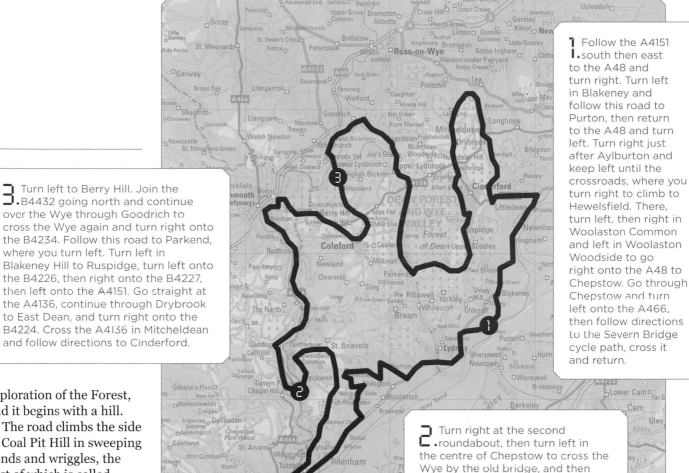

1. Follow the A4151 south then east to the A48 and turn right. Turn left in Blakeney and follow this road to Purton, then return to the A48 and turn left. Turn right just after Aylburton and keep left until the crossroads, where you turn right to climb to Hewelsfield. There, turn left, then right in Woolaston Common and left in Woolaston Woodside to go right onto the A48 to Chepstow. Go through Chepstow and turn left onto the A466, then follow directions to the Severn Bridge cycle path, cross it and return.

3. Turn left to Berry Hill. Join the B4432 going north and continue over the Wye through Goodrich to cross the Wye again and turn right onto the B4234. Follow this road to Parkend, where you turn left. Turn left in Blakeney Hill to Ruspidge, turn left onto the B4226, then right onto the B4227, then left onto the A4151. Go straight at the A4136, continue through Drybrook to East Dean, and turn right onto the B4224. Cross the A4136 in Mitcheldean and follow directions to Cinderford.

2. Turn right at the second roundabout, then turn left in the centre of Chepstow to cross the Wye by the old bridge, and then turn left onto the B4228 in Tutshill. Follow this road to Coldharbour, turn left and descend to Brockweir. Turn left onto the A466, then right next to the hotel and follow this road to a T-junction, where you turn right down a steep hill to turn left onto the A466. Follow this road to Monmouth, turn right onto the A4136 and then right onto the B4228 to Coleford.

exploration of the Forest, and it begins with a hill.

The road climbs the side of Coal Pit Hill in sweeping bends and wriggles, the first of which is called the Fiddlers Elbow. The Forest's second big town, Coleford, comes next, then Berry Hill, before a long descent back to the Wye opposite Symonds Yat for two crossings of the Wye where it makes a huge sweep across a suddenly wider valley bottom. Then there's another climb into the trees.

This is Worral Hill, which takes you through Lower and Upper Lydbrook and on into the thickest part of the Forest. There are abandoned mines here, and you might notice the road verges have been rooted up in many places by wild boar. You leave this straight road in Parkend, and I've saved the best till last.

The final leg rides one of the most beautiful roads I've seen. It winds along tiny, steep-sided stream valleys, then explores the hills around Cinderford. It's a world of its own, a world sealed from outside by the forest, so you only hear the sounds of water, birdsong and the rhythmic swish of a cyclist's tyres.

'IT'S A WORLD OF ITS OWN, A WORLD SEALED FROM OUTSIDE BY THE FOREST'

START AND FINISH: Cinderford

GETTING THERE: Cinderford is just west of the A48, 11 miles west of Gloucester and 17 miles north-east of Chepstow and the end of the old Severn Bridge.

BIKE SHOP: Winner Bikes on Forest Vale Road

CAFE: Sadie's Cafe on the High Street

LOCAL DELICACY: Elvers from the River Wye

BATH AND THE MENDIPS

RIDE FACTS

Rating
Hard

Total climbing
1400 metres

Killer climb
Cheddar Gorge

'HUGE CLIFFS TOWER ABOVE YOU, AND THE ROAD WRIGGLES AND SQUEEZES UPWARDS BETWEEN THEM'

T he Mendips are a steep-sided limestone block with an undulating top that stretches from its widest part near Frome in Wiltshire, south of Bath and Bristol, to a narrow point at the Bristol Channel just south of Weston-super-Mare. This ride explores how the character of the Mendips changes from east to west, and it climbs one of the most famous hills in Britain.

It starts in historic Bath. Founded by the Romans, made famous, or notorious, during Regency times, Bath looks a bit faded now but the bone structure of a great city is still there. The Mendips are on its doorstep, and once you've climbed the two and a half miles from the centre to Odd Down you are in them.

The route heads for Frome, home of the Cobble Wobble. This is a time-trial bike race held each year on the town's cobbled Catherine's Hill, where serious and not so serious competitors take part. Fancy dress is a regular option, so why not have a go? It's usually held in September.

You visit Chewton Mendip next, then descend to Chew Valley Lake, one of several reservoirs on the north side of the Mendips serving Bristol. This is huge, though, the fifth biggest artificial lake in the country. You ride across the dam and climb Felton Hill past Bristol Airport, before descending to the base of the Mendips.

The next climb uses a feature that has made the Mendips famous. The limestone block is cut into by several steep-sided valleys, and one whose sides are vertical.

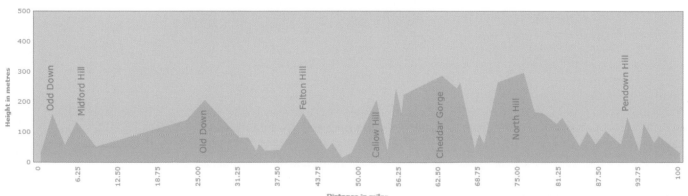

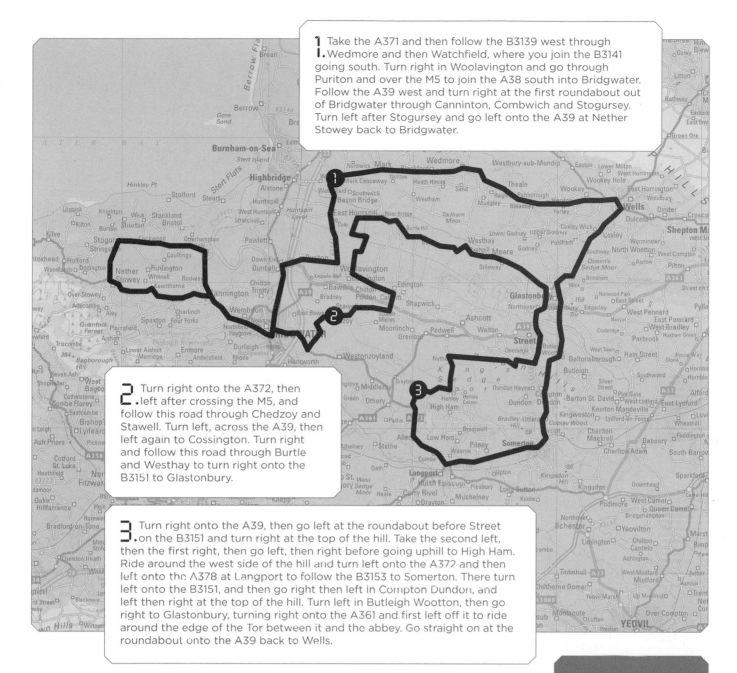

1. Take the A371 and then follow the B3139 west through Wedmore and then Watchfield, where you join the B3141 going south. Turn right in Woolavington and go through Puriton and over the M5 to join the A38 south into Bridgwater. Follow the A39 west and turn right at the first roundabout out of Bridgwater through Canninton, Combwich and Stogursey. Turn left after Stogursey and go left onto the A39 at Nether Stowey back to Bridgwater.

2. Turn right onto the A372, then left after crossing the M5, and follow this road through Chedzoy and Stawell. Turn left, across the A39, then left again to Cossington. Turn right and follow this road through Burtle and Westhay to turn right onto the B3151 to Glastonbury.

3. Turn right onto the A39, then go left at the roundabout before Street on the B3151 and turn right at the top of the hill. Take the second left, then the first right, then go left, then right before going uphill to High Ham. Ride around the west side of the hill and turn left onto the A372 and then left onto the A378 at Langport to follow the B3153 to Somerton. There turn left onto the B3151, and then go right then left in Compton Dundon, and left then right at the top of the hill. Turn left in Butleigh Wootton, then go right to Glastonbury, turning right onto the A361 and first left off it to ride around the edge of the Tor between it and the abbey. Go straight on at the roundabout onto the A39 back to Wells.

edge of the Quantock Hills for some glimpses of the sea and the nuclear power station at Hinckley Point, and then returns through Bridgwater and back onto the levels. You ride over another raft of low hills, then wander through a string of quiet villages towards Glastonbury, a place that looks all the more magical if you approach it from this direction.

Glastonbury Tor is a conical hill with a church on it that you can see for miles; add in a bit of mist or low cloud and it gains an ethereal air. Legend has it that this is Avalon of King Arthur fame, and that Joseph of Arimathea, washed across the levels towards Glastonbury by a flood, stuck his staff into the ground here and a holy thorn bush grew. There are many

more mystical legends, and Glastonbury is a centre of New Age culture today. Their alternative-style shops certainly liven up the town centre. The Glastonbury Festival is held near Pilton, on the other side of town.

You skirt the town, then head south for another level loop, this time around King's Sedge Moor, before riding back to Glastonbury over a sharp ridge called Collard Hill. The route goes through the centre of town, from where there's a straight run back to Wells. This is a great ride for a first 100-miler. There are some gentle hills to break any monotony, and you can really bowl along the flat sections on a magical ride full of history, mystery and legend in a quiet backwater of Britain.

START AND FINISH: Wells

GETTING THERE: Wells is 15 miles east of Junction 22 of the M5 using the B3139. The nearest rail station is Shepton Mallet, which is six miles away.

BIKE SHOP: Bike City on Union Street

CAFE: Fenney Castle House on Castle Street in Wookey Hole

LOCAL DELICACY: Somerset cider

THE BLACKDOWN, BRENDON AND QUANTOCK HILLS

RIDE FACTS

Rating
Hard

Total climbing
1550 metres

Killer climb
Elworthy Barrows

The Blackdown, Brendon, Quantocks ride, call it the BBQ for short, is a lovely ride over striking hills and through spectacular valleys. You even catch a glimpse of the sea. It starts in Taunton and the first of the day's long climbs begins as you leave town.

The road wriggles upwards for two and a half miles, and then you ride along the spine of the Blackdown Hills. The first section of this ridge run goes through an avenue of trees, which in summer looks like the vaulted nave of a giant, leafy cathedral. And when the trees thin out the view from up here is amazing.

The ridge run ends at the Wellington Monument, which is shaped like a bayonet used by Wellington's troops at the Battle of Waterloo. You head south now along a lower ridge, then descend steeply into Hemyock to ride along the first of the valleys.

The Culm is a gorgeous little river that lends its name to the Culm grassland that used to cover much of Devon and is preserved in places because of its biodiversity. It's the product of a badly draining acid soil, but it supports a wide variety of flora as well as butterflies and birds. You leave the river at Culmstock, riding up a shallow climb, while on your right there's a reconstructed hilltop beacon that was built to give advance warning of the Spanish Armada.

The next section goes along some heavy roads typical of inland Devon. They undulate constantly and are made from granite chippings. The combination of their rough surface and gravity seems to drag at your wheels, but don't despair, just dig in and take your time, gearing down and spinning your legs. Try not to fight your bike; work with it instead.

Eventually you'll reach the second valley, that of the River Bathern, where you start to climb Haddon Hill at Bampton. It's a long one, over four miles, and it rises in distinct steps, with the steepest coming just after Morbeath, and there's another very steep pitch close to the summit. Again, gear down and spin up. The top is another ridge, then there's a short descent before you climb Brendon Hill for the final ridge run of the day.

This is fantastic. There are incredible views across the Bristol Channel to Wales on your right, with Mid Devon rolling away to the English Channel on your left. The ridge goes on for six miles, until a

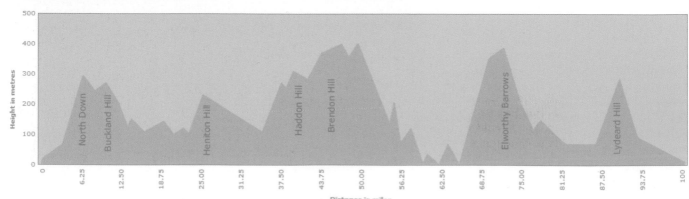

Height in metres — North Down — Buckland Hill — Heniton Hill — Haddon Hill — Brendon Hill — Elworthy Barrows — Lydeard Hill

500 — 400 — 300 — 200 — 100 — 0

0 — 6.25 — 12.50 — 18.75 — 25.00 — 31.25 — 37.50 — 43.75 — 50.00 — 56.25 — 62.50 — 68.75 — 75.00 — 81.25 — 87.50 — 93.75 — 100

Distance in miles

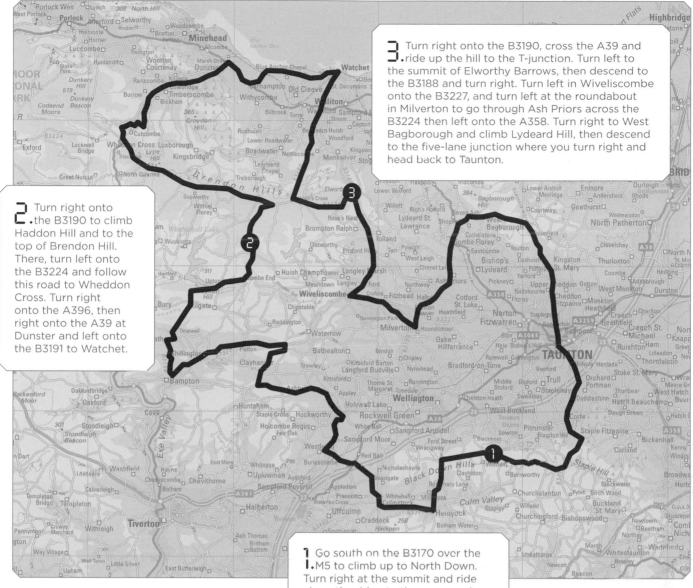

3. Turn right onto the B3190, cross the A39 and ride up the hill to the T-junction. Turn left to the summit of Elworthy Barrows, then descend to the B3188 and turn right. Turn left in Wiveliscombe onto the B3227, and turn left at the roundabout in Milverton to go through Ash Priors across the B3224 then left onto the A358. Turn right to West Bagborough and climb Lydeard Hill, then descend to the five-lane junction where you turn right and head back to Taunton.

2. Turn right onto the B3190 to climb Haddon Hill and to the top of Brendon Hill. There, turn left onto the B3224 and follow this road to Wheddon Cross. Turn right onto the A396, then right onto the A39 at Dunster and left onto the B3191 to Watchet.

1. Go south on the B3170 over the M5 to climb up to North Down. Turn right at the summit and ride along the ridge to the crossroads just before the Wellington Monument. Turn left to Hemyock. Turn right onto the B3391 and go through Culmstock, over the M5, and cross the A38 to turn right in Westleigh. Follow this road, keeping the canal on your left, then turn left over the River Tone and climb up to Crosses Farm, where you turn right to go through Clayhanger to the B3227. Turn left to Bampton.

steep descent leads to the final valley and one of the prettiest A-roads in Britain.

You hit the A396 at its watershed, the point where the Quarme, which later becomes the Exe, flows south and the Avill goes north. You follow the Avill, on a road twisting this way and that between impressive valley sides, past the striking yet homely Dunster Castle to begin the sea section through Watchet.

Another climb onto the Brendons follows, then there's a quick sprint across Taunton Vale to the last hills, the Quantocks. Their ridge road is a bit bumpy, and the way up is very steep, so because they come late in the ride I've routed you over Merridge Hill at their eastern end, from where there's a short descent back to Taunton. You should come back and explore the Quantocks with fresh legs.

'A STEEP DESCENT LEADS TO THE FINAL VALLEY AND ONE OF THE PRETTIEST A-ROADS IN BRITAIN'

START AND FINISH:
Taunton

GETTING THERE:
Taunton is right by Junction 25 of the M5, with good access to the national rail network through its station.

BIKE SHOP: Six Cycles on Pegasus Court just off St James Street

CAFE: Olio and Farina is right next to Six Cycles and is a great Italian-style cafe

LOCAL DELICACY: Taunton honey

WEST CORNWALL

RIDE FACTS

Rating
Medium

Total climbing
1430 metres

Killer climb
Chywoone Hill

'YOU ARE RIDING OVER HEADLANDS WITH THE SEA ON ONE SIDE AND A MASS OF EMPTY MOORLAND ON THE OTHER'

This ride goes as far south and as far west as you can go in mainland Britain. Some Cornish people would like their county to be a country, and it does feel different. The feeling increases the further west you go. The tip of Cornwall is called Penwith, and it's attached to the rest of Britain by slightly less than four miles of land. It feels like an island, and it even has a unique flora because plants grow outdoors in Penwith that struggle elsewhere.

But that's for later in the ride; it starts in a very different part of Cornwall. Redruth was the centre of Cornish tin mining, and there still are mineral-rich rocks underground here, created by Cornwall's geology, in which existing rocks were heated and altered by lava intrusions below ground.

The first leg heads south past the chimneys of silent engine houses, with empty eye-socket windows, that were once the hearts and lungs of the mines. This part of the county used to be an industrial wasteland, with spoil heaps from the mines and giant china-clay quarries, but various initiatives have restored it to the lovely rolling countryside it once was.

You ride through Helston, home of the Floral Dance and gateway to the Lizard peninsula. Lizard Point is the southernmost part of Britain, Lizard being a corruption of the Cornish Lys Ardh, meaning High Court. The route passes RNAS Culdrose on the outward and return leg, and you also pass the back

of Goonhilly Earth Station, where a radio dish called Arthur was the first satellite communication antenna in Britain. The site is owned by BT today and is partly a communication centre, while part of it is dedicated to deep-space research.

The Lizard is home to the chough, one of Britain's rarest birds and a symbol of Cornwall. The peninsula is also known as the Graveyard of Ships, because of its rocky coast, and more specifically a group of rocks called the Manacles, lurking just below the surface about a mile east of Dean Point. On the way back from Lizard Point you ride through Mullion to the idyllic beach at Poldhu Cove before returning to the main road and heading for Penzance.

You pass into Penwith at Marazion, where St Michael's Mount dominates the bay from its regal position at the end of a tidal causeway. The killer climb starts in Newlyn, the fishing town on the southern edge of Penzance, and the ride is hard now all the way to St Ives. As you pass Land's End and Cape Cornwall the road is never flat, climbing over the fingers of a granite block that extends into the sea. This section is a magnificent experience; you are riding on an undulating shelf of road over headlands with the sea on one side and a mass of empty moorland on the other.

St Ives is stunning, bathed in a soft light that has attracted generations of artists and still does. There's a Tate Gallery here and four wonderful beaches. The sand continues on the other side of

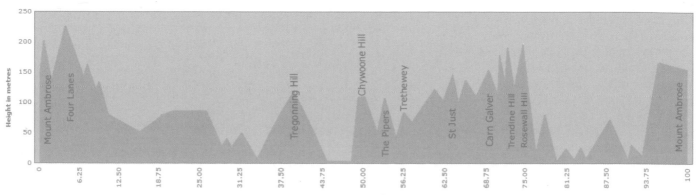

Height in metres

Distance in miles

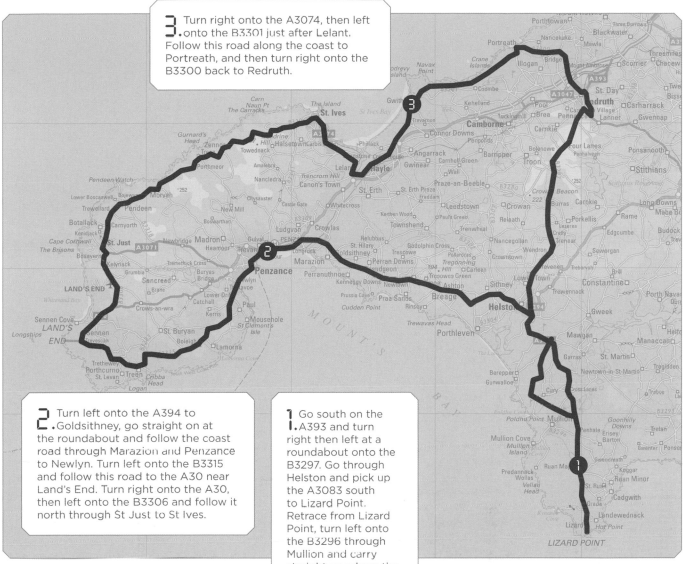

3. Turn right onto the A3074, then left onto the B3301 just after Lelant. Follow this road along the coast to Portreath, and then turn right onto the B3300 back to Redruth.

2. Turn left onto the A394 to Goldsithney, go straight on at the roundabout and follow the coast road through Marazion and Penzance to Newlyn. Turn left onto the B3315 and follow this road to the A30 near Land's End. Turn right onto the A30, then left onto the B3306 and follow it north through St Just to St Ives.

1. Go south on the A393 and turn right then left at a roundabout onto the B3297. Go through Helston and pick up the A3083 south to Lizard Point. Retrace from Lizard Point, turn left onto the B3296 through Mullion and carry straight on where the B3296 turns sharp left to Mullion Cove. Follow the road past the beach at Poldhu Cove, turn right, then keep left to go left on the A3083 to Helston.

the River Hayle, eventually giving way to the rolling Cornish landscape in which this ride started as you ride the north-coast leg to Portreath, where Atlantic waves crash onto a surfers' beach. The last bit inland to Redruth is a long, steady climb.

START AND FINISH: Redruth

GETTING THERE: Redruth is on the A30, 28 miles south-west of Bodmin. It is on the London Paddington to Penzance rail line.

BIKE SHOP: Bikechain Ricci in Mount Ambrose, Redruth

CAFE: Bissoe Bike Hire is just outside Redruth and a little bit off this route, but it has a fantastic cafe run by real cycling enthusiasts, and they've got an amazing collection of cycle-racing memorabilia.

LOCAL DELICACY: Stargazy pie